TANKS

TANKS

FROM WORLD WAR I TO THE PRESENT DAY

MARTIN J. DOUGHERTY

METRO BOOKS
NEW YORK

This 2008 edition published by Metro Books,
by arrangement with Amber Books.

Metro Books
122 Fifth Avenue
New York, NY 10011

Editorial and design by
Amber Books Ltd

Project Editor: Sarah Uttridge
Picture Research: Anthony Cohen
Design: Terry Forshaw and Kate Green

ISBN 13: 978-1-4351-0123-4
ISBN 10: 1-4351-0123-5

Printed and bound in China

10 9 8 7 6 5 4 3 2 1

Picture acknowledgements:
Art-Tech/Aerospace: 26, 34, 45(r), 48, 60, 63, 75, 78, 85, 98(r), 104-106, 115, 116, 119, 128, 134, 135, 142, 152(both), 154, 160, 170, 176, 177, 180(l), 181, 183, 184, 188, 200(r), 201, 207, 208, 211, 218, 219
Art-Tech/MARS: 35, 36
Cody Images: 6, 11, 12, 16(t), 18, 19, 21, 24, 25, 27(l), 32, 33, 37, 38, 42, 43, 46, 49, 52, 53(r), 55, 58, 62, 64, 68-70, 72, 73, 79, 80(l), 81-83, 88-91, 93, 97, 98(l), 99, 107, 112, 122, 124, 125(r), 126, 127, 129, 130, 143-146, 148, 153, 155-157, 164-167, 171(both), 182, 185, 189-191, 194, 206(r), 209, 216
Corbis: 27(r)
Christopher Foss: 203, 206(l), 210
Terry Gander: 47
Getty Images: 31
Library of Congress: 9(b), 20, 125(l), 147
Photoshot: 8, 9(t), 10, 13, 67(b), 30
Tank Museum: 41(both), 45(l), 53(l)
Ukrainian State Archive: 66, 96, 100, 101, 108, 114, 137-140, 161, 163
US Department of Defense: 173-175, 192, 195, 198(r), 199, 200(l), 214, 215

Artwork credits
Alcaniz Fresno's S.A.: 40, 44, 50, 51, 54, 56, 57, 59, 71, 74, 77, 80(r), 84, 86, 87, 92, 102, 103, 111, 113, 120, 121, 131-133, 149, 150, 196, 205, 217
Amber Books: 61, 65, 94, 95, 123, 136, 159, 168, 169, 172, 178, 180(r), 186, 187, 198(l), 202, 204, 212
Art-Tech/Aerospace: 14, 15, 22, 23, 28, 29, 76, 109, 110, 118, 141, 151, 158, 162, 179
Ray Hutchins: 197, 213

CONTENTS

C.15.

INTRODUCTION

The function of an armoured fighting vehicle (AFV) is threefold: to move, to fight and to protect the crew and weapon system, so that it can continue to do its job whatever the enemy might do to try to stop it.

There is nothing new about this concept. A tribal warrior of 5000 years ago, marching on foot, had exactly the same three attributes: combat power, protection and mobility, as provided by his spear, shield and feet. Advancing technology, however, has allowed the creation of combat vehicles of almost unbelievable power. Capable of high speeds, they can cross harsh terrain, carry weapons of tremendous power and are all but invulnerable to most attacks. There are many variations on the theme, but in the end the concept is much the same.

First and foremost, an AFV must be able to fight. It needs a weapon that can harm whatever opposition it is designed to go up against, ammunition to feed the weapon and some means to aim the weapon at the target. These requirements may necessitate the creation of turrets or other mountings, and those in turn need a chassis strong enough to support them.

A British Male Tank Mk 1. The trailing wheels were deleted from later models. The rooflike structure is a mesh-covered framework intended to cause grenades to roll off.

Second, the vehicle must be able to move. A source of power is required, and some means to deliver that power to the ground – in other words, a final drive system of some kind. If the vehicle is to go anywhere other than on good roads, it will need suspension and ground clearance sufficient to cope with rough terrain. It has long been known that tracks are better than wheels for moving across rough ground or spreading out the weight of a heavy vehicle.

The vehicle also needs protection of some kind. At its most basic, this means plates of metal to keep out bullets and shell fragments. As the capability of weapons has improved, so better protection has evolved to match it. Thicker armour is an option, though there is a practical limit to how much metal can he hung onto a given vehicle before it stops moving effectively. The elimination of 'shell traps', as well as the use of sloping armour and of advanced or composite materials to get better protection from the same weight of armour, is part of good design. Yet this is where the matter gets complicated and tradeoffs become necessary. A greater weight of armour requires a stronger chassis and either slows down the vehicle or necessitates a more powerful engine. Larger engines need more fuel and weigh more, which may reduce the amount of space available for the crew or weapon system – and require another redesign.

Even when the basic parameters of an AFV have been established, the design is far from complete. Peripheral but vital equipment must be fitted to enable the vehicle to do its job. A tank needs to be able to communicate, or at least to receive orders. Its crew must be able to see out while still being protected as far as possible. Its gun must be aimed, the turret traversed, and fumes from expended ammunition extracted.

And then there is the crew to consider. Several otherwise good tank designs have underperformed on the battlefield because they exhausted their crews by being hard to operate, or brutalized them by

The earliest combat vehicles were horse-drawn chariots. True cavalry later replaced chariots, just as armoured vehicles have replaced horsemen.

harsh cross-country performance. Tanks must therefore be able to do more than move, shoot and keep out bullets to be efficient on the battlefield. They need to be reliable, maintainable and operable.

Today's frontline Main Battle Tanks (MBTs) are fast, comfortable, well-protected, computerized, reliable, mobile, efficient – and even air-conditioned. Some can drive on the bottom of rivers; most can operate in the dark. Many can score a first-shot kill at 3km (1.9 miles) on the move, and are ready to fire again just seconds later. This level of excellence was not achieved overnight. Indeed, today's AFVs have developed as the result of a painful and often violent process of evolution. The terrain is littered with failed experiments and the burning hulls of vehicles that were not quite up to the job. It has taken a century to produce the tank of today – and the origins of the AFV go back further than that. Much further.

The Rise and Fall of Cavalry

The first combat vehicles were chariots pulled by horses (or occasionally oxen), from which the crew could shoot bows or throw javelins, or at least fight with spear or sword. Chariots developed because the horses of the time were not strong enough to bear a rider in combat, and chariot forces fulfilled the role that cavalry later undertook. Once the practice of riding horses into battle began and suitable mounts were bred, the chariot was supplanted and its function largely usurped by mounted warriors. Two main functions then developed for the horse soldier to carry out: reconnaissance and combat.

Throughout history, reconnaissance has tended to be the work of light cavalry. Their combat power was reasonable but they were more suited to screening, outpost duty and searching for the enemy than to shattering his formations – though they were excellent at exploiting a victory and chasing down an enemy in flight. The destruction of the enemy on the battlefield is traditionally the function of heavy cavalry, better protected by armour and mounted on bigger and stronger horses. The weapons of the heavy cavalry might not differ from those of their lighter cousins. Although horse archers and the like have been used by various nations to deliver firepower, cavalry have traditionally been a 'shock' arm, intended to smash the enemy like a battering ram rather than nibble at him from a distance. These roles have at times blurred into one another, and the issue is further complicated by the creation of dragoons. These were originally mounted infantry, but in many nations eventually evolved into true cavalry. Once that happened, mounted infantry tended to reappear under a different name.

The parallel between traditional cavalry and modern armour is obvious – lighter vehicles to conduct screening and reconnaissance tasks, MBTs to shatter an enemy force by shock action and vehicle-mounted infantry ready to move up in support. Indeed, it was the inability of horse cavalry to carry out their traditional functions that prompted the invention of the AFV. There was no instant changeover, of course; both existed side by side for many years.

Cavalry had been in decline for a long while before the AFV made its appearance. Against musket-armed infantry a mounted charge had every chance to reach the target, though breaking a disciplined infantry formation was a problem. Once rifle-muskets became commonplace, however, and infantry could conduct accurate fire to 450m (1476ft) instead of 150m (492ft), matters changed considerably.

There is a certain amount of mathematics involved in the dynamics of a cavalry charge. Horses tire rapidly at the gallop and formations can become too confused to deliver an effective charge if they must cover too much ground at top speed. Thus against infantry that now had an accurate range of 450m (1476ft), the danger to the cavalry was much worse than the 3:1 increased range might imply. Against muskets, most of the ground in the danger zone could be covered at a high speed. Against rifle-muskets, it could not. A longer period spent in the danger zone meant more rounds incoming. In turn, that led to more casualties and greater disruption. So it was that during the American Civil War (1861–65) and the European wars of the same period, notably the Franco-Prussian War of 1870, cavalry tended to be shot to pieces before they could reach the enemy. The advent of true cartridge-fed rifles and, a little later, machine guns, made matters even worse.

Despite the fact that cavalry in the American Civil War was most effective as mobile mounted infantry and that there was only one really effective cavalry charge in the Franco-Prussian War (which succeeded but at a high cost in casualties), the adherents of mounted warfare continued to believe that cavalry could achieve a decisive result on the modern battlefield. Thus it was that large numbers of cavalry divisions were deployed at the outbreak of World War I (1914–18).

In the early days of the war, when the situation was still very fluid, cavalry formations did engage in traditional actions at times. Where they were able to operate on their own terms – conducting reconnaissance and screening operations and engaging in sharp-fought encounter skirmishes – they were effective. When they were forced to go up against even sketchily prepared enemy positions, the story was very different. Barbed wire was a virtually impassable obstacle to cavalry, and there are several heartbreaking accounts of cavalry formations mown down by machine guns while unable to move forward or even to find their way out of the wired area. Hence the British Dragoons, who had recently been issued with the finest sword ever used by British cavalry, were shot down in droves by riflemen and machine-gunners. The gallant French *cuirassiers* met the same fate as they rode forward in their shiny breastplates and helmets, just as had been worn at Waterloo. The 'Uhlan Parties', as the British riflemen described the massacre of attacking German lancers, were similarly grim. The age of cavalry was over, penned up for slaughter by barbed wire and swept from the field by automatic guns. Now obsolete, some cavalry units found a role as mobile reserves, but many divisions simply waited behind the lines, hoping for the chance to do something useful. The day of the horse soldier was over, but his roles

French *cuirassiers* (heavy cavalry) went into action in 1914 looking little different from their counterparts at Waterloo.

The American Civil War showed that increasing infantry firepower left the cavalry almost impotent on the battlefield.

– screening, reconnaissance, shock action and the exploitation or pursuit of a broken enemy – still existed. These were still vital roles, but until the way was found to carry them out, the infantry and artillery would have to carry on the war, grinding the opposition down but unable to achieve a victory. Fortunately, work on a replacement for the horsed soldier was already underway.

Early Experiments

The idea of a mobile fighting platform, all but impervious to enemy action, has always appealed. Early moves in this direction used animal or human power. Armoured elephants, horse- or ox-drawn 'war wagons', siege towers on wheels, and mobile *ballistae* mounted on carts had been tried at various times in history. None of these was a true combat vehicle, but they all indicate the direction that military thinking was headed.

Later medieval experiments included an armoured wagon driven by hand-cranks, from which the crew could fire arquebuses, and in the nineteenth century Gatling guns were mounted on camels. However, thhe concept of using well-protected artillery weapons to reduce enemy positions (which is one role that tanks perform), was explored in the 1870s by British colonel C. B. Brackenbury. Brackenbury's idea was to create a battery of 'assault artillery' by fitting field guns with defensive shields of metal impervious to small-arms fire. The guns could then be manhandled forward by their crews, destroying enemy positions as they went. Relying on manpower meant that the guns, whose armour added to their already not inconsiderable weight, were not very mobile. However, the idea of an artillery-sized weapon protected by armour and able to move to new firing positions is the same as the concept of a tank.

The first true self-powered armoured combat vehicle was patented in 1855, during the Crimean War (1853–56). This was a steam-powered vehicle mounting artillery guns and protected by steel armour. Designed for the assault role, the vehicle used carronades – short guns with a limited range but capable of firing 6.4kg (14lb) shot – and had a set of scythes for anti-personnel use. Whether or not the design was practicable, it was considered uncivilized and there was no official interest. As a result, the prototype was

Roman chariots

The Roman army made little use of chariots for most of its history, but they were used in ceremonies and raced in sporting events for many years. A Roman general leading a procession in his chariot was much like the cavalry escorts at modern British state occasions – a reminder of the martial traditions of the nation and a link to a glorious past.

Steam-powered traction engines began to be used for engineering works, and to pull artillery pieces, in the late nineteenth century.

not built and the Crimean War was fought without such barbarous devices.

Steam Tractors and Armoured Cars

Two separate streams of development led to the tank becoming a reality. The practical considerations of movement over rough ground were first tackled by steam-powered agricultural vehicles, while the question of whether an armed vehicle could be useful in combat was answered by the armoured car.

It was the internal combustion engine that really solved the power problem for armoured vehicles. What was needed was an engine that could deliver suitable amounts of power without being so heavy itself, or requiring such quantities of fuel, that it could not drive a heavy vehicle for a useful distance. Development was inhibited, however, because in the latter years of the nineteenth century, British law did not permit mechanically propelled vehicles (other than steam-powered traction engines) to operate on the roads. The law was finally changed in 1896, the same year that the first usable British motor car design was exhibited.

Just four years later, an armoured version of this vehicle appeared, designated the Pennington Armoured Car. Where some inventions have names that do not precisely reflect their origin or function, the armoured car was exactly that – a civilian road car with armour of steel plate 6.4mm (0.25in) and two Maxim machine guns mounted in the back. It was, quite simply, a car to which armour had been added and like all such experiments, its performance was marginal.

Two years later, in 1902, the Simms armoured car appeared. This was an interesting concept, whose wheels were protected by a curtain of chain mail hanging from the bottom of the armoured belt. Armament was increased too – the Simms had two Maxim machine guns augmented by a 1-pounder pom-pom (an early automatic cannon). There was still a civilian car underneath all this, however, which was not a suitable base for a combat vehicle. An updated Simms, in 1903, was the first land vehicle with a rotating turret. Actually, it had two of them, one for each machine gun. The driver used a periscope to see out from behind the armour. Unfortunately, the improved Simms used the same 12kW (16hp) engine as the civilian road car from which it was developed, and was therefore barely able to move under the weight of its armour.

Similar vehicles were under development in other nations, in some cases with a slightly different emphasis. In France, the Charron-Giradot et Voight armoured car made its appearance in 1902. This was not so much a true AFV as a mobile machine-gun emplacement. Although there was a gun shield and some armour to protect the gunner, the driver and engine were exposed. Early German armoured cars used a truck chassis rather than that of the more usual touring car. Designs ranged from mobile anti-observation-balloon gun mounts (with and without armour) to oversized machine-gun-armed vehicles.

Development during the years immediately prior to World War I was rapid, but showed varying degrees of success. Several nations managed to produce a workable touring-car-based, machine-gun armed vehicle with light armour. Some attempted to field heavier vehicles with multiple guns, heavier guns, or both. Heavy armoured cars tended to fail, however. Some designs were so overloaded that they could break their own axles on a bumpy road. The problem with armoured cars of this kind was that they offered no off-road performance. They were useful for security operations such as airfield defence and so forth, and perhaps scouting along roads, but designs that were at all effective in the open field were the exception rather than the rule.

During the first months of World War I, armoured cars did give good service and some designs even proved that they could operate in open country. After this, they were largely unable to contribute to the fighting on the Western Front. Shell-torn mud, with barbed wire and trenches running across it, was inaccessible to even the best armoured car designs.

Nonetheless, armoured cars served, sometimes with distinction, in other theatres. In Russia and the Middle East, armoured car squadrons were useful assets in their own right, often acting as a sort of cross between mobile artillery or support weapons and cavalry units. The ability to bring heavy firepower to bear at a given point, then move on to another location, was very useful and demonstrated the effectiveness of the AFV beyond question. Armoured car operations also demonstrated other important concepts. For example, some early designs had an open top and hence their crews were vulnerable to snipers or shell fragments. The need for all-round armour was shown in the first weeks of the war, when many cars were disabled by snipers firing from nearby hilltops or church towers.

Such was the fate of many of the cars operated early in the war by the Royal Navy, which created an armoured car squadron to protect the Admiralty Air Base at Dunkirk. There was at the time no separate Royal Air Force (RAF), and so operations over the Western Front were carried out Royal Navy pilots. The armoured cars were intended as a mobile force that served a dual role: defending the air base and also picking up downed pilots. Presumably, they were also tasked with rounding up any enemy pilots who were forced down behind the Allied lines.

The experiences of the Admiralty Air Department with open-topped armoured vehicles in 1914 had far-reaching consequences for vehicle design. Top armour tends to be thinner than that of

Armoured cars and motorcycles made their combat debut during World War I.

Armoured Cars

Early armoured cars were built on commercial car and truck chassis, sometimes as private ventures by manufacturers who hoped to win a defence contract. The usual concept was simply to bolt sheets of metal over an existing vehicle, overburdening its chassis and engine. Custom-designed armoured vehicles made much more efficient use of their weight capacity and achieved better results in both the marketplace and the field.

the main hull, especially the front of the vehicle where most enemy fire is likely to strike, but it is always present in tanks and usually in other armoured vehicles.

In all, the early armoured cars demonstrated that AFVs could be effective if their problems were resolved, and also indicated what those problems were. They also carved out their own niche, which still exists – modern armoured cars have more in common with tanks than their 1902-vintage ancestors, but there is a new generation of lightly protected armoured vehicles in operation today, still carrying out internal security and patrol operations along the roads and in less difficult terrain.

If the armoured car maintained an interest in creating AFVs, it fell to the humble steam tractor to show how their problems could be overcome. Steam power was well proven by the middle of the nineteenth century. It was in use on the railways and in industry, and was being introduced for shipping. Steam-powered vehicles came along a little later and were at first extremely clumsy. These early vehicles had a limited output and range, but they were found useful for pulling loads and were sent off to far corners of the world for engineering work and to pull artillery pieces. The big steel wheels of traction engines were not ideal for operations on rough ground, however, and eventually something better was invented – the caterpillar track.

Armoured cars were primarily useful for internal security and the protection of installations.

Tracks were developed by the British firm Richard Hornsby & Sons, a manufacturer of agricultural machinery. They were intended for use on farm machines, to enable them to handle soft ground. It was not long, however, before the military applications became obvious (to Hornsby at least) and so the firm demonstrated a track-laying vehicle for use as an artillery tractor, to pull guns and ammunition limbers. The performance of this vehicle was good – in a demonstration it was able to cross ground that a team of horses could not, and also rescued the stuck horses into the bargain – but this was not enough to prompt the government to place an order. Hornsby therefore sold the patent to the Holt Caterpillar Company, an American firm, and over the next few years it developed what became known as the 'caterpillar' track, for agricultural applications.

HEAD TO HEAD: *Tank MK V MALE* VERSUS

British tanks in World War I were clumsy and prone to a range of mechanical problems. However, they were built with a specific task in mind and did that job reasonably well. The Mk V benefited from being a developed model, which allowed some of the Mk I's faults to be eliminated. Equally importantly, they were deployed in sufficient numbers to make a difference.

MK V MALE

Crew: 8
Weight: 29,600kg (65,120lb)
Dimensions: length 8.05m (26ft 5in); width over sponsons 4.11m (13ft 6in); height: 2.64m (8ft 8in)
Range: 72km (45 miles)
Armour: 6–14mm (0.24–0.55in)
Armament: two 6-pounder (57mm/2.24in) guns, four Hotchkiss machine guns
Powerplant: one 150hp (112kW) Ricardo petrol engine
Performance: maximum road speed 7.4km/h (4.6mph)

STRENGTHS

- Excellent obstacle and trench-crossing capability
- Second-generation design eliminating many basic problems
- Efficient design for its intended combat environment

WEAKNESSES

- Unreliable and prone to breakdowns
- Exhausting and stressful to drive or crew
- Poisoned its crew with carbon monoxide

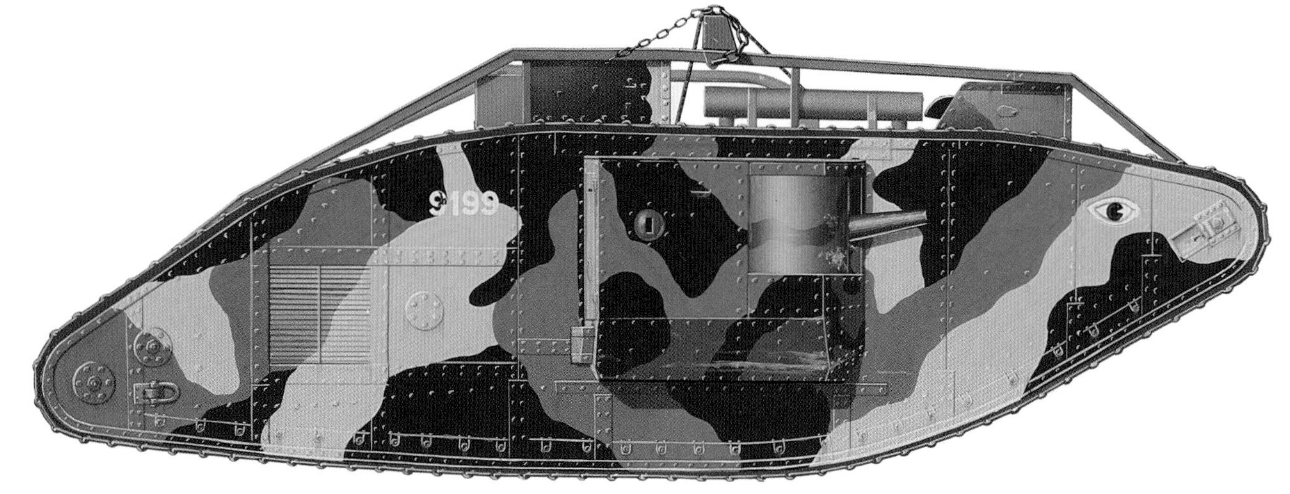

Sturmpanzerwagen A7V

It is hard to imagine what sort of task the German designers of the A7V had in mind for it. Incapable of crossing any sort of obstacle, this tank had no chance of contributing usefully to the war. In addition, there were simply not enough A7Vs to make any real difference, even on a local level. Overall, the German tank was big, impressive and useless while the British fielded large numbers of much less imposing vehicles, which were nevertheless entirely superior.

A7V

Crew: 18
Weight: 33,500kg (73,700lb)
Dimensions: length 8.0m (26ft 3in); width 3.05m (10ft); height 3.3m (10ft 10in)
Range: 40km (25 miles)
Armour: up to 30mm (1.18in)
Armament: one 57mm (2.24in) gun; six or seven 7.92mm (0.3in) MGs
Powerplant: Two Daimler-Benz, 4-cylinder 100hp (74.5kW) petrol engines
Performance: maximum road speed 12.8km/h (8mph)

STRENGTHS

- Huge and impressive
- Powerful armament
- Protected against small-arms fire

WEAKNESSES

- Very poor obstacle crossing capability
- Hard to coordinate the large crew
- Huge target with numerous weak points

At the outbreak of World War I, all the vital ingredients of the AFV were in existence – tracks, engines, armour, weapons and, most of all, a proven concept. In 1912, an Australian by the name of L. E. Mole designed a track-laying combat vehicle and sent it to the British War Office. The concept did not attract interest and was ignored even when it was resubmitted in 1915 since, by then, a design was under development. In the event, the first tanks built bore a considerable resemblance to the Mole combat vehicle, but were later admitted to be inferior in some ways. Mole had the right idea at just slightly the wrong time, for the critical catalyst was still missing at the time of his first submission – the desperate need to find a weapon that could replace cavalry on a shell-torn, wire-strewn battlefield.

As the early months of World War I ended and the deadlock began; as cavalry were swept from the field and infantry driven under cover; as artillery was reduced to long-distance shelling, so at last the need was seen. And then, unreliable, hellish to operate and prone to breakdowns as it was, came the tank.

The Development of the Tank

Tanks were a British invention, though they represented a coming-together of ideas rather than a sudden stroke of brilliance. There are many names associated with the development of the tank in one capacity or another, but one of the most important is that of E. D. Swinton, then a lieutenant-colonel.

Swinton knew about caterpillar tracks from reports he had seen, and had witnessed both the promise of armoured cars and their inability to cross the trench combat zone. He proposed developing a vehicle that was much like an armoured car but which could run on tracks rather than wheels. This, he argued, would be able to function in the mud and wire, and thus contribute usefully to the conflict. The War Office decided to try out Swinton's idea, and obtained a Holt tractor for trials. The vehicle never had any chance of succeeding in its allotted task – to complete a very muddy course dragging a load of some 2.54 tonnes (2.5 tons) – which was supposed to simulate the eventual service weight of the combat vehicle.

Naturally, the tractor failed to impress the officials, and interest waned once more. Swinton remained convinced, however, and began again, this time targeting the Admiralty. He gained the support of the First Lord of the Admiralty, no less a

Early Aircraft

Aircraft made their combat debut as reconnaissance and strike platforms, and soon began to fight one another. Within 30 years, aircraft would be supporting tank attacks and flying tank-busting missions, and specialist anti-aircraft tanks would be integrated into armoured formations.

Without the internal combustion engine, neither aircraft nor tanks would have been possible, and World War I was the proving-ground for both weapon systems.

A Whippet tank of this type, named *Musical Box,* made the world's first armoured exploitation, rampaging behind enemy lines for 11 hours before being disabled.

figure than Winston Churchill. The Admiralty formed a Landships Committee to look into the idea and obtained its own test vehicle. This time it was a Killen-Stuart tractor, which used the patented caterpillar track, as had the Holt unit purchased by the army.

Experiments were carried out with this vehicle and all seemed favourable. It was fitted with a wire-cutting device adapted from the same net cutter that was used by naval vessels. However, by July 1915 armoured cars had passed their useful phase on the Western Front, and the Admiralty was considering disbanding its armoured car units. Interest in the whole AFV concept was once more on the wane. Swinton pointed out, however, that tracked vehicles were being successfully used as prime movers for artillery and ammunition. Assisted by urgings from others, he was able to convince the Admiralty that it was worth continuing with the project.

The Admiralty decided to keep No. 20 Armoured Car Squadron, the unit that was conducting the tracked-vehicle experiments, in existence for a while longer. Development continued, and the War Office came back to take another look.

Swinton created a specification for an armoured combat vehicle to suit the needs of the Western Front. He considered crew, armament and propulsion, but also practical matters such as protection and obstacle-crossing capability. His suggestions became the benchmark for a workable design, and the Killen-Stuart tractor was able to demonstrate capabilities that matched the specifications.

The trials were observed by War Office officials, government ministers and representatives from what had been the Naval Landships Committee, but which now was becoming a joint military/navy concern. Although the army had finally become involved in the development of the new weapon, it was a civilian, Mr W. Tritton, and an officer of the Royal Naval Air Service (RNAS), Lieutenant W. G. Wilson, who came up with the design for the very first workable tank. The task of building it was given to William Foster & Company, a firm that was already building tracked agricultural vehicles.

Little Willie

The prototype was rolled out in late July 1915. Known as 'Little Willie', this rather primitive vehicle was originally designed to carry a turret on top, and it bore many similarities to more modern vehicles rather than the 'lozenge' tanks that followed.

Little Willie was driven by two men sitting side by side. The man on the right operated the gearbox and used foot pedals to control the 78kW (105hp) Daimler engine, which could drive the vehicle at up to 3.2km/h (2mph). He could also make minor direction corrections by the use of a pair of tail wheels, which were steered by cables. Larger changes of direction were accomplished by the left-hand man braking one track or by throwing a track out of gear.

Little Willie could climb a 30cm (12in) obstacle and cross a 1.2m (3ft 11in) trench as first built. While not bad for an initial attempt, this performance was obviously inadequate for combat use, so Tritton worked to develop and improve the design. Modifications included new tracks, and these improved performance considerably. Little Willie could now scramble up a 1.2m (3ft 11in) obstacle and cross a 1.5m (4ft 11in) trench.

Little Willie was developed in great secrecy and showed considerable promise. The combat version would have carried either two or four gunners, depending on the armament fitted. This was to include a 2-pounder (40mm/1.57in) cannon, a Maxim machine gun and possibly a number of Lewis machine guns. However, while Tritton was working to improve Little Willie, Wilson had produced a new design of his own.

Mother, or Big Willie

Wilson departed from the Little Willie design considerably when he designed his new tank. The idea of steering using trailing wheels was retained, but much else changed. In order to be able to climb the sort of obstacles its specifications required, this tank, which was named 'Big Willie' at times and 'Mother' at others, was given a rhomboid or 'lozenge' hull form with the tracks running around the outside.

The task of building this new prototype was given to Foster's again, and the new design rolled out for trials on 16 January 1916. The actual vehicle used in the tests was a mockup, as the actual prototype was not ready in time. It met the specified requirements of being able to climb a 1.37m (4ft 6in) obstacle and cross a 2.44m (8ft) trench, and sufficiently impressed the observers that discussion moved to how the vehicle was to be armed and protected.

Swinton recommended that the tank's armour be capable of defeating a reversed rifle bullet from 10m (32ft). Reversed bullets had recently been found to penetrate armour better than standard rounds. The protection decided upon was 10mm (0.39in) in front (later increased to 12mm/0.47in), 8mm (0.31in) on the sides and 6mm (0.24in) on top. The latter reflected the need to protect the crew and internal components from shell splinters as much as from small-arms fire.

The new tank was to be capable of 6.4km/h (4mph) if possible; the final version came close at 5.95km/h (3.7mph). Armament was more of a problem due to the vehicle's considerable height. Rather than perch a turret atop the hull, some 2.41m (7ft 11in) high, weaponry would be carried in sponsons along the side of the hull, and possibly mounted on the front of the hull between the 'horns' created by the projecting tracks.

Armament presented a problem. Tritton's Little Willie had been developed with either a 2-pounder (40mm/1.56in) gun or a 75mm (2.95in) quick-firing mountain gun as its main armament. The former proved too light for use aboard Wilson's 'Big Willie' design and the mountain gun was not available in quantity. A substitute, a naval 6-pounder (57mm/2.24in), was tried out and proved effective; it was also available in suitable quantities.

Big Willie was difficult to operate and required a large crew. The driver and commander sat side by side in a turret at the front of the hull. The commander, sitting on the left, operated the brakes as well as commanding the vehicle. The driver sat on the right; between him and the commander was a machine gun. There was a second turret at the rear of the hull, containing a machine gun and semaphore apparatus for signalling.

The generals of World War I had trained in an age before mechanized warfare.

In the main hull were four gunners and two gearsmen, who received orders by hand signal from the commander and used their gearboxes to assist the driver in steering. The term 'landship' was used to describe this new vehicle, and was appropriate – the crew had to work together in a way more akin to a warship than anything ever seen in land combat. The men climbed in and out through doors on the rear of each sponson and another at the rear of the hull, and a hatch on the top of the tank. The total armament on this version was two 6-pounder (57mm/2.24in) Hotchkiss guns and four Hotchkiss machine guns.

After the first trials, modifications were made and the tank was presented to a distinguished audience, including King George V. Lord Kitchener, the British Secretary of State for War, was not convinced, but the king was. After a ride in the prototype a few days later, he suggested that the British Army would benefit from having large numbers of these vehicles available.

Big Willie passed its trials and an initial order of 100 was placed with Forster's as well as the Metropolitan Carriage & Finance Company. The order was quickly increased to 150, and the specifications changed slightly. Instead of one type of tank, there would be two. Both were identical but for armament. The 'male' version would carry as its main armament two 6-pounder (57mm/2.24in) guns for destroying strongpoints, and the 'female' would carry only machine guns for anti-personnel work, including the protection of the 'male' tanks from infantry close assault.

The first Tank Mark Is, as these vehicles became known, went into production in early 1916 and were ready for action in September. They were still a great secret at that time, and a suitable cover name needed to be created. Such huge objects, even covered with tarpaulins and netting, were sure to attract notice when parked or passing by on a train.

It was decided to claim that they were bulk water tanks for the eastern theatre of war, and to refer to them as cisterns or containers. However, somone decided that the vehicle bore a close resemblance to the fuel tank of a make of motorcycle that was popular at the time, so the tarpaulin-draped objects became 'tanks'.

Early tanks were referred to as 'landships', and in many ways they operated like a naval vessel.

The First Tank Actions

Swinton was given command of the first tanks to arrive in the theatre of war, but as the theorist behind their development he was placed in an administrative and training capacity rather than that of battlefield commander. He was permitted to recommend an officer for that role, and put forward Lieutenant-Colonel H. J. Elles of the Royal Engineers, who had been involved in tank development.

Elles took command of the first operational tank unit in September 1916. At this time, tank doctrine was based on Swinton's thinking that the tank was essentially an infantry weapon and should be treated as part of the infantry force. A year later, the then Major J. F. C. Fuller, one of the greatest exponents of armoured warfare, would describe the tank as an 'armoured, mechanical horse'. Fuller realized that tanks were, in fact, cavalry returning to the battlefield having donned armour and been rendered bulletproof. In 1916, however, the tank was not seen as a decisive weapon or an independent arm.

While the tanks sought their identities, various issues remained to be settled. One was what to call their units, especially since secrecy had to be maintained. Elles' force was constituted as the Tank Detachment and briefly became the Armoured Car Section of the Motor Machine-Gun Service. That title was sensibly shortened to Heavy Section, Machine-Gun Corps. As the formation expanded, 'Section' became 'Branch'. It was in the guise of Heavy Branch, Machine-Gun Corps, that tanks first saw action. In 1917, when secrecy was no longer so vital, the name changed again to the more accurate Tank Corps. In late 1916, the Heavy Branch, Machine-Gun Corps was organized into six companies, each of four sections. A section contained six tanks; three 'male' and three 'female' with another tank in reserve as a source of spares.

At this time, the city of Verdun was under terrible pressure from German forces and the Allies had launched their own offensive along the River Somme to try to relieve some of the pressure. The Somme offensive was soon bogged down, and it was decided to see if tanks could help at all.

The first assault by tanks was launched at Flers-Courcelette on the Somme. It took place on 15 September 1916, a fortnight before Elles assumed command. The odds were against success from the start. Because the operation was hurried, there had been no training whatsoever for cooperation between infantry and armoured forces, and even within the tank force itself training had been on a very small scale. Nobody knew how to handle large numbers of tanks, or how to fit them into a battle plan. Nor was there any clear idea what a tank should carry into battle. As well as eight human beings and all their personal gear, the tanks were to carry an entire spare machine gun, a spare Hotchkiss barrel and four barrels for their Lewis machine guns, wire-cutting gear, signalling equipment including lamps and flags, a drum of cable, one of engine oil and another of gearbox oil plus cans of grease for the tank and water for the crew or the vehicle. There were also 16 loaves of bread, 30 tins of rations, two boxes of revolver ammunition and a field telephone.

The tanks of this time were difficult to operate. Fumes from the engine and the heat inside the fighting compartment took their toll on the crew

Developments in Protection

The open hatches give an indication of how thick the armour of early tanks was. As metallurgy and construction techniques improved, it became possible to provide better protection for the same weight of armour.

Early tanks were protected only against small arms and machine-gun fire. Even then, spallation represented a problem: rivet heads or fragments of armour being knocked off the inside and injuring crew members as they bounced around inside.

even without hot splinters of armour flying about inside as a result of non-penetrating hits. Driving the tank was exhausting work, and none of the crew could see much of what was going on. The tanks were also less than reliable. Forty-nine were detailed for the operation, and of them just 32 reached the start point.

The 32 tanks actually able to take part went forward through country unsuited to tank operations. Sodden mud and shell holes from months of bombardment made the going even harder than usual. Five tanks ended up ditched – stuck in mud or trapped while attempting to cross an obstacle. Nine broke down after the operation started and thus made no contribution. Another nine were so badly slowed by various problems that they were left behind by the infantry, though they were able to take part in mopping-up operations to good effect.

Just nine tanks of the 49 – not 20 per cent of the assigned force – were where they were supposed to be, advancing ahead of the infantry to suppress opposition. Despite their small numbers, however, the tanks were wildly successful, especially at Flers. There, three tanks led a division of British and a division of New Zealand infantry into the village, which had been a German strongpoint, and advanced through it almost without opposition.

Here was the first recorded case of 'tank terror'. Infantrymen, seeing the mechanical monstrosities rumbling slowly towards them, impervious to anything the infantry could fire at them and shooting back with machine guns and light artillery weapons, became demoralized and fled their positions. In some cases, units broke and ran before the tanks even came into range. The reaction is understandable. The defenders did not know how unreliable the tanks were, and could not see how much the crews were suffering at the hands of their own vehicle, let alone those enemy shots that did have telling effect. All they saw was something new, frightening and apparently unstoppable.

The press made much of the capture of Flers, though it was only a tactical success. After months of desperate slogging on the Somme, even a small victory was something to celebrate. And in this case the press were entirely right – Flers was the shape of things to come. The action at Flers-Courcelette included another first. Tank D1 was hit on the sponson by a shell, the first serious damage done to a tank by enemy action.

Despite the limited nature of the success at Flers-Courcelette, it *was* a success, and this encouraged the War Office to expand the tank force. In October 1916, it was announced that the tank companies would be expanded up to battalions, each of three tank companies with a workshop company attached. A tank company would now comprise four sections of five tanks (later reduced to four). A later reorganization made the fourth section a repository for spare tanks rather than a fighting unit.

By the beginning of 1917, the tanks were, therefore, theoretically organized in battalions of three tank and one workshop companies, with the tank companies consisting of three fighting sections of four tanks and one 'spare' section with, again theoretically, four more tanks. There was also a battalion headquarters section of four tanks. This was a workable setup, but although many quarters recognized that tanks needed to be used *en masse* in fairly well-drained country for best effect, this was not how they were used for the remainder of 1916. Indeed, the opposite was the case. Tanks were scattered along the front in 'penny packets' or even solo, making it difficult to supply and maintain them. Tanks contributed to a number of actions, but always in a small way. Breakdowns, ditching and other problems meant that often the entire tank strength of an operation might fail to get into action at all. Tanks were lost where they might easily have been recovered after a successful operation.

There were no specialist antitank weapons to oppose the early tank attacks, just field guns firing over open sights.

Meanwhile, the battalions grew into brigades at the beginning of 1917, and modifications were made to the tanks being produced. Hotchkiss machine guns were replaced with Lewis guns, and the trailing wheels were removed as unnecessary. Operational experience had shown that a redesign was needed but large numbers of tanks were required, and quickly, so although a Mk II and Mk III appeared they were only very slightly different from the Mk I. The Mk IV Tank, designed by Wilson (who was now a major), finally made its

HEAD TO HEAD: *Char d'Assaut Schneider* VERSUS

Controversy dogged French efforts to create a tank arm and resulted in two poor designs being fielded in large numbers. Both were based on the same vehicle and had similar armament, and both underperformed in action. The Schneider's armour was not very good and could be penetrated by rifle rounds. Its fuel tanks were particularly prone to being holed, leading to disastrous fires.

Char d'Assaut Schneider

Crew: 7
Weight: 18,800kg (32,560lb)
Dimensions: length 6m (19ft 8in); width 2m (6ft 7in); height: 2.39m (7ft 10in)
Range: 48km (30 miles)
Armour: 11.5mm (0.45in)
Armament: one 75mm (2.95in) gun, two additional machine guns
Powerplant: one 55hp (41kW) Schneider four-cylinder petrol engine
Performance: maximum road speed 6km/h (3.7mph)

STRENGTHS

- 75mm (2.96in) main gun armament
- Body designed to help clear obstacles
- Relatively small crew (7 men)

WEAKNESSES

- Poor armour protection
- Caught fire easily
- Poor obstacle-crossing capability

Char d'Assaut St Chamond

The St Chamond was better armoured but even more prone to getting stuck as its front and rear ends greatly overhung its tracks. An extra 5.1 tonnes (5 tons) of needless weight was added by the electric transmission system, despite which it was faster than the Schneider – when it was not hung up on something and entirely unable to move.

Char d'Assaut St Chamond

Crew: 9
Weight: 23,400kg (51,480lb)
Dimensions: length with gun 8.83m (28ft 11.75in); length of hull 7.91m (25ft 11.5in); width 2.67m (8ft 9in); height 2.34m (7ft 6in)
Range: 59km (36.7 miles)
Armour: 17mm (0.67in)
Armament: one Modele 1897 75mm (2.95in) gun; up to four machine guns
Powerplant: one 90hp (67kW) Panhard four-cylinder petrol engine powering a Crochat-Collardeau electric transmission

STRENGTHS

- Thick armour
- 75mm (2.95in) main gun
- Faster than Schneider design

WEAKNESSES

- Very poor obstacle-crossing capability
- Excessively heavy
- Unstable and prone to tip over

appearance in mid-1917. It was a big improvement on the Mk I, though it was still highly unpleasant to be inside and hard on its crews. It was less likely to immolate them, though. Fuel was still petrol, and thus highly flammable, but this was carried in an armoured tank at the rear rather than inside the driver's compartment. The Mk IV was also better protected than its predecessor. The Mk I was fitted with glass prisms for the crew to see through, but these would shatter if hit. The new tanks used perforated steel plates that offered better protection, but probably reduced visibility even further than before.

For some months, German forces had been receiving armour-piercing ammunition, which could punch through a Mk I's plate on a clean hit. The Mk IV was impervious to this new ammunition. The Germans did not find this out until the end of the war, a fact that proved something of a double-edged sword. On the one hand, they did not know their anti-armour measures were ineffective and replace them with something better. On the other hand, troops who thought, rightly or otherwise, that they could stop a tank were more likely to stand and fight than those who knew they could not. The ineffective armour-piercing bullets served to stiffen the morale of troops facing tanks, if nothing else.

One advantage of the new design was logistical – the Mk IV had smaller sponsons than earlier models, and these could be swung inboard for transport by rail rather than having to be removed and refitted at the far end. The incorporation of an 'unditching beam' was useful too. This was nothing more complex than a wooden beam longer than the width of the tank and carried across the top. If the tank became stuck, the beam could be released to be dragged under the tracks, thus providing extra purchase.

Machine Gun

The machine gun was the main threat to an assault. This Lewis gun team has several ammunition drums ready and would be able to maintain a high rate of fire for some time. Tanks were largely tasked with the elimination of machine-gun positions, which would allow infantry to advance without being mown down.

The battle of Arras, which began on 9 April 1917, was a second attempt to use tanks in a large-scale action. The plan was to use tanks and infantry to smash a hole in the enemy lines, into which the cavalry could advance. Here was a chance for the horsed soldier to finally make a contribution.

It was not to be. The offensive opened with the usual massive artillery bombardment, which ripped up the ground and made it difficult for the tanks to get forward. The tanks themselves were deployed in small units rather than *en masse*. They did their best and some local successes were gained, but eventually the infantry outran their artillery support (as had always happened in the past), and became exhausted, then stalled against the still-resisting rear enemy lines.

Two British Mk I tanks were captured by the Germans after the battle of Arras, which confirmed that the armour-piercing ammunition issued to their infantry was effective, and a general order soon after guaranteed that quantities were available to riflemen and that machine gunners were issued several hundred rounds. Casualties among the crews of Mk I tanks rose sharply thereafter, though the Mk IVs were immune.

Enter The French

The French equivalent to Colonel Swinton was Colonel J. E. Estienne, who recommended to his superiors that a Holt tractor could be fitted with a gun and used on the battlefield to good effect. Estienne had similar difficulties in getting anyone to listen to him, but was finally permitted to approach the Schneider Creusot company for a detailed design. The French government then had a sudden fit of enthusiasm for armoured vehicles and placed an order for no less than 400 Schneider tanks, even before the design was ready. They then ordered 400 tanks of a different design from St Charmond. Both designs were based on the Holt agricultural tractor.

The Schneider was armed with a short 75mm (2.95in) howitzer carried on a sponson on the right side, plus two Hotchkiss machine guns on the left.

Developments in Protection

One of the earliest standards for tank armour was that it had to withstand a hit from a reversed bullet of rifle calibre. Reversed bullets penetrated better than standard ones, which were more likely to glance off.

Armour-piercing rifle and machine-gun ammunition was quickly issued to German troops when it became apparent that standards small arms could not stop a tank. However, by then armour protection had advanced to the point where these, too, were ineffective.

The 'horns' of a British Mk V tank as an enemy infantryman might see them.

It also had its petrol tanks in the sides, and caught fire readily when penetrated by rifle fire. This happened quite often as the armour of 11mm (0.43in) in the front and 8mm (0.31in) elsewhere was not up to the job.

The Schneider was not well designed and was hard to maintain, resulting in long periods out of service. It did incorporate some interesting ideas, such as the shiplike front prow and steel spades at the rear to assist in obstacle crossing, but overall it was a poor design, rushed into service, and it performed badly. The Schneider is sometimes designated CA1 (Char d'Assault), and there was also the experimental CA2 mounting a 47mm (1.85in) gun in a turret. This came to nothing, and indeed many CA1s were delivered without armament as armoured supply vehicles.

The St Charmond was no better. Its body was much longer than the tracks of its Holt chassis, creating an unstable vehicle that was poor at obstacle crossing. This was a severe drawback on the Western Front. It also tended to tip over sideways on relatively gentle slopes. Its armament was a front-mounted 75mm (2.95in) gun and four

French tanks halted near the front. Early French armour was very poor and had not improved greatly by World War II.

Hotchkiss machine guns. St Charmond tanks went into action in May 1917, or rather, they tried to. All 16 tanks committed became stuck at the first trench they tried to cross and contributed nothing to the battle. French tank warfare was off to a rather poor start.

Validation at Last

It was 1917 when the tank first showed its true capabilities. It was also the year when Fuller (now promoted to lieutenant-colonel) wrote a paper that showed the way forward for the tank. Although largely ignored in Britain, Fuller's work was instrumental in the formulation of German armoured strategy between the wars.

The first real hint of what tanks could achieve came at St Julien on 19 August 1917. An infantry attack had become bogged down, pinned by a nest of well-sited pillboxes. Artillery was unable to shift the obstruction and the infantry commanders thought that if they could be taken at all, it would cost up to a thousand casualties.

Tank assistance was requested, and nine tanks were detailed to make the assault. The armour commander asked for smoke to conceal his advance, but no artillery barrage, which might make the ground impassable. Each tank was assigned an infantry platoon to follow close behind in support. Each platoon was to move in single file behind its tank, thus receiving protection from its armour. After a flanking approach, the composite assault units made their attack. One pillbox was deserted by its garrison as soon as the tanks were sighted. The others put up a fight but the troops inside were killed, driven out or captured for the cost of two British soldiers killed and 27 wounded.

St Julien demonstrated how tanks could achieve decisive results. Striking by surprise without a lengthy artillery preparation, with infantry in support, they could destroy whatever enemy forces they did not simply chase away, and do it for a very low cost in lives. St Julien was a demonstration on a small scale, but something much grander was already being planned.

In June 1917, the administrative commander of the British Tank Corps, Major-General Sir John Capper, visited the headquarters of Elles, who was at that time a brigadier-general. There, Fuller (who was on Elles' staff) presented him with a copy of his paper on how he thought tanks should be employed the following year. Capper was impressed and intrigued, and he and Fuller worked together to plan a massed tank attack between St Quentin and Cambrai.

The area was highly suitable for a tank attack, and a couple of days later Capper presented the paper and his plans to his superiors. At a conference a month later everyone but the chairman of the committee considering the scheme, General Kiggel, was in favour. Kiggel won in the end and the plan was not implemented.

Pillbox

A bunker, or 'pillbox', was a severe obstacle to infantry, and could cost many lives to eliminate. However, without antitank weapons such an emplacement was powerless to prevent the approach of armoured vehicles, which could then eliminate the position with their heavy guns.

At St Julien, this is exactly what happened; a nest of pillboxes was eliminated by armour and infantry operating together, for very few casualties.

The impressive obstacle-clearing capabilities of 'lozenge' tanks are demonstrated here. Sometimes an entire crew was rendered unconscious by the impact when the front end crashed down on the far side.

Fuller then came up with another scheme to use tanks to capture St Quentin, and after some input from Elles the area around Cambrai was chosen instead. Elles fought for the plan all the way to the commander-in-chief, but again Kiggel derailed it.

Yet somehow the idea had taken root, and plans were put in motion for a major operation near Cambrai, to be undertaken in November. Fuller had conceived a large-scale tank raid, but this plan was to be more than that – high command wanted a decisive battle, and the landscape was not suitable for one. Fuller had selected the area because canals on either side would help protect his flanks. This was valuable in a raid, but the same canals would channel a major attack and make it difficult to expand the hole made in the enemy line.

HEAD TO HEAD: *Tank MK A 'Whippet'* VERSUS

The very first tanks were designed to create a breakthrough and needed to be able to cross No-Man's Land in the face of heavy fire. Their role was to destroy machinegun nests and other strong positions and allow infantry to move up. However, soon a need was perceived for light tanks to exploit the breakthrough and get into the enemy rear area. The British Whippet and the French FT17 were two approaches to this concept.

Tank MK A

Crew: 3 or 4
Weight: 14,300kg (31,460lb)
Dimensions: length 6.10m (20ft); width 2.62m (8ft 7in); height 2.74m (9ft)
Range: 257km (160 miles)
Armour: 5–14mm (0.2–0.55in)
Armament: two Hotchkiss machine guns
Powerplant: two 45hp (33.6kW) Tylor four-cylinder petrol engines
Performance: maximum road speed 13.4km/h (8.3mph)

STRENGTHS

- Fast compared to most other tanks
- Good combat range
- Separate fighting and engine compartments

WEAKNESSES

- Light armament
- Limited gun traverse
- Obstacle-crossing inferior to Mk V tank

Renault FT 17

The FT17 was the best French tank of the war – which is not saying much. It was unreliable and awkward to work on, resulting in a lot of vehicles being out of action for maintenance. Despite this, the FT17 was successful, mainly because it was deployed in large numbers. So many were built that some were used by the German army in 1944.

Renault FT 17

Crew: 2
Weight: 6600kg (14,520lb)
Dimensions: length with tail 5m (16ft 5in); width 1.71m (5ft 7.33in); height 2.133m (7ft)
Range: 35.4km (22 miles)
Armour: 16mm (0.63in)
Armament: one machine gun or 37mm (1.45in) gun
Powerplant: one 35hp (26kW) Renault four-cylinder petrol engine
Performance: maximum road speed 7.7km/h (4.4mph)

STRENGTHS

- Turret-mounted weapon
- Small crew (2 men)
- Good armour protection

WEAKNESSES

- Unreliable and hard to maintain
- Slow even compared to breakthrough tanks
- Commander overworked by also acting as gunner

Nor was the timing good for a major battle. All the available infantry reserves had been used up by the third battle of Ypres. A raid was doable; a major breakthrough was beyond the capabilities of the forces available. Nevertheless, the plan was approved and the forces began to assemble.

They faced a formidable task. The ground was open and offered good going for tanks, but the enemy positions were largely situated on reverse slopes. There were three lines of trenches, which had been widened and built up in front and behind to create gaps too wide for tanks to cross. The wire defences were also formidable. Tanks would be able to break through wire without difficulty, but the infantry might struggle.

Crossing these wide trenches was a particular problem for the tanks. The agreed solution went back to an earlier age of warfare, when troops would drop fascines (bundles of sticks) into a ditch or moat to enable them to get siege engines across and up to a castle wall. Each tank was to carry a fascine made from 75 brushwood bundles of the sort used by field engineers to repair roads. They were held together with chains and carried atop the tank, weighing about 10.2 tonnes (10 tons) each.

Some of the tanks were modified for the operation. Thirty-two were fitted with grapnels to catch wire and drag it away. Others would pull sledges loaded with supplies. More important were the tactics to be used: Fuller suggested a doctrine that was used with success by all formations but the 51st Division, whose commander had his own ideas. Fuller's plan was for the tanks to operate in groups of three, advancing in a wedge formation. The 'advanced tank' at the point of the wedge was to suppress the enemy while the other two, the 'main body tanks', would attack the trenches. Each main body tank would have a platoon of infantry in close support and others following behind.

An alternative to sandbags, these wickerwork frames are ready to be filled with earth and arranged as a wall to protect personnel from incoming fire.

Each tank wedge had a specific objective assigned to it, usually a segment of trench. The advanced tank was to break through the wire and then turn left along the parapet of the front trench, moving along it and firing in at the unprotected occupants. The main body tanks would cross at a single point, thus using only one fascine. The left-hand tank would then turn left and move along behind the trench, firing into it while the right-hand tank advanced to the support trench, turned left and made its own attack along the front.

The operational plan was to smash a hole in the enemy line between the two canals and permit cavalry to advance into the enemy rear, where it could exploit the breakthrough in the old style. There would be no lengthy artillery preparation, but smoke would be put down to assist the assault. The initial plan was to hold some tanks in reserve, but in the event all were committed.

Movement up to the battlezone was conducted in great secrecy; so much so that many of the infantry units detailed to take part in the attack did not know the tanks were there. In fact, a great many tanks had arrived. A total of 324 tanks were

Cambrai

One reason for the success at Cambrai was the maintenance of operational security. Getting more than 300 tanks to the front without attracting attention was a considerable feat in its own right.

By this time in the war, it was common to prepare the way for an assault with several days of artillery bombardment. At Cambrai, this practice was not followed, meaning that surprise was achieved. Had the attack been followed up aggressively, a decisive result would have been likely.

assembled for the attack, with 54 in mechanical reserve to replace breakdowns before the start of the operation. There were also 18 supply tanks, 32 tanks converted to drag wire aside, three tanks converted to carry wireless equipment and two carrying bridging material. Army headquarters also had a tank adapted to lay field telephone cables. The attack was led by Brigadier-General Hugh Elles in a tank named *Hilda*. His command tank was at the centre of the line, like a medieval king going to battle on his charger. In a similar manner, Elles displayed his own banner. It was held up by a walking-stick projecting from *Hilda*'s top hatch. The flag was red, brown and green, signifying the intent of the attack and indeed of the Tank Corps in general. They plan was to advance 'through mud and blood to the green fields beyond.'

A brief but savage artillery barrage drove the defenders under cover at 0620 on 20 November 1917, 10 minutes after the tanks had started forward from their positions. Smoke covered the assault as the tanks smashed through the wire and dropped their fascines in the trenches.

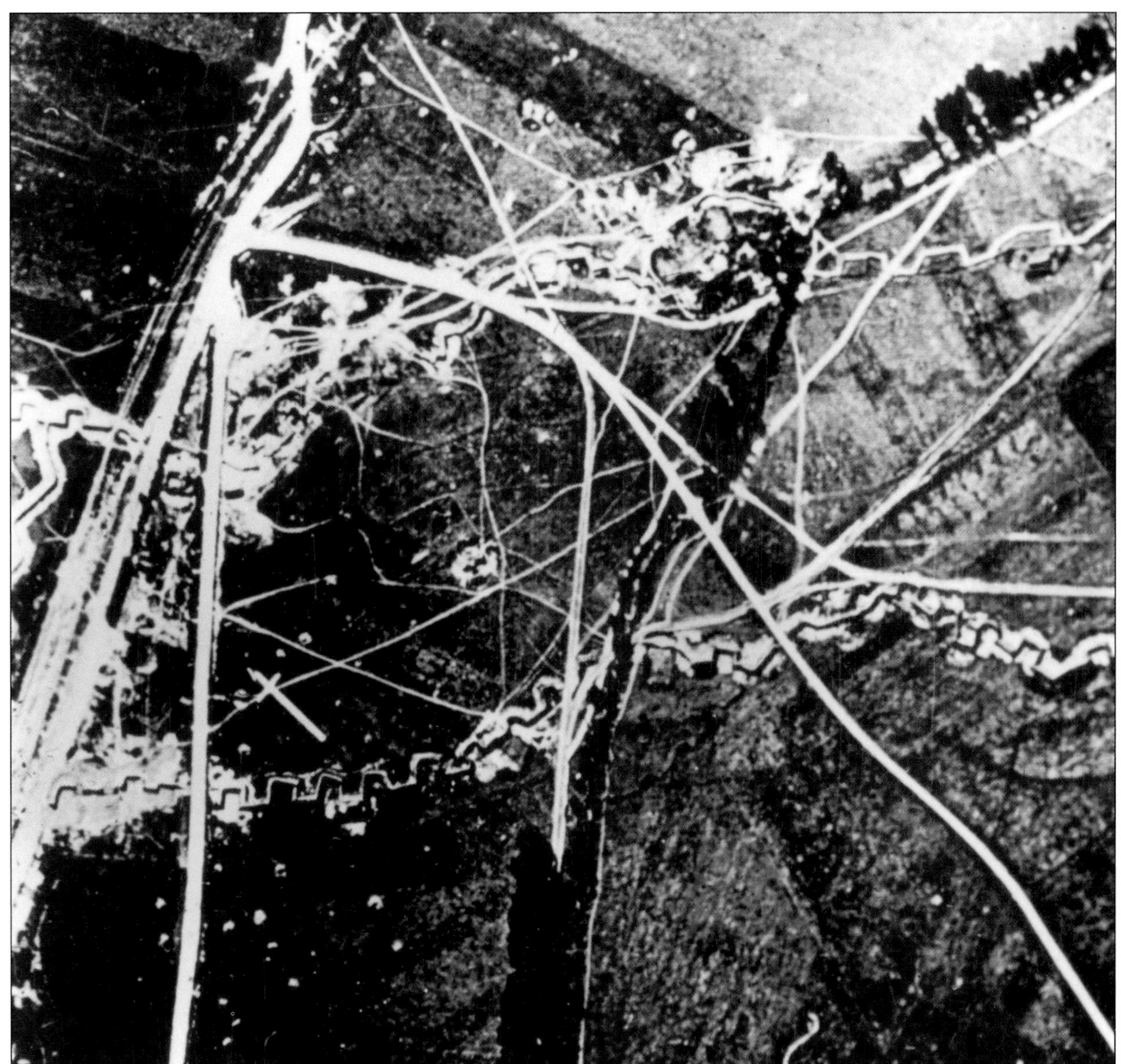

The Hindenburg Line was a well-fortified position adopted by the German army. Aerial reconnaissance revealed concealed secondary positions behind the main line, which would otherwise have surprised assaulting troops.

The prototype 'Little Willie' armoured vehicle proved the concept was viable. A turret was later mounted on top of the hull.

With infantry in close support, the tanks punched through the stunned defenders of the first line, then the second, and finally breached the Hindenburg line in the rear. The tanks had done as planned – for the first time since the beginning of trench warfare, the line was broken and the lead troops could see the 'green fields beyond' the combat zone.

The German high command was stunned and desperate, and began formulating emergency plans for a withdrawal. There was simply no other option; the line had been blasted wide open and reinforcements could not be in the area for three days at least. There was nothing to stop the British from widening the breach, flinging troops through it and shattering the German armies – except that the British had nothing with which to exploit the victory.

The operation at Cambrai succeeded beyond the wildest expectations of the British commanders, but they had failed to plan for success. There was no infantry force in reserve to carry on the advance, and no armoured reserve either. The cavalry were available and had just been presented with a splendid opportunity to validate their existence by bursting through the gap and causing mayhem. But they could not act quickly enough. Perhaps made complacent after years of waiting around behind the lines, cavalry HQ was slow to react and too distant from the front to take rapid advantage of the opportunity. The moment passed before the corps commander could give the order to advance, and so the cavalry missed the best chance to make a difference that it would ever have.

The hammerblow had cost the British 65 tanks from combat damage, 71 broken down and 43 ditched, requiring rescue. Many more were in need of servicing due to wear or minor damage. The crews were wrung out after a day of hard fighting. Renewed attacks were made over the next few days, but tank support was greatly reduced and the assault gradually wound down. The advance that had begun so promisingly eventually returned to stalemate.

A counterattack by German forces on 30 November retook some ground and was doing very well in one sector when the tanks of 2nd Tank Brigade came to the assistance of 1st Guards Brigade, which was holding under severe pressure. The tanks were in the process of being dismantled for train transportation, but were flung back together and sent off into action as fast as they could be readied. The tanks alone did not restore the situation, but the value of an armoured reserve to counterattack a breakthrough was amply demonstrated.

Towards a Modern Doctrine

As 1917 turned to 1918, tank warfare was increasingly seen as the way forward, but there were many questions to be answered. Most important was the question of how best to use tanks, both in offence and defence. The issue of defence in particular was gaining importance, since the Revolution in Russia and the country's subsequent withdrawal from the war presented an advantage to the Germans. Fresh offensives were to be expected, and it was hoped that tanks might offer significant advantages in meeting them.

Once again, it was proposed to disperse the tanks into 'penny packets' along the front, either dug in (and thus effectively doing no more than serving as expensive immobile pillboxes) or hiding in dugouts to rush out as the enemy approached. Each of these 'savage rabbits' would effectively conduct its own armoured counterattack as necessary.

The dispersal had serious consequences. It was simply not possible to maintain or refuel all the tanks while they were scattered about the countryside. By the end of March 1918, more than half the tanks assigned to the frontline to oppose the new German offensive had been lost – about 120 in total – and many of those for the simple reason that they ran out of fuel. Fuller had proposed something very different, of course. He wanted tanks to operate in a concentrated mass, ideally supported by infantry riding in their own armoured vehicles, meaning that they were able to keep up with a breakthrough. Unfortunately, this was a practice that would first be implented only 20 years later.

Although mechanized infantry was a long way off, the arrival of the light tank was a move in the right direction. The British light tank of the day was the Whippet, about half the weight of a Mk IV though almost as well protected. It was designed by William Tritton, and bore a marked resemblance to 'Little Willie', his first design.

Whippets carried four machine guns but no larger weapons, as they were designed for anti-

Mounting the Whippet's armament in a fixed superstructure was technically simpler but limited the tank's firing ability.

personnel work only. Trench and obstacle crossing was not as good as that of the 'lozenge' tanks, and the Whippet's armament had very limited traverse in its solid superstructure. A rotating turret had been planned, but the added complexity was considered undesirable.

The Whippet's main advantages were speed and range: it was twice as fast as a Mk IV and had more than twice the operational radius. It could also be crewed by three men, and driven by just one. Perhaps its greatest contribution to armoured warfare was the creation of separate fighting and engine compartments, which reduced the amount of fumes inhaled by the crew. To date, carbon monoxide poisoning had killed at least as many crew members as enemy action.

The Whippet was designed for armoured exploitation; in other words, it was intended to accomplish the task that cavalry had been given at Cambrai. Moving up behind the 'breakthrough' force, the Whippets would then burst out into the enemy rear to cause maximum havoc. In this, the Whippet was highly successful. In their very first action on 26 March 1918, 12 Whippets routed two entire battalions of German infantry near Colincamps. Whippets were deployed for the battle of Amiens in August 1918, and there the world's first true armoured exploitation was made by a lone Whippet tank, whimsically named *Musical Box.*

The FT17 was more modern than the Whippet, but it was also more of a mobile infantry support vehicle than a tank.

Following up an initial attack by the heavier tanks, *Musical Box* outran them and got into the enemy rear. After smashing an artillery battery, the little tank rampaged around the countryside for 11 hours, shooting up everything it encountered and causing total chaos. Infantry retreating from the main battlezone were attacked, and transport assets were machine-gunned or even rammed to destruction, until finally the Whippet was immobilized and disabled by field artillery. Two of the three crew survived to become prisoners. The Whippet impressed the German Army, and though it never saw combat with them it may have influenced later tank development. Whippets fought in the last tank battle of the war and saw action in Russia as well.

Different Roles

In France, the tank was considered very much an infantry support weapon. After the dismal performance of the initial designs, Colonel Estienne came up with something better. This was the Renault FT-17. It did well in trials in early 1917 and a large order (initially 1000, quickly raised to 4000) was placed.

Early Tank Roles

In 1918, the tank was just beginning to explore its role. Some saw it as a slow-moving gun platform to support infantry while others were becoming aware that tanks could do more than crawl across the trench lines knocking out machinegun posts.
Many thinkers went down the blind alley of considering tanks as 'landships' and trying to operate them as fleets of 'cruiser' and 'battleship' tanks, with light 'frigate' tanks for screening, exploitation and pursuit. This thinking led to a number of highly impractical designs.

The Renault might be considered a forerunner of the armoured assault gun. It was essentially intended as a well-protected mobile artillery emplacement rather than a tank in the sense of those developing in Britain. Despite this, it had what became the classic tank form – a tracked body topped by a rotating turret mounting the main armament. Armament was to be either a single machine gun or a short 37mm (1.45in) gun. A 75mm (2.95in) version was also considered, but was not implemented on a large scale.

The Renault was crewed by two men: a driver and a commander/gunner, the latter who had to load, aim and shoot the main gun himself as well as directing the tank. This doubling up was a drawback, but otherwise the Renault was effective in its intended role. It was protected against small-arms fire and capable of keeping up with advancing infantry, which was all the designers had intended. Renaults saw action at the very end of the war, in an unglamorous but effective role as infantry support vehicles. The design was widely copied all over the world and French Army Renaults served on distant colonial stations for many years. No less than eight battalions of FT-17s were still in service with the French Army in 1940.

The little Renault was built to do a particular job, and did it well. It demonstrated one of the roles that tanks might take and some important concepts of tank design. Its success also worked against the French since it encouraged them to think of tanks as infantry weapons and thus perhaps blinded them to what tanks might be capable of as the arm of decision.

Meanwhile, the forerunner of another armoured vehicle, the tank destroyer, was under development. The appearance of tanks caused great alarm in Germany, and a countermeasure had to be found quickly. Armour-piercing machine-gun bullets, antitank rifles and grenades, and the use of field artillery batteries in direct-fire mode, offered some hope, but there was a need for an armoured vehicle to fight and destroy the enemy tanks as well as one to assault enemy positions as the British were doing so successfully.

One solution to the tank problem was the LK II light tank. The concept was to build a very simple

German A7Vs moving towards the front. Huge, clumsy monsters, these vehicles were very primitive and had numerous defects, including very poor obstacle clearance.

An A7V cresting an obstacle. Low ground clearance often resulted in these huge vehicles becoming stuck.

vehicle based on the chassis of a Daimler car, mounting a 57mm (2.24in) gun in a revolving turret. Two prototypes were built and a variant with twin machine guns was also planned before the war ended. The LK II was a cheap, light, stop-gap weapon unsuited to the role of armoured assault over the trenches. It might have been effective against British tanks, however, by dint of sheer weight of numbers. Although more lightly protected, LK IIs might have been able to launch an armoured counterattack and knock out the enemy spearhead of tanks while the static entrenched defences withstood the infantry assault.

This kind of 'sword and shield' defence has been used successfully since. However, experience has shown that one of the best antitank weapons is another tank. It was not until 1918 that tanks first fought other tanks in battle.

Endgame: Tank vs. Tank

The German Army received a number of captured British tanks that were pressed into service, but it was not until October 1917 that it got one of its own – the A7V Sturmpanzerwagen. Like its British opponents, it was based on a Holt tractor chassis.

The A7V was essentially a huge armoured box containing the powerplant, the crew of 18 men and an armament of up to seven machine guns plus a 57mm (2.24in) gun. It was hard to operate, however, and had many defects. Breakdowns were common and ground clearance was so low that minor obstacles immobilized it. Worst of all, it was a huge target with many weak areas in its armour.

Only 20 A7Vs were delivered. Their replacement would have more closely resembled British tanks, but the war ended before this vehicle, the K-Wagen heavy tank, could be delivered. However, the A7V did make history by participating in the first tank-versus-tank duel.

On 24 April 1918, the German Army was trying to push British and Australian troops from the village of Villiers-Bretonneux. A number of A7Vs and captured British Mk IVs were operating in the area. They had been very successful, breaking the Allied line at several points. The village had been shelled for some time and the situation was perilous, so a section of three British tanks was ordered to join the fight, even though gas had disabled some crew members. The section consisted

Male and Female Tanks

The tank-versus-tank action at Villiers-Bretonneux demonstrated an important concept – tanks must be able to fight other tanks. The British female tanks were unable to do much to the enemy vehicles and were disabled by the heavier guns of the A7V. The male, on the other hand, was a more credible threat to its opponents and succeeded in driving them off, even though its guns did not penetrate the enemy vehicles.

of two female tanks armed only with machine guns and a male with two 6-pounder (57mm/2.24in) guns. The latter was Tank No. 1 of No. 1 Section of A Company, 1st Battalion, Tank Corps.

As the British tanks advanced, they encountered a German A7V. The females were closest and opened fire, but to no effect. While the A7V had many points on its armour that would 'trap' a bullet and assist penetration, or cause 'bullet splash' inside as pieces broke off the inside of the armour and bounced around the fighting compartment, the giant mobile fortress was not seriously harmed. It fought back with its 57mm (2.24in) gun and lighter armament. Both females were disabled.

Meanwhile, Tank No. 1, the male, had worked around to the flank. The A7V's frontal armour was good enough to stop a direct hit from field artillery, provided the range was not too short. From the side, however, the tank made a better and less well-protected target. A direct hit from one of the male's 6-pounders failed to disable the A7V, but caused it to run onto a steep bank and tip over, which had the same effect.

Two more A7Vs then joined the fight. After an exchange of fire, one crew abandoned their vehicle and fled, and the other retired. The engagement was somewhat inconclusive, but it demonstrated a vital need for future tanks – they were going to have to be able to fight other tanks.

The Armistice

Despite the end of the war in 1918, both sides had new tank designs in the pipeline and orders for large numbers of vehicles already placed. Many of these designs were promptly dropped and forgotten about, such as the monstrous breakthrough tanks designed for a German 1919 offensive. Based on British concepts, they were bigger and more heavily armed.

A MK VIII 'International' tank jointly designed for British and American forces.

More advanced British tanks were planned, some with international cooperation. The Mk VIII 'International' was the first ever joint project to build an armoured vehicle. The tank would have served in British and US forces, but only a handful were built by the end of the war. The Mk VIII was a 'lozenge' tank, however, and the days of those were already over. The US 6-Ton Tank, the French Char 2C and the first of Walter Christie's designs all show a move towards the design used by the Whippet or Renault FT-17 – or even the very first tank of all, Little Willie. The days of all-round tracks were ending. Tanks were adopting their modern form; a tracked hull with a turret on top. They had proven their worth and taken their place in the panoply of weapons available to the combatant nations.

Now began 20 years of uneasy peace, a period of evolution before the great armoured struggle of World War II.

THE END OF THE GREAT WAR

As World War I came to a close, large numbers of tanks were on order in Britain, France, and, to a lesser extent, Germany. These orders were cancelled or scaled right back once the need for huge tank offensives was no longer perceived.

The large numbers of tanks already in service meant that new orders were unlikely to be placed. As is the case after all large-scale conflicts, military procurement dropped off rapidly as budgets were cut and the funds turned to rebuilding the peacetime economy. This meant that the armies of Britain and France had large numbers of tanks at the dawn of the 1920s, but these were early designs rushed into mass production as a wartime expedient. Little money was available for the development of replacement designs, and it was inevitable that progress would be slow for a time.

In Germany, all projects were shelved. Denied tanks by the terms of the Armistice, the country was allowed armoured cars, and these were found useful for internal security duties, but German tank development halted in 1918. The abandoned projects included the K-Wagen heavy tank, a very large and powerful 'breakthrough tank' based on British lozenge-shaped vehicles. It was to mount four 77mm (3in) guns and seven machine guns, requiring a crew of 22 men. The K-Wagen was a typical artefact of the war. It was slow-moving but capable of crossing large obstacles and wide trenches, designed to crawl across No-Man's Land and smash a hole in the entrenched positions of the enemy, rather than conduct fast-moving warfare in the open as later German tanks would be intended to do. It did, however, foreshadow the German fascination with super-heavy tanks, which would re-emerge in later years. Moreover, the need to rearm from the ground up when the Armistice was repudiated did allow a more deliberate approach to be made than in nations where large stocks of wartime 'legacy' equipment remained.

Left: A Japanese Type 95 light tank, developed in the 1930s. Japanese armoured vehicles were inferior to Western designs of the same period.

France ended the war with the Renault FT-17 in service. While a decent enough tank this, too, was a concept intended for slow-moving infantry support rather than cavalry-style operations. FT-17s were still in service in the French Army in 1940, and the thinking behind their use had not changed all that much in the previous 20 years.

The French also finished the war with a heavy 'breakthrough' tank design. This was the FCM Char 2C heavy tank, designated a 'Fortress Tank' by the designers. It was driven by a petrol-electric system despite problems with the electric transmission in the earlier St Charmond tank. The Char 2C was the world's very first multi-turreted tank. Multiple turrets became something of a fad in the 1920s and '30s, but the concept was never successful. The Char 2C mounted the usual 75mm (2.95in) gun in the main turret and had a rear turret with a machine gun. There were also three hull-mounted machine guns.

The 75mm (2.95in) guns mounted by French tanks in this period seem impressive compared to the smaller calibre pieces mounted by later designs of other nations, but it must be noted that these were essentially field artillery pieces firing explosive shells to destroy infantry positions, rather than high-velocity penetrators intended to disable tanks. The same is true of the guns carried by the tanks of other nations. The move in Britain, for example, from a converted 6-pounder (57mm/2.24in) naval gun to the smaller guns of the early years of World War II was not really a retrograde step. As tanks moved from being mobile artillery emplacements to track-laying cavalry, they increasingly needed to penetrate hard targets. A smaller projectile, moving fast and well shaped for penetration, was better for this purpose than a simple high-explosive shell. Eventually the mobile-artillery role was assumed by lightly armoured assault guns.

In Britain and the United States, a joint project to produce the Mk VIII 'Liberty' or 'International' tank was cancelled at the end of the war with just eight of the 4500 intended tanks built. A handful of another design, the Mk IX, was built. This machine was not really a tank at all but the first custom-designed armoured personnel carrier (APC). It did not arrive in time to be very useful, but it proved one important concept – the Mk IX was amphibious.

While the Mk VIII was very much a developed version of the World War I tank, two designs under development in Britain showed the beginnings of progress towards something more advanced. The Medium Mk C tank was designed to a specification put forward by tank crews themselves. Two dozen of the design, which had an armoured superstructure built on a semi-lozenge body, were built at the time of the Armistice. This was the last British tank without suspension and had male and female variants with different armament.

The Medium Mk C was promising. It had the range of a Whippet and the speed of a Mk VIII, but was more manoeuvrable. Armour and armament were decent, and best of all it had a crew of only four men, who all rode in the same fighting compartment and could communicate with one another effectively. Five hundred Medium C tanks had been ordered, out of an intended total of 6000 (4000 female and 2000 male). On the day after the ceasefire, however, it was decided that no more tanks would be built but for those already underway. Fuller, by then a general, realized that the Medium C was a decent enough tank, but did not have the cross-country performance he wanted since it lacked suspension.

The Medium D, designed by Lieutenant-Colonel P. Johnson, would deliver what Fuller wanted. Its specifications appeared fanciful: it had to be well armoured but able to climb large obstacles, cross wide trenches and traverse slopes at speed, as well as offer a range of 322km (200 miles). On top of all that, it had to be able to cross a normal bridge and, Fuller decided, should be comfortable for the crew and able to float.

The Medium D's development was funded by the courageous decision to divert money from the construction of Mk Cs and, amazingly, it achieved all that was wanted of it. Fuller was very impressed. He went so far as to propose that the army needed this tank plus only two other designs – one for infantry support and the other a supply carrier. However, although Fuller and a few others like him were proposing a new kind of fast-moving warfare

FM CHAR 2C

Crew: 12
Weight: 69,000kg (152,119lb)
Dimensions: length 10.27m (33ft 8ft); width 2.95m (9ft 8in); height 4m (13ft 1.5in)
Range: 100km (62.1 miles)
Armour: 45mm (1.7in)
Armament: one 75mm (2.95in) gun; four 8mm (0.315in) Hotchkiss MGs
Powerplant: two Daimler or Maybach, 6-cylinder petrol 520hp (388kW) engines
Performance: Maximum speed 12km/h (7.5mph)

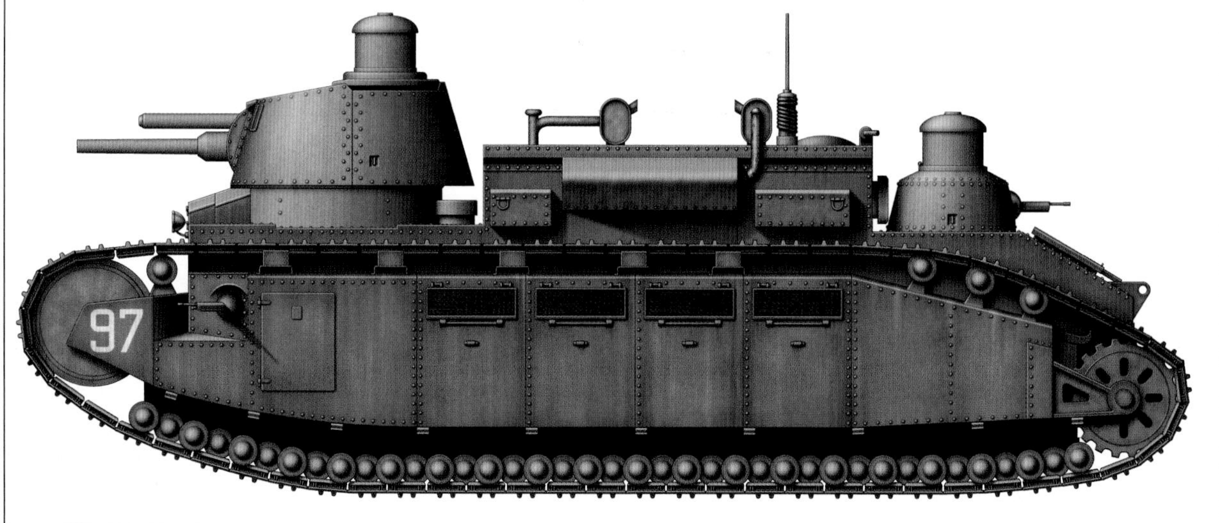

'Lozenge' tanks

A Medium Mark C tank, designed at the very end of the Great War on trials. 'Lozenge' tanks could cope with very large obstacles, but without suspension they were prone to injure their crews by throwing them about inside.

The Mk IX 'tank' was, in fact, an armoured personnel carrier or logistics vehicle.

that used tanks like armoured cavalry, to be followed up and supported by infantry, conventional thinking was expecting a repeat of World War I. The overall experience of that war had been one of trench deadlock, and it was this that was remembered rather than the notion that such deadlock could be broken and mobility restored by tanks.

There was still good work going on in Britain at that time, however. Johnson had been put in charge of the nation's first formal tank design department and given the task of creating a new light tank for the Northwest Frontier and similarly remote theatres. Johnson produced a design and the prototype seemed to deliver everything that could be wanted from it, but for some reason the British government bought a Vickers model without bothering to first consult Fuller, Johnson or anyone else who might have raised objections. Budgetary considerations required that this tank be put into production immediately, and in due course the army received a tank that was a decent enough vehicle but which offered a fighting ability that was unimpressive.

Meanwhile, the Medium Mk D and Light Infantry Tank, as Johnson's design was known, needed more development time to iron out the kinks and turn them into first-rate combat machines. This would have cost money and was vetoed. The tank design department was closed

A US M1921 medium tank undergoing trials in the 1920s – one of several obsolescent US designs of the period.

down and the prototypes destroyed. At a stroke, Britain lost the lead in tank technology.

Faulty Concepts in the 1920s

Although Fuller and a few others were expressing their vision of rapid armoured warfare, smashing through the enemy's lines and causing chaos in the rear, there was still a strong feeling in many nations that the tank was an infantry weapon or a mobile artillery emplacement. The French Army, in particular, followed this view and that in turn influenced many other nations. The French had used tanks in war, as very few nations had done, and they had a lot of them in service, which suggested that they knew their business. The French tank force consisted largely of Renault FT-17s in an infantry support role. Thus it was easy to assume that this was indeed the right way to do things.

French influences were felt in the United States, which abolished its fledgling tank corps in 1920 and established the tank as an infantry weapon. There was, at the time, no suitable tank for this role, though the US military had experience with both light and heavy tanks. US light tank concepts left over from the Great War included the 3-Ton Tank, which was more of a support vehicle than a true tank, and the 6-Ton Tank, which was an Americanized FT-17. These were considered too light for their intended role. Meanwhile, the heavy tank of US experience was the International Mk VIII, which was too big and clumsy for the needs envisaged.

This situation resulted in the decision to investigate medium tanks, and various designs were tried out. The first was the Ordnance M1921 medium tank, armed with a 57mm (2.24in) gun and two machine guns. Although it was not a 'lozenge' tank, this design owed a lot to thinking from World War I. Its secondary machine gun was carried in a second turret and the construction used outdated methods. The M1921 was not up to much and a developed version, designated M1922, was little better. This version was used as the basis for the next incarnation, designated T1. It too was found wanting, and interest in medium tanks waned for a time.

The depth of the identity crisis faced by the tank in the 1920s is clearly shown by the US situation. The infantry had been given the tank, and the cavalry were not allowed to try to develop or obtain one. Thus the curious practice arose of designating cavalry-owned tanks 'combat cars' to get around the prohibition. The US Cavalry evaluated a number of designs and eventually adopted one that suited its needs. The result was the M1 combat car of the mid-1930s, which influenced a number of later designs. After a few years of claiming its tanks were in fact something quite different, the cavalry was able to stop pretending in 1940, when the Armoured Force was created and all tanks were assigned to it.

While the Americans were claiming that some of their tanks were actually 'combat cars', certain other nations regarded them as ships. Ever since the original 'landships' concept, tank development was inspired by nautical thinking. Tank warfare was considered as something akin to naval combat on land, with frigate, cruiser and battle tanks for the reconnaissance, general combat and assault roles respectively. Such thinking was flawed for several reasons, but some of the concepts were retained. The 'cruiser' designation was used in Britain for several years, for example.

The 'landship' idea was taken to an extreme by the idea of the multi-turreted tank. The whole point of turrets was that they gave a weapon all-round capability, so a vehicle could carry less guns and still be effective in combat. It is understandable that early tanks would need several weapon mounts. They were large and awkwardly shaped, and needed to defend themselves from infantry assault with secondary armament while attacking targets with their main guns. However, as tanks moved towards their classic form of a low hull with an armoured turret on top, there was little need to festoon every vehicle with weaponry.

Multi-turreted tanks were something of a fad in the interwar years. The saner versions had only two turrets, but designs with up to five were put into production.

The idea of a multi-turreted land-battleship, blazing away in all directions with a weapon for every occasion, must have appealed to a lot of designers because there was a positive fad for such designs. The first was a French tank appearing at the end of World War I, and others followed.

The A1E Independent Tank from Vickers, seemed like a good idea on paper: while the E stood for Experimental, the name 'Independent' implied an ability to conduct single-tank warfare and achieve great things on the battlefield. Appearing in 1925, this tank had several features that were advanced for their time. Indeed, its layout is remarkably similar to that of modern tanks: engine at the back of the low hull, driver at the front and the crew in a central fighting compartment. However, in other ways the A1E was rather flawed. It needed a crew of eight to man the five turrets, which held a 37mm (1.45in) gun and four machine guns, and coordinating all these people and weapons was a challenge. The turrets and their occupants pushed weight and hull size up, which in turn affected performance. The A1E was not the all-powerful force its designers had hoped it to be.

Russia obtained a few foreign machines at the end of the war, but did not begin to develop tanks of its own until the late 1920s. There, too, the multi-turret bug had bitten. Along with some rather poor conventional machines, the Soviet design bureaus came up with the T-28 medium tank. This was the first Soviet attempt at a medium tank and in some ways it was a decent enough vehicle. It was mobile cross-country and despite its unsophisticated appearance the suspension worked well to create a good firing platform. Once again, however, the T-28 had too many turrets. Two on the bows contained machine guns (in some early versions, one of them mounted a 45mm/1.7in gun instead) and the main turret contained a short 76mm (2.99in) gun and a third machine gun pointing backwards. This was a lot of firepower, but operating it required jamming a crew of six into a medium tank hull.

Aside from crew numbers, control issues and the difficulty of bringing the right weapons to bear, the extra turrets, guns and crew added to the vehicle's weight. The subsidiary turrets needed armouring, which also added to the weight that must be propelled by the engine.

The end result of this was a tank that was both slow and underprotected. T-28s suffered badly against the Finns during the Winter War of 1939–41, even though the Finnish Army was very short of antitank weapons. The survivors were pushed into the breach to fight the German invasion in 1941, but achieved very little against the altogether better tanks fielded by the *Wehrmacht.*

In 1935, the same year that the T-28 was beginning its career of underachievement, the Soviets produced another multi-turreted tank. This was the impressive-looking T-35 heavy tank, a true 'land battleship' equipped with no less than five weapon turrets. The main turret mounted a short 76mm (2.99in) gun. It was surrounded by four smaller turrets, two mounting 45mm (1.7in) guns and two with machine guns. The bigger guns were placed at opposite corners of the square made by the turrets, with the machine guns on the other corners so that one 45mm (1.7in) and one machine-gun turret could bear in any direction.

Despite this apparently impressive armament, the T-35 was a very poor tank. It required a crew of no less than 11 men, making it hard to control. It was also prone to break down, it was slow and difficult to drive, and on top of all that its armour was entirely inadequate. Although T-35s looked good in Red Square parades, their combat value was negligible. As an AFV, the T-35 failed in all areas – it was poorly protected and not much good in a fight even if it could get to the battle area. It is likely that its operators knew the inadequacy of the tank. It was in production for five years, in which time only 61 were built. This was plenty to impress people with on May Day, and in reality there was no other use for this tank.

Yet the multi-turret mania would not go away. The final folly was another Soviet heavy tank, designated T-100. Its original specification called for five turrets, but this was reduced to three and finally two. The front turret mounted a 45mm (1.7in) gun on a low-mounted turret, superfired by the main armament in its own turret. This was a short 75mm (2.95in) gun. There were, of course, three machine guns as well.

T-28 MEDIUM TANK

Crew: 6
Weight: 28,509kg (62,720lb)
Dimensions: length 7.44m (24ft 4.8ft); width 2.81m (9ft 2.75in); height 2.82m (9ft 3in)
Range: 220km (137 miles)
Armour: 10–80mm (0.39–3.15in)
Armament: one 76.2mm (3in) gun; three 7.62mm (0.315in) MGs
Powerplant: one 500hp (373kW) V-12 petrol engine
Performance: maximum road speed 37lm/h (23mph)

The T-100 design was accompanied by a very similar machine, with the same turret layout and more or less the same armament but for an additional machine gun. This was the SMK heavy tank. Both the SMK and T-100 needed a crew of seven, but at least they were better protected than the T-35. All the same, the prototypes performed very poorly in combat trials, and after an attempt to use the T-100 hull as a mount for a 130mm (5.1in) naval gun, both designs were scrapped. With their demise, the multi-turret concept was finally laid to rest.

Another flawed 1920s concept was the idea that if a tank could be made small and fast, it would be very difficult to hit and thus would need only very light armour. This appealed for cost reasons, and thus was born the idea of the tankette.

Tankettes were one- or two-man vehicles with light armour and an armament of one or sometimes two machine guns. A number of variations on this theme were tried, including some curious-looking half-tracked vehicles such as those invented by the then Major Martell. Tankettes aroused interest for several reasons. Some nations felt they were a reasonable substitute for tanks, others considered them for a reconnaissance role. Never viable as a true combat vehicle, tankettes nevertheless went into production in several countries.

Soviet multi-turreted tanks included the T-100, which was sent to fight in Finland in the Winter War in 1939.

Bren Carrier

The Universal Carrier was developed from the Carden-Loyd tankette and was used in vast numbers as a radio vehicle, personnel carrier, ambulance, artillery tractor, logisitics vehicle – and a mobile machinegun carrier, from which it derived its more famous name, the Bren Carrier. Versions also saw service with antitank guns or mortars carried aboard.

Thus one of the most useful military vehicles of all time was developed from a badly flawed concept; tankettes were almost completely worthless on the battlefield.

British Vickers Mk 6 light tanks on exercise. Within a few years, tanks would become less high-sided and block-like.

The tankette concept was explored by two British civilians, Messrs Carden and Loyd, who built an all-tracked-topped machine-gun carrier. It was a better concept than most tankettes – a mobile infantry support vehicle rather than a tank. These 'machine-gun carriers' went into production in 1927 and were exported to several countries.

The 'Carden-Loyd' found a role for itself as a weapons carrier armed with a machine gun or mortar, as a tractor for light artillery or antitank guns, and as a general utility vehicle. Some armies used it as a miniature tank. In any serious conflict, it would have suffered terribly in this role, but as a peacetime security vehicle or a means of gaining experience of armoured operations it was a big success. Later vehicles such as the Bren Carrier were heavily influenced by the Carden-Loyd, which seemed to have found its niche. It is notable that tankettes as true combat vehicles passed away quickly once they were forced to fight in a real war. Some tankettes were used in World War II, for example by the Polish Army. They performed as poorly as might be expected.

New Technologies For The 1930s

Towards the end of the 1920s, tank development was proceeding at a slow pace in most nations. In Britain, Vickers-Armstrong had produced a series of medium tanks. The Mk I was the first tank to mount its main armament in a turret that both rotated and elevated. Designed for service in remote areas, which might include the deserts and barren terrain that formed much of British overseas territories, the Mk I Medium was air-cooled rather than water-cooled, but this was not a very successful concept.

Christie M1931

The Christie M1931 Medium Tank was a big improvement on earlier designs, using Walter Christie's suspension system. Although some components were unreliable, its advanced suspension allowed it to move fast over rough ground and deal with very difficult terrain. The world-beating T-34 could trace its lineage back to this tank, as could some British tank designs.

Christie Suspension System

Starting with a tank designated T3 or M1928, Walter Christie developed a family of tanks with vastly improved suspension compared to contemporary models. Christie used large bogie wheels, which were mounted on individually sprung bell cranks. Curiously, Christie's tanks were designed to run on wheels with their tracks removed as well as with them fitted. This allowed higher speeds on good roads and might have had benefits for strategic mobility, but the idea never really caught on.

Next came the Mk II Medium, which was the first 'fast tank' in the world. Capable of 48km/h (30mph) flat out, the Mk II was lightly armoured and somewhat mediocre as a combat vehicle. It was followed by the Mk III Medium, which was known as the '16-tonner' even though it weighed a little more than that. The Mk III was, like its predecessors, lightly armoured, though it was also fast. Armament consisted of a 3-pounder gun in the main turret and two machine guns in subsidiary turrets. Multi-turret madness had returned, as a result of the influence of the 'Independent'. The Mk III did have some of the Independent's better features, such as stability and cross-country performance. The main problem with this design was that it was expensive. As the world's economies nose-dived, budgets were cut and only the prototypes were built.

Interest in light tanks was at this time considerable, perhaps in part because they were cheap. The British model of note was the Vickers-Armstrong '6-Ton' tank. The design influenced American thinking and found favour in several countries, including the Soviet Union, Finland, Bulgaria, Romania, China and Thailand. It was exported widely overseas and copied in some nations, but in Britain there was no money for tanks and the design was not picked up by the military.

In the United States, however, money was available. The military was looking for a light tank design that could be carried on a standard 5.1-tonne (5-ton) truck. This specification resulted in a light tank designated T1 and referred to as a 'Combat Car' – remember, the US Cavalry was not allowed to develop or have tanks. It was a little heavy at 6.8 tonnes (6.7 tons) but it was a reasonable effort, armed with a 37mm (1.45in) gun and a machine gun. However, its armour was light and its performance sluggish for a light tank.

The T1 was not taken into service, but it was the basis for some experimentation which, if nothing else, showed weaknesses that a new design must avoid. This new design was the revolutionary T3, designed by J. Walter Christie. Christie had produced a design as early as 1919, which could run on wheels or tracks. Yet the early days of peace after World War I were not fertile ground for new tank designs, and after a half-hearted look over the design the US military took no further interest.

The T3, also designated M1928 or 'Convertible', was a second attempt to create a tank that could run on wheels as well as tracks. It could be converted between the two modes in the field, but more importantly it was the first vehicle to use the Christie suspension system. This used individually sprung bogie wheels to allow each wheel to react to an obstacle as it reached it, rather than the whole track assembly reacting. The Christie suspension greatly smoothed out the ride the tank crew experienced, enabling tanks to manoeuvre at higher speeds than before and giving at least a vague chance for a hit when firing on the move. The T3 was a 'technology demonstrator' rather than a combat design. When an impressed military made an offer to purchase it, the designer refused and a project to produce a fighting tank was implemented, using a developed version of the M1928 as its basis.

Christie's M1931 design had teething troubles, including engine defects, but it was bought by the US military, which took it into infantry service as the T3 medium tank. Identical vehicles went to the cavalry as T1 (Christie) Combat Cars, creating some confusion with earlier designs using a very similar designation. The infantry tank was armed with a 37mm (1.45in) cannon and the cavalry combat car with a machine gun. The initial model was followed by an improved version designated T3E2, with better armour, an improved engine and more machine guns. The T3E2 was faster than the basic design and could reach 97km/h (60mph) on wheels. Christie tended to tinker with designs even when they were in production, making adjustments and improvements along the way. One slightly adapted version was bought by the British and two by the USSR, influencing tank development in both countries. The first Soviet Christie-based tank was the BT-2, a mobile and fast, if unreliable, little tank with a crew of three. It was originally

The Christie suspension system allowed for much greater speeds, which in turn enabled tanks not only to leave the ground but return to it with their crews still conscious.

armed with a machine gun, but quickly gained a 37mm (1.45in) gun. After some experimental models, the Soviets produced the BT-5, using versions of the Christie suspension and the M1931's Liberty engine.

The BT-5 was a good tank, and its resemblance to later Soviet battle tank designs is not coincidental. It was the forerunner of the T-34 and served with distinction in the Spanish Civil War (1936–39) as well as against the Japanese in Manchuria. Armed with a 45mm (1.7in) gun and a machine gun, armour was light but the tank was very fast, robust and effective in action.

The Rise of the Panzer Divisions

It was not until 1926 that Germany began to work towards developing an armoured force of its own. In some ways this was an advantage. Having no large stocks of 'legacy' equipment left over from the last war, there was no temptation to create a doctrine to suit what was available. Instead, the German military could decide what it wanted its tanks to do and develop designs to suit that need.

Tank experiments began in 1926, at a secret location in Russia and with the agreement of the Soviet government. Within two years, there were two experimental types under testing: a light tank with a 37mm (1.45in) gun and a medium tank with a short 75mm (2.95in) gun as its main armament. There were about 10 tanks in all.

Experiments in armoured warfare were undertaken more openly elsewhere, using mock-up tanks based on civilian wheeled vehicles. These caused little alarm, which might not have been the case had the world known that Germany was developing a tank force to make use of the findings of these exercises.

General Guderian

General Heinz Guderian, one of the foremost exponents of tank warfare in the interwar years and author of the classic *Achtung – Panzer!*. Guderian was an extremely successful panzer general in the World War II, where his theories were proven correct.

There was still no consensus on how tanks should be organized and used, and the practice of scattering them around infantry formations was common. However, the British took a step in the right direction with the formation of the Experimental Armoured Force (EAF) in 1927, and no doubt the German Army watched with interest. The EAF was built around a battalion, three companies strong, of Vickers Mk II Medium tanks. A second armoured battalion comprised a company

HEAD TO HEAD: *Vickers Light Tank* VERSUS

Light tanks were popular in the interwar years for several reasons. They were cheap, allowing a nation to establish a tank force for relatively little cost and to gain experience in armoured operations on a large scale. Their combat value was not great, though they proved useful for reconnaissance and infantry support in difficult terrain. The Vickers Light Tank was based on the Carden-Loyd tankette and was a decent reconnaissance vehicle but a failure on the battlefield.

Vickers Light Tank

Crew: 3
Weight: 4877kg (10,729lb)
Dimensions: length 3.96m (13ft); width 2.08m (6ft 10in); height 2.235m (7ft 6in)
Range: 201km (215 miles)
Armour: 10–15mm (0.4–0.6in)
Armament: one Besa 7.92mm (0.3in) MG; one Besa 15mm (0.6in) MG
Powerplant: one Meadows ESTL six-cylinder petrol engine developing 88hp (66kW)
Performance: maximum road speed 51.5km/h (32mph); fording 0.6m (2ft)

STRENGTHS

- Capable of carrying a radio
- Inexpensive to produce
- Reliable under most conditions

WEAKNESSES

- Thin armour
- Tracks prone to breakage
- Light armament

BT-5

The BT-5 was developed from Christie tanks bought by the Soviet Union. It had the ability to run on wheels rather than tracks, though this was not a very useful feature. More importantly, the Soviets gave their tank a 45mm (1.7in) gun and good protection for its size. Coupled with good general reliability and excellent mobility, this created the best tank of its type in the interwar period.

BT-5

Crew: 3
Weight: 11,700kg (25,794lb)
Dimensions: length 5.48m (18ft); width 2.23m (7ft 4in); height 2.2m (7ft 3in)
Range: 200km (124 miles)
Armour: 6–13mm (0.236–0.51in)
Armament: one 45mm (1.7in) Model 1932 gun, one 7.62mm (0.3in) DT MG
Powerplant: one M-5 12-cylinder 350bhp (261kW) petrol engine
Performance: Maximum speed 70km/h (43mph)

STRENGTHS

- Christie Suspension
- 45mm (1.7in) main gun
- Robust and reliable

WEAKNESSES

- Thin armour
- Outmatched by 1941 designs

LEICHTTRAKTOR VK-31

Crew: 2 or 3
Weight: approx 9650kg (21,275lb)
Dimensions: length 4.32m 914ft 2in); width 2.26m (7ft 5in); height 2.27m (7ft 5.4in)
Range: no data available
Armour: 14mm (0.55in)
Armament: one 37mm (1.45in) gun; one 7.92mm (0.312in) MG
Powerplant: one 100hp (74.5kW) petrol engine
Performance:maximum speed 35km/h (21.75mph)

of tankettes and two companies of armoured cars. The Armoured Force, to which its name was quickly changed, was a combined-arms formation. The infantry component was a motorized machine-gun battalion and there was a regiment of artillery, some of it self-propelled.

After a year of experimentation, the Armoured Force was broken up in 1928. It reappeared in 1931 as the 1st Armoured Brigade, but this was not the same kind of force. It was instead a grouping of four armoured battalions into an all-tank brigade. However, the idea of an all-arms force based around tanks had been demonstrated, and even though the British were not pursuing the idea the German Army decided to do so.

The first permanent armoured division anywhere in the world was created in 1934 by the French. This was the *Division Légère Mécanique* and was built around a tank brigade, supported by three 'dragoon' battalions, comprising motorized infantry and a company of light tanks. There were also artillery and armoured reconnaissance regiments. The formation had a lot of promise, but was never used in a manner recommended by Fuller or by Basil Liddel Hart, another great British exponent of armoured warfare.

French military planners also created the *Division Cuirassée,* a heavy armoured formation with four battalions of heavy tanks and two of motorized infantry. A reorganization later reduced the capabilities of this formation, and in any case it was still an infantry-centric force designed to support an attack by footsoldiers rather than to make an armoured assault with infantry support.

The British had pioneered the tank and both Liddel Hart and Fuller had expounded at great length about what should be done with it, but now the most important developments were taking place in a country that was not even allowed to possess tanks at all.

The German general Heinz Guderian expounded his own ideas in various publications, of which his work *Achtung – Panzer!* is the most famous. He agreed with Fuller and Liddel Hart that tanks should be concentrated to strike hard, smash a hole in the enemy's line and get into the rear to cause maximum damage. He also believed that tanks needed to be supported by fast-moving infantry and artillery. Having created a doctrine for tanks, Germany now needed to develop the vehicles to implement it.

Early experiments included the Leichttraktor VK-31 and Grosstraktor 1. The former was a light tank armed with a 37mm (1.45in) gun. It was ordered in slightly different variants for evaluation

Within a few years of developing a tank force, German designers began working on huge vehicles like the Grosstraktor 1.

purposes. Orders for a few hundred were placed, but later cancelled as better designs became available. The Grosstraktor 1 project was intended to provide the German Army with a heavy tank. Designs from various manufacturers were solicited. One was amphibious, another was to have had two turrets. The main mounting was to carry a 75mm (2.95in) low-velocity gun with little antitank capability and a coaxial machine gun, or a 105mm (4.1in) howitzer as a variant. The rear turret was for vehicle defence and contained a machine gun. There was another one mounted on the hull.

The Grosstraktor 1 harked back to World War I in more ways than its multiple armament. It had all-round tracks as well, though the hull was a lot lower than the lozenge tanks of a decade before. The project was terminated in 1933, in favour of a new attempt, the Neubaufarzeuge V and VI heavy tank designs.

The new heavy tank was another multi-turret machine, with a main armament of either coaxial 75mm (2.95in) and 37mm (1.45in) guns or a 105mm (4.1in) howitzer, superfiring two small turrets (one in front and one behind the main

Battle Tanks

The PzKpfw I should never have been used in combat. However, the need for tanks in sufficient numbers meant that designs had to be pushed into roles they were not designed for. There were not enough Panzer III combat tanks and Panzer IV fire support tanks available, so the Panzer II, which was really a reconnaissance vehicle, and the Panzer I, which was to have been used for driver training, were both elevated to the status of battle tanks. This diluted the fighting power of the panzer divisions somewhat but ensured that there were enough of them to make a difference. With intelligent and aggressive handling, the lighter tanks could still contribute, dealing with personnel targets and distracting attention from the heavier tanks. Against primarily infantry forces the lighter tanks were entirely adequate.

mount) each containing a machine gun. A handful of prototypes were built, using mild steel instead of high-grade armour. None of the designs were taken up by the military, though the prototypes remained in service long enough to take part in fighting in Norway in 1940.

Developing a workable battle tank was taking time, and in the interim the German government decided that a light tank would be designed and built as a training machine. This was the Panzerkampfwagen (PzKpfw) I, whose prototypes began testing in 1934. Panzerkampfwagen translates to English more or less as 'armoured fighting vehicle', the term by which modern tanks are properly known.

The PzKpfw I was not intended as a serious combat vehicle and, in keeping with its training role, many of the initial machines had no turrets as they were simply driver-training platforms. The PzKpfw I Ausf ('model') A suffered from a number of teething troubles and an enlarged Ausf B design was created soon afterwards.

The PzKpfw I was armed only with a pair of machine guns in its small turret, and despite the original intentions of the designers it was built in large numbers. More than 6000 of the standard combat model, Ausf B, were built, along with a number of variants that included specialist reconnaissance units, command tanks and an infantry support vehicle. The chassis was used as a base for the world's first tank-destroyer and an air defence tank. Although the PzKpfw I was never intended for combat, it was there when tanks were needed in large numbers, and was pressed into service to fill out the Panzer divisions in the first 18 months or so of the war. The model was withdrawn as soon as sufficient replacements became available.

PZKPFW I

Crew: 2
Weight: 5893kg (12,992lb)
Dimensions: length 4.42m (14ft 6in); width 2.06m (6ft 9in); height 1.72m (5ft 8in)
Range: 153km (95 miles)
Armour: 13mm (0.51in)
Armament: two 7.92mm (0.3in) MGs
Powerplant: one 100hp (74.5kW) Maybach NL38TR, 6-cylinder petrol engine
Performance: Maximum speed 40km/h (24.8mph)

The Panzer divisions of the early months of World War II were predominantly armed with PzKpfw Is and another light tank design, designated PzKpfw II. At 7.6 tonnes (7.5 tons) initially, increasing by 2.03 tonnes (2 tons) as more armour was added, this machine was a fair bit heavier than the PzKpfw I. It also differed in that it was intended from the outset to go to war.

The PzKpfw II was envisaged as a light armoured reconnaissance vehicle rather than a battle tank, and mounted a 20mm (0.78in) gun coaxial with a machine gun. In keeping with its intended role, its armour was light. Despite this, the tank was effective in the light combat role, and almost 2000 were built, including variants that featured a bridgelayer and a flamethrower.

Panzer IIs. Primarily a reconnaissance vehicle, the PzKpfw II was forced to become the backbone of the German forces.

Creating A Tank Arm

With no stocks of legacy equipment from the Great War, Germany was forced to gain experience of armoured warfare using armoured cars and mock-up tanks. However, this did allow the creation of a custom-designed tank force rather than an evolution of existing designs. The first step was to build large numbers of simple, light training tanks while more combat-worthy models were under development. The resulting PzKpfw I was intended as a training vehicle but ended up in the front line.

The tank that came to be designated PzKpfw IV was ordered in 1936, before the PzKpfw III. This was a medium tank with good armour, armed with a short 75mm (2.95in) gun. It was intended for fire support, but became one of the mainstays of the Panzer divisions, with various models serving right through the war. Germany's allies received many of these tanks, and large numbers were used for ad-hoc conversions to fit a local need. The PzKpfw IV gained a longer gun and more armour as the war went on, and variants appeared that included powerful tank destroyers. It was a very effective and serviceable vehicle that remained a credible threat to Allied tanks right to the end of hostilities. It was the most numerous of all German tanks, with more than 9000 built.

Ordered in 1937, after the IV with which it had a lot in common, the PzKpfw III was originally intended to be a light combat tank, offering strengths that complemented the PzKpfw IV. However, during development the III grew from 15.2 tonnes (15 tons) to 19.8 tonnes (19.5 tons) and became a more powerful combat vehicle. Early

HEAD TO HEAD: *Panzer II Light Tank* VERSUS

The Panzer II was the standard German light tank at the outbreak of World War II and was better suited to armoured reconnaissance than the combat role. Handled with dash and aggression it gave good service.

Panzer II

Crew: 3
Weight: 10,000kg (22,046lb)
Dimensions: length 4.64m (15ft 3in); width 2.30m (7ft 6.5in); height 2.02m (6ft 7.5in)
Range: 200km (125miles)
Armour: (Ausf version) 20–35mm (0.8–1.38in)
Armament: one 20mm cannon; one 7.92mm machine gun
Powerplant: one Maybach six-cylinder petrol engine devleoping 140hp (104kW)
Performance: maximum road speed 55km/h (34mph); fording 0.85m (2ft 10in); vertical obstacle 0.42m (1ft 5in); trench 1.75m (5ft 9in)

STRENGTHS

- Available in large numbers
- Good armour for a light tank
- Easily converted to other roles

WEAKNESSES

- Forced into a role it was not suited for
- Obsolete by 1943
- 20mm gun had limited antitank capability

7TP

The best Polish tank at the time of the 1939 invasion was the 7TP, based on a British design from Vickers. Versions armed with two machine guns or with a 37mm (1.45in) gun were fielded. The 7TPs put up a good fight but there were too few of them to make much difference.

7TP

Crew: 3
Weight: 9550kg (21,054lb)
Dimensions: length 4.6m (15ft 1in); width 2.16m (7ft 1in); height 2m (6ft 7in)
Range:160km (100 miles)
Armour: 5-17mm (0.197-0.67in)
Armament: one 37mm (1.45in) gun and one 7.92mm (0.312in) MG, or two 7.92mm (0.312in) MGs
Powerplant: one Saurer 110bhp (82kW) 6-cylinder diesel engine
Performance: maximum speed 32km/h (20mph)

STRENGTHS

- 37mm (1.45in) gun
- Good armour on later versions
- Diesel engine reduced flammability

WEAKNESSES

- Insufficient numbers available
- Early versions had two turrets
- Obsolescent design

models were subject to a variety of problems, and the version that went into mass production was the Ausf E, followed by the F.

The PzKpfw III borrowed a number features from the PzKpfw II. Its turret was an enlarged version mounting a 37mm (1.45in) gun and a coaxial machine gun. Another machine gun was mounted in the hull. Armour was lighter than that of the PzKpfw IV, but battlefield experience resulted in heavier armour as well as other modifications. A 50mm (1.97in) gun replaced the 37mm (1.45in) from the Ausf G model onwards. Although this was a design that was updated frequently, the PzKpfw III eventually fell behind Allied tanks and antitank equipment and it was therefore phased out of the battle tank role. The chassis was well regarded, however, and so a host of variants and conversions emerged right up to the end of the war.

These four designs equipped the Panzer divisions of the first part of World War II. As has been noted, much of the Panzer strength that rampaged across Europe was made up of thin-skinned and lightly armed vehicles suitable, on paper at least, only for armoured reconnaissance. What made them so effective was the combination of tactics, training and aggressive handling that became the hallmark of the German armoured forces.

The first tank battalion was formed in Germany in 1934, at a time when the only tank in

Heavily armoured, the Panzer IV was intended as a fire-support tank but evolved into a Main Battle Tank.

production was the PzKpfw I. A year later, as the PzKpfw II became available, there were three armoured divisions in existence. These were not at their projected strength and were mainly equipped with the PzKpfw I. A 1935 Panzer division was spearheaded by a tank brigade. This contained two Panzer regiments, each of two battalions. The infantry component comprised a motorized infantry brigade. The supporting artillery regiment was also motorized and, significantly, there was an antitank battalion assigned to each Panzer division.

Expansion was rapid from this point. In late 1937, a showpiece operation was mounted as part of army manoeuvres that involved 800 tanks. The principle of close air support was also demonstrated, with 400 aircraft taking part in the exercise. By 1938, there were six armoured divisions, and other armoured formations were appearing.

In 1937, the German Army created a tactical formation known as a light brigade, which included some tanks. It was soon expanded and redefined as a light division, and three more were created in 1938. The composition of these forces varied, though they were all built around a core comprising a battalion of tanks and four of motorized infantry.

As the political situation deteriorated and general war in Europe threatened, the German military was to some extent going out on a limb. It was spending a lot of time and money creating a combat arm that was essentially untried. Early tanks had been successful in action, but armoured warfare was still in its infancy. Germany was staking a lot on its Panzer divisions and there was no guarantee that Fuller, Guderian or any of the other advocates of armoured warfare were correct.

The outbreak of the Spanish Civil War in 1936 provided a live-fire opportunity to test some of the concepts of tank warfare, as well as the vehicles themselves. Germany supported the Nationalist faction in Spain and sent them assistance in the form of the Condor Legion. This included 120 PzKpfw I tanks.

The PzKpfw I performed well enough in Spain, though it was badly outmatched by more combat-worthy designs such as the Soviet BT-5. It was found to be inadequately protected for a combat role and lacked a heavy enough armament. This was hardly surprising, given that the vehicle was never intended to fight. Some PzKpfw I tanks were refitted with 20mm (0.78in) guns, though the added weight reduced performance considerably.

German involvement in the Spanish Civil War provided a great deal of experience of modern warfare, albeit a confused and messy sort of war, as civil conflicts tend to be. The understanding gained

PZKPFW III

Crew: 5
Weight: 19,500kg (42,990lb)
Dimensions: length 5.38m (17ft 4.5in); width 2.91m (9ft 11in); height 2.44m (7ft 12in)
Range: 165km (103 miles)
Armour: 30mm (1.18in)
Armament: one 37mm (1.45in) gun; two 7.92mm (0.312in) MGs
Powerplant: one Maybach 300hp (224kW) petrol engine
Performance: maximum speed 40km/h (25mph)

Renault R-35

A column of French Renault R-35 light tanks. Designed as a replacement for the venerable FT-17, the R-35 was similar in concept. It was an 'infantry' tank intended to act as a fire support platform rather than make sweeping armoured attacks. Thus its speed was low but armour was sufficiently good that the standard 37mm (1.45in) antitank gun of the period could not penetrate its forward arc. The R-35 was the most numerous French tank at the time of the 1940 invasion, and a great many were captured by the German army. Some were used to make up numbers in the Panzer divisions.

The remainder of the R-35 tanks were converted to a range of roles, including tank destroyers, artillery tractors and training vehicles.

of trying to operate a tank force under actual combat conditions was invaluable, and in this the PzKpfw I fulfilled the intentions of its designers – it was created to enable Germany to gain experience of armoured operations, and that is what it did.

The Road To War

Europe was a volatile place in the late 1930s, and it was becoming obvious that those nations that had not yet begun to re-arm in earnest needed to do something, and fast. In France, there were several battalions of FT-17s still in service and even a handful of 1918-vintage Char 2Cs. In the first days of the German invasion of France in the summer of 1940, the latter would be destroyed while still entrained and achieved nothing.

French tank design had languished in the 1920s and early '30s, and the theory of tank operations had not advanced at all. The 1931 vintage Char D1 was an infantry support tank. It had a cast steel turret, which was advanced for its time, and a 47mm (1.85in) gun capable of penetrating any contemporary design. However, it was a poor design with many mechanical faults and, more importantly, it was designed as an infantry weapon – in contrast to the Panzers being created just over the border.

Another infantry support tank emerged in 1935. This was the Renault R-35 and was intended to replace the venerable FT-17 in a similar role. It mounted a 37mm (1.45in) gun and was well armoured, though slow. Its speed, however, was not considered a disadvantage considering the tank was supposed to accompany infantry.

Tank production began to be seen as critically important in France, and large orders were placed.

CHAR B1 HEAVY TANK

Crew: 4
Weight: 31,500kg (69,446lb)
Dimensions: length 6.37m (20ft 10.7in); width 2.5m (8ft 2.4in); height 2m (9ft 1.8in)
Range: 180km (112 miles)
Armour: 60mm (2.36in)
Armament: one 75mm (2.95in) gun; one 47mm (1.85in) gun; two 7.5mm (0.3in) MGs
Powerplant: 300hp (224kW) Renault 6-cylinder petrol engine
Performance: maximum speed 28km/h (17.4mph)

It may be that the wrong tanks were ordered; some 1100 R-35s were constructed and delivered before the outbreak of war, but there were only a little over 400 SOUMA S-35s in existence.

The S-35 was designed by the Société d'Outillage Mécanique et d'Usinage d'Artillery (SOUMA), and was a very good tank. It was the first to have both a cast hull and turret, and had sloped armour faces that helped deflect incoming fire and increased the effective thickness of the tank's armour. The S-35's 47mm (1.85in) gun and coaxial machine gun were mounted in an electrically powered turret, while speed and mobility were both good. The S-35 had a few drawbacks, but overall it was a solid design with the capability to put up a decent fight. Unfortunately there were not enough of them in the French battle area to make much difference, and those that were there were hamstrung by French tank doctrine – or rather, the lack of one.

The other main French design at the outbreak of the war was the Char B1-bis heavy tank. Although it entered service in 1935, this design dated from much earlier. The main armament was a 75mm (2.95in) gun mounted on the front of the hull and thus only able to fire forwards. Secondary armament of a 47mm (1.85in) gun was mounted in a turret identical to that of the S-35.

In appearance the B1-bis seemed to be halfway between a lozenge tank, with its all-round tracks, and a more modern turreted design. Armour was good and in theory the B1-bis was a formidable opponent, but it too, fell foul of doctrine. Instead of being concentrated for armoured counterattacks, the French tank forces were dispersed with infantry formations and under their orders, which denied tank force commanders the flexibility to hit back to the best effect. By the time France was invaded in 1940, the French Army had more tanks than their German opponents, and a greater proportion of tanks armed with guns that could kill other tanks. These powerful forces were hamstrung by policy rather than capability and were not able to effectively respond to their fast-moving enemy.

Italian tank development began relatively late, and was heavily influenced by French thinking. Indeed, the first Italian tank was built by Fiat to a design derived from the French FT-17. About a hundred of the latter had been bought from France. The Italian version, which was something of an improvement, served up to 1943. In the meantime, designers experimented with everything from tankettes to heavy tanks. Experiences in the Spanish Civil War convinced the Italian military that tankettes were not viable in the frontline combat role, but they made up the majority of Italian armoured strenght at the outbreak of war.

It was not until the eve of the war that a battle tank design went into production. This was the Carro Armato M11/39 medium tank, designed in response to the underperformance of tankettes in combat. However, it was not up to the task either, with thin armour and high sides that made it an easy target. Armament was initially two machine guns in the turret and a hull-mounted 37mm (1.45in) gun, but these were swapped around in some versions.

It was with these inadequate tanks and a large number of tankettes that the Italian army began World War II. Its armoured formations were quickly overmatched by their opponents.

Elsewhere in the world, large numbers of tanks were being built, but construction programmes were not always implemented soon enough. In other cases, obsolete or inadequate designs had remained in production for too long. In the Soviet Union, the BT-5 had shown itself to be a formidable tank, but was outnumbered in service by lighter or badly designed vehicles.

Inadequately armoured and making a big target with their high sides, the M11/39 was the main Italian tank in 1939.

One of the best light tanks in Soviet service was the BT-7. It used the excellent Christie suspension system and had sloped frontal armour for additional protection, although its armour was light to start with. The BT-7 mounted a 45mm (1.7in) gun and two machine guns. It was designed for a 'light cavalry' role, making deep penetrations and exploiting breakthroughs made by the heavier tanks. It was a very good tank, but underprotected, and lessons learned with it in the Spanish Civil War were carried over into the design of what became one of the best tank designs of all time, the T-34.

There were few tank operators outside Europe and the United States, but in the 1930s Japan was assembling an armoured force. Japanese tanks were poor by European standards, but when war broke out in the region they demonstrated the truth of the adage that any armour is better than no armour. Against opponents that lacked tanks and even antitank weapons, even fairly poor tanks were a huge advantage.

The first Japanese tank was the Type 89, a light tank based on the Vickers Mk C. It originally mounted a 57mm (2.24in) gun in the turret, plus two machine guns. The gun was upgraded to 57mm (2.24in) early in production. One of the machine guns was mounted in the bow and the other at the rear of the turret for infantry defence. This concept appeared from time to time in various nations. Armour was very thin, but this tended not to matter against most of the Type 89's opponents.

A column of Italian L6/40 light tanks. Although clumsy in appearance, these vehicles were an enormous improvement on the tankettes whose chassis they utilized.

Variants on the Type 89 appeared. The most significant was a diesel-engined version. This vehicle was a response to experiences in Manchuria, where petrol engines malfunctioned due to the cold. The Type 89 was the first tank to use a diesel engine. It was followed by a couple of tankettes, which were more appropriate for service in the Far East than Europe. As already noted, there were a lot less anti-armour weapons facing Japanese tanks, at least before 1939, and so tankettes tended to survive their encounters as well as being small and light enough to function in the close terrain the Japanese Army often had to fight over.

Not a tankette, but a light and thinly armoured tank developed from one, the 1935-vintage Type 95 Ha-Go was armed with a 37mm (1.45in) gun and two machine guns. It went into service in 1939 and was effective against light opposition, but suffered badly when it came up against an enemy trained and equipped to fight tanks.

Just before Japan became embroiled in World War II (Japanese troops had been fighting the Chinese, amongst others, for years at that point), a medium tank design was implemented. This was the Type 97 Chi-Ha. It was delayed by arguments about whether many cheap tanks were more desirable than smaller numbers of better ones, an argument that was influenced by the fact that existing cheap, light tanks were performing well in Manchuria and the army did not perceive a need for something newer and heavier. It was not until World War II proper began that the limitations of existing Japanese armour were perceived.

Meanwhile, in the United States moves were afoot to concentrate armoured vehicles in armoured formations, doing away with the infantry tanks/cavalry combat cars distinction that had existed for some time. Most of the tanks under development were light designs and just as doctrine was in a period of transition so American tank design was evolving towards the classic models that would emerge during World War II.

The most important US tank of this period was the M2 light tank. Armed with a 37mm (1.45in) gun and no less than four machine guns, one of which was mounted atop the turret for air defence, the M2 was the first US tank to go into war production. It was gradually developed and formed the basis for the M3 Stuart. The T5 medium tank was also significant, even though only about a dozen were actually built. It was used as a testbed for experimentation with a new suspension system using paired sprung bogie wheels, a system that was later used on a large number of US designs. A number of variations appeared, including one with a hull-mounted howitzer which became the basis for the M3 Lee/Grant tank

In Britain, finally, work was underway to produce an effective tank force. This effort came not a

Heavy Cruiser Tank

A British A10 Cruiser Tank in the desert. The designation A10 refers to the specification number. The A10 was heavily armoured and slow like an infantry tank, and was redesignated a 'Heavy Cruiser Tank' during its development.

moment too soon; virtually all the tanks in service were obsolete and there were too few of them in any case. In 1938, Britain possessed just four battalions of obsolete medium tanks, and the programme delivered the first new machines just in time.

The intention was to create a force of heavy 'infantry' tanks with good armament and protection, which need not be fast. Their role was to be infantry support, creating a breakthrough in the enemy lines. The infantry tanks would be supplemented by less well protected but faster 'cruiser' tanks with similar armament to the infantry tanks. Cruisers would exploit a breakthrough once it was made. The lights would provide reconnaissance and support wherever they could.

Here was '1917 thinking'; the planners wanted tanks to refight World War I, casting infantry tanks in the role of the Mk I and IV and cruisers as Whippets to break through static defensive lines and disrupt the enemy rear. Even the projected deployments – one battalion of infantry tanks to every infantry division – reflected the experience of World War I.

The first move towards a modern tank force was the Vickers Mk VI light tank. It was not intended for heavy combat, being primarily an armoured reconnaissance vehicle. However, as in Germany, there was a shortage of heavier tanks, which had to be made up with whatever was available. Meanwhile a suitable medium tank was long overdue, and a specification designated A9 had already been issued by the War Office. Another, designated A10, was created and development on both proceeded. The A9 was intended to be a cheaper, lighter vehicle than existing mediums, and it was decided that it would fit the bill of a cruiser tank well enough. The A10 would be heavier and fulfil the infantry tank role. However, the experience of Sir Hugh Elles, commander of the very first large-scale tank action and now Master General of Ordnance, suggested that the A10 could not fulfil the requirements of an infantry tank. It was too lightly protected, so it was eventually decided that the A10 would be a cruiser tank instead. There was another problem with the A9 and A10, too. They did not have the Christie suspension system. It was not until British officials observed a Soviet BT-5, which did have the Christie system, manoeuvring at high speed on very rough ground, that they realized what was missing from their designs.

Hydraulic turret traverse

The two tanks went into production anyway. Both mounted a 2-pounder (40mm/1.57in) gun as main armament. The A9 was the first British tank with hydraulic turret traverse, and was powered by a commercially available engine, which kept costs down and eased maintenance. Yet it was too thinly armoured to be survivable and too slow for the cruiser role.

The A10 was also too slow – far too slow – to be an effective cruiser tank, though its protection was better than that of the A9. The armour was of

CRUISER MK IV

Crew: 4
Weight: 15,040kg (33,158lb)
Dimensions: length 6.02m (19ft 9in); width 2.54m (8ft 4in); height 2.59m (8ft 6in)
Range: 145km (90 miles)
Armour: 6–30mm (0.23–1.2in)
Armament: one 2pdr (40mm/1.57in) gun; one 7.7mm (0.3in) Besa MG
Powerplant: Nuffield Liberty V-12 petrol, 340bhp (254kW)
Performance: maximum speed 48km/h (30mph)

composite construction, with additional plates added in some areas. The A9 and A10 were better than their predecessors, but they were outclassed by foreign designs and in addition needed further development work to eliminate a number of faults.

Meanwhile another flawed design had gone into production. This was specification A11, nicknamed 'Matilda' after a cartoon duck. The Matilda fulfilled one of the requirements of an infantry tank, in that it was amazingly tough. However, its only armament was a machine gun, rendering it more or less useless on the battlefield other than for shooting up infantry and soft targets like supply trucks.

A much more capable Matilda appeared just in time for the war. Specification A12 was another attempt at an infantry tank, and became known as the Matilda Mk II. It was extremely heavily armoured and armed with a 2-pounder (40mm/1.57in) gun plus a machine gun. A close support variant mounting a howitzer was also implemented. The design was difficult to build quickly and few were ready at the outbreak of war.

Also known as the Cruiser Mk III (and later Cruiser Mk IV), Specification A13 called for a cruiser or medium tank with Christie suspension. Developing this machine required that a Christie tank be purchased for study. Obtaining it was a problem, as US law made the export of war materiel illegal at that time. The tank was smuggled from the United States to Britain under the guise of a tractor, hidden beneath crates of grapefruit.

Having finally obtained the tank for study, the British government decided to proceed and purchased the rights to built a tank with the Christie suspension system. It was designed and put into production in just two years, and the British Army took the first deliveries in 1939.

More specifications appeared, this time for medium tanks, but it was then decided that the A13 was what the army needed and the mediums were shelved. Other design work went on, but it did not bear fruit until after the war had begun.

In 1939, a new organizational structure emerged for Britain's one and only armoured division. It would now consist of a light armoured brigade with three mixed regiments of light and cruiser tanks, a heavy armoured brigade equipped exclusively with cruiser tanks and a support group with a motorized infantry battalion, an artillery regiment and a company of engineers. Nevertheless, it was just one division. As the war opened and the massed tank strength of the *Wehrmacht* crushed first Poland and then France, it would seem that the tank was to be the decisive weapon of this new age of warfare. And the enemy had far more tanks than the British.

2

EARLY WORLD WAR II TANKS

At the outbreak of World War II, the combatants fought with what they had, often fielding inadequate designs that had been developed before the importance of the tank was really appreciated.

Japan's first tank, the Type 89, was based on the Vickers Mk C. Like many Japanese tanks, it was not really up to the task of fighting on the modern battlefield, though it and even lighter vehicles such as the Type 94 tankette performed well enough in the small-scale actions of Japan's gradual annexation of China. The poorly equipped Chinese could not put up effective opposition against Japanese mechanized forces, and after the fall of Beijing the Japanese Army was able to advance rapidly across northern China.

Normally facing only small arms and light support weapons, the vehicles' light armour was adequate to protect them and their weaponry was up to the job. This situation meant that a handful of tanks or even tankettes could overthrow a much larger force or drive it from prepared positions. Their small size was an advantage in that they could operate in close terrain where larger, more capable tanks could not pass.

Left: The vast tank battles of the Eastern Front established once and for all that the tank's most serious enemy is another tank.

Japan then came into conflict with the Soviet Union. The 1938 Changkufeng Incident was in some ways a precursor of what would happen in Europe a little later. Japanese attacks spearheaded by tanks and other armoured vehicles were met by an armoured counterattack.

In May 1939, a border incident escalated into large-scale combat. The Soviet Union sent General Georgi Zhukov to take command of its forces, and for a time the fighting took the form of skirmishing and minor raids. Late in June, however, the Japanese launched an operation intended to be decisive. Forces including two regiments of tanks committed in a double envelopment attack that brought about what is now known as the Battle of Khalkhyn Gol. The Japanese attack was initially successful and there were hopes of encircling and destroying large numbers of Soviet troops and their Mongolian allies. One prong of the Japanese assault was fought to a standstill, but the other got across the Khalkhyn Gol River and drove off the nearest enemy forces. It began to advance along the river as planned.

Zhukov, however, responded in a highly aggressive manner, making an armoured counterattack with over 400 vehicles. He had available a mix of tanks and armoured cars, but no infantry support. Zhukov trusted his armoured forces to win the battle on their own, and after several days of hard fighting they drove back the Japanese force, destroying most of its tanks.

After a period of skirmishing and another Japanese attack, also unsuccessful, Zhukov took the offensive. Overcoming severe logistical difficulties, he was able to muster a force of almost 500 tanks supported by 250 aircraft and large forces of infantry, cavalry and artillery. Zhukov's assets included three armoured (tank) brigades and two mechanized brigades comprising a mix of armoured cars and infantry.

Zhukov's offensive was a classic armoured operation, using modern weapons to execute a tried and tested battle plan. In the centre his ground and air forces attacked the unprepared Japanese, who had only light armoured forces available. With the centre gripped, fast-moving armoured forces slashed around the flanks and executed a pincer attack, or double envelopment, which surrounded the Japanese 23rd Division. Japanese counterattacks failed to rescue the 23rd Division, which declined to surrender and was ground down to nothing by air attacks and artillery bombardment. Soon afterwards, on 15 September, peace was signed between the Soviet Union and Japan. This outcome freed the Soviet Union to invade Poland, but it also permitted more Japanese resources to be turned southwards for the conquest of Southeast Asia in an escalating world war.

Obsolete by Western standards, the Japanese Type 97 Chi-Ha medium tank was still a respectable combat vehicle. The rails around the turret top are ring aerials for the tank's radio.

The tanks taken into action in these advances were unimpressive by European standards. The Type 95 Ha-Go was the main Japanese tank throughout World War II. It was a decent enough light tank, armed with a 37mm (1.45in) main gun and a machine gun in the bow and another offset at the rear of the turret. Powered by a diesel engine, it had a good power-to-weight ratio and thus both speed and mobility, once problems with its suspension were ironed out. However, even the up-gunned 45mm (1.77in) version was unable to deal with serious opposition. Its armour was simply too light for a battle tank.

There were two vehicles bearing the designation Type 97. One was a tankette with a 37mm (1.45in) gun that had been designed to double as a logistics vehicle. It had a front-mounted diesel engine and an armoured cargo area at the rear. The other Type 97, called the Chi-Ha, claimed to be a medium tank, but despite being bigger and having a four-man crew it was really only a large light tank. A range of variants were built, including a 47mm (1.85in) gun version and command, recovery and bulldozer versions.

During 1941, the Type 1 Chi-He medium tank appeared, in response to the underperformance of the Type 97 Chi-Ha against armoured opponents. Fitted with a higher-velocity gun and thicker armour, the Type 1 was a true medium tank design.

In late 1941 and early 1942, Japanese forces overran most of Southeast Asia and commenced hostilities against Britain and the United States. At first, things went well. In the advance down the Malay Peninsula towards the critical British fleet base at Singapore, Japanese tanks appeared in places where conventional wisdom said tanks could not go, causing chaos and dismay among the defenders. Some of the operations undertaken by Japanese forces during the advance on Singapore went beyond audacious and into the realms of sheer cheek. Extremely small forces of tanks several times undertook recklessly aggressive attacks or went plunging off into the defenders' rear without any form of support available. Had a coherent response been made, these forces would have been doomed from the outset. However, they got away with it.

One reason for the success of these operations was their sheer audacity. Even a handful of tanks, appearing where the enemy does not expect, can cause immense damage and, more importantly, can have a devastating effect on morale. The British defence of Malaya and the retreat to Singapore was fraught with errors, including a gross underestimation of enemy capabilities and a fixation with organizing neat lines of defence, establishing liaison with friendly units on the flanks, and similar 1917-vintage concepts. Meanwhile, the Japanese were demonstrating how things could be done in the new age of mobile warfare. Their tanks seemed to be everywhere, traversing apparently impassable terrain and smashing up defensive lines before they had a chance to become properly established. The British forces were kept thoroughly off-balance and demoralized by the constant attacks of what turned out to be a very small armoured force that had outrun its support – and its orders.

The Japanese advance on Singapore was greatly assisted by the aggression shown by a very small force of tanks.

The result of this massively aggressive campaign was the total collapse of the British defence and ultimately the fall of Singapore, which had far-reaching consequences for the war and the British Empire. Tanks were only a part of the picture, of course. Air and naval forces played a critical part alongside the other ground-combat arms.

Nevertheless, aggressive handling of what might appear to be an inadequate tank force paid huge dividends and made it unnecessary to fight large set-piece infantry battles to push through the defensive lines.

The Invasion of Poland

Tanks played an important part in the expansion of Germany even before combat became necessary. As a symbol of military power and prestige, they rolled into Czechoslovakia and Austria in the late 1930s, taking part in parades rather than armoured assaults. Their presence was important, however; weapons are the tools of political will, and had Germany not possessed a large and impressive tank force the annexations and political union with Austria might not have gone so smoothly, even if they had been accepted at all.

Having grabbed all he could without a shot being fired, Hitler turned his attentions towards Poland. The Poles were not caught unprepared, though their mobilization was incomplete at the time of the invasion, which began on 1 September 1939. The Poles were badly outmatched in terms of armour. The heaviest armoured vehicle in service was the 7TP light tank, a modified version of the Vickers 6.1-tonne (6-ton) tank. Heavily armoured for a light tank and equipped with a good 37mm (1.45in) gun, the 170 or so 7TPs available to the Polish Army put up a good fight, but were beaten by numbers as well as the superior tactics of the German armoured forces.

Most of the Polish armoured strength was made up of tankettes, about 700 of them in total. The TK-3 and TK S tankettes in service were developed from the British Carden-Loyd and were mostly armed with single machine guns. Some were fitted

The tank was a potent symbol as well as a military tool. Armoured vehicles rolling through the streets graphically demonstrated the invaders' power to the conquered population.

with a 20mm (0.78in) gun, which enabled them to take on the Panzers with at least a slight chance of success. One TK S is credited with knocking out seven German tanks in a single engagement.

The bulk of the Panzer forces were machine-gun-armed PzKpfw Is, themselves little more than tankettes. They were accompanied by PzKpfw IIs with 20mm (0.78in) guns and smaller numbers of PzKpfw III and IV machines. The Panzer II was really an armoured reconnaissance vehicle, but was able to take on Polish tankettes with confidence, while the Panzer I could supply anti-personnel fire support. During the campaign, there were few armoured vehicles to offer hard targets, so these tanks were able to perform well enough.

Yet it was the PzKpfw III that really showed what was to come. At the time only early versions (Models A to D) were available and these had many defects, but their 37mm (1.45in) guns and good armour made them formidable opponents. They were not invulnerable; the 20mm (0.78in) guns of some Polish tankettes could penetrate and disable a PzKpfw III, but they were nevertheless a potent force on the battlefield.

German tactics in the invasion of Poland were more conventional than is often thought. There was no breakneck *Blitzkreig* advance. Instead, the six Panzer divisions were used as spearheads to break through the enemy, assisted by tactical air power. The ability of the German Army to bring motorized artillery to bear quickly was also decisive. Artillery and infantry then moved up in support, completing the destruction of the enemy. All-arms cooperation of this sort allowed strong positions to be eliminated without heavy losses.

The offensive took longer than expected, not least because it was conducted with a fair amount of caution. German commanders were reluctant to unleash the armoured divisions and let them run since this risked their destruction and they were attempting an untried form of warfare. The outcome was never in any doubt, but losses were heavy. This was partly due to the fact that large numbers of very light tanks were in use, but also pays tribute to the stubborn defence put up by the Poles.

On 17 September, two days after signing a peace deal with Japan, the Soviet Union invaded from the east. This new assault came in through an open back door and wrecked the Polish defence plan. Some Polish units escaped to other countries and carried on the war, but the battle for Poland was lost. The Allies did not come to Poland's aid, perhaps sensibly, as there was

TKS TANKETTE

Crew: 2

Weight: 2600kg (5732lb)

Dimensions: length 2.67m (8ft 6in); width 1.78m (5ft 10in); height 1.36m (4ft 5in)

Range: 200km (125 miles)

Armour: 10mm (0.39in)

Armament: one 7.92mm (0.312in) MG or one 20mm (0.79in) cannon

Powerplant: one Fiat 40bhp (30kW) 4-cylinder petrol engine

Performance: maximum speed 40km/h (25mph)

Panzer I Glory

Panzer Is taking part in a demonstration of German military power. In a nation recovering from economic collapse, such spectacles assured the populace of renewed glory under the Nazi party.

nothing that could be done, and although organized resistance continued for a time the campaign was over by 6 October.

Germany was now at war with Britain and France. Hitler had not wanted to fight Britain so soon, if at all, but there could be no turning back. The next target had to be France, so the Panzer divisions transferred west ready for invasion.

The 'Sitzkrieg'

Although Britain and France had declared war on Germany, neither was in a position to do much and over the next few months there was little in the way of prosecution of the war. This period was known as the 'Phoney War', though once the term *Blitzkrieg* was coined, the months of inactivity became known as 'Sitzkrieg' in some quarters.

The lull between the invasion of Poland and the attack on France was vital to the Allies. British forces had been promised to defend France, but they were still being created. The British Expeditionary Force (BEF) in France was badly understrength and lacking in transporters to give what tanks it possessed strategic mobility. Its light units were still using Vickers Mk VIs and all kinds of equipment were lacking. Britain's only armoured division was still at home, having been scattered all over the country in small formations as part of hurried defensive preparations. When it finally got to France in March 1940, it had no artillery and only about half its specified number of tanks.

At least some thought was being given to stopping the expected German armoured thrusts. Allied generals had noted how the Panzers operated in Poland and proposed that in the event of a breakthrough the intact units on the flanks should hold their ground, attempting to prevent the enemy infantry and supporting troops from moving up after the armour. The Panzers would then effectively eliminate themselves by running out of fuel and munitions.

This was not a bad idea in principle, though it assumed that any penetration would be on a very

narrow front. The other dangerous assumption was that the attack would come via Belgium, where the flat terrain necessary for armoured operations was to be found. There were, after all, few other options. Terrain and the vast fortification chain of the Maginot Line (and the German equivalent, the Siegfried Line, facing the other way) surely ruled out armoured operations anywhere else.

Not everyone was fooled. Whether or not he knew about Japanese tanks operating in the jungle, General William Ironside, commander of the British Imperial General Staff, suggested that a German thrust through Luxembourg and the Ardennes Forest was possible. The French high command decided that this was not practical and since it was their country that was being defended, this appraisal was used as the basis of defensive deployments. The deployments made were indeed defensive. Although French doctrine had for many years stressed offensive action, the French military mindset was in practice inclined in the opposite direction. The Maginot Line is clear evidence of defensive thinking at the strategic level, and the practice of using tanks as infantry supports was not well suited to offensive operations of any sort. French planners of the time felt that tanks would be highly vulnerable to artillery and antitank weapons and were not inclined to risk them in hard-charging actions. Instead they would be kept safe from risk as part of infantry formations.

The Maginot Line contained an extensive tunnel system, allowing supplies to be moved about in secrecy and safety.

German generals had been similarly cautious about tanks' vulnerability before the invasion of Poland, but were becoming more inclined to be aggressive despite the losses in that campaign. The Panzer force to be committed to the invasion of France was expanded and improved. Many PzKpfw Is and some PzKpfw IIs were replaced with better tanks – PzKpfw IIIs and IVs, and also the newly available Panzer 35(t) and 38(t).

The latter were Czech designs. The 35(t) was in service and the 38(t) had been in the last stages of development when Czechoslovakia was annexed by Germany. The 35(t) was taken into German service in time for almost 300 of them to take part in the invasion of Poland. It was a light–medium tank armed with a 37mm (1.45in) gun and a coaxial machine gun in the turret, with a second machine gun in the bow.

Most of the Panzer 35(t)s gained from Czechoslovakia went to fill out German armoured units as it was more capable than the PzKpfw I and II, but some were sent to Germany's allies in Slovakia. After the fall of Poland, some examples were transferred westward. Many others remained in service with the forces covering the new German–Soviet border. Most new production went to Bulgaria, Romania and Slovakia; production was curtailed in 1940.

Those 35(t)s that remained in German service were gradually phased out. They were obsolete by 1942 and, unlike some other designs, the chassis was not converted to other roles. Existing vehicles were adapted as artillery tractors and armoured transport or recovery vehicles.

The other Czech vehicle taken on by the German Army became designated the Panzer 38(t). It was in many ways equivalent to the PzKpfw III, and tests on the prototypes indicated that it was all-round a very good tank. The German Army ordered large numbers and by January 1940 about 30 per month were reaching the Panzer divisions, of which there were now ten.

The Panzer 38(t) was a light–medium design armed with a 37mm (1.45in) main gun and two machine guns. Armour was reasonable to start with and was enhanced over time. The chassis was used for a range of vehicles such as tank destroyers even after the tank itself had become obsolete for frontline service. A handful of Panzer 38(t)s had taken part in the fighting in Poland, but it was in France that they really showed their worth. The 200 or so available tanks were assigned to the 7th and 8th Panzer Divisions, which were still awaiting deliveries of PzKpfw III and IV tanks.

The Panzer formations also received another armoured vehicle that was to be very important in the years to come. This was the Sturmgeschütz (Stug) III assault gun. Conceived in 1937, the Stug III was built on the chassis of a PzKpfw III and mounted a 75mm (2.95in) gun in a limited-traverse mount. Well armoured and low, it was a difficult target and excellent for infantry support. In many ways, assault guns of this type fulfilled the original role of the tank – to assist infantry in penetrating enemy positions. However, later versions gained a longer gun with good antitank

PANZER 35(t)

Crew: 4
Weight: 10,670kg (23,523lb)
Dimensions: length 4.9m (16ft 1in); width 2.16m (7ft 1in); height 2.21m (7ft 3in)
Range: 190km (120 miles)
Armour: 15–25mm (0.59–0.98in)
Armament: one 37mm (1.45in) cannon, two 7.92mm (0.312in) MGs
Powerplant: Skoda 120bhp (89.5kW) T-11 6-cylinder petrol
Performance: maximum speed 35km/h (22mph)

capability and were pressed into service as tank destroyers as well as being used to fill out understrength tank formations. They were less well suited to this role – a rotating turret allows engagement in any direction as well as firing from a hull-down position, while the assault guns had to slew the whole vehicle to engage a target.

At the opening of the offensive against France, the available Panzer strength stood at about 1500 PzKpfw Is, 1200 PzKpfw IIs, 100 PzKpfw IIIs and 230 Panzer 38(t)s plus 200 PzKpfw IVs. Most of the Panzer Is had been pulled out of frontline units and were in reserve to act as reinforcements. Against these approximately 3300 German tanks, most of them lights, the French Army could theoretically muster about 3500 tanks. It had far more medium and heavy tanks available, including good designs like the SOUMA S-35, the well-armoured Renault R-35 and the powerful but clumsy Char 1. However, the French deployments were not well suited to repel an armoured assault. The only formations capable of meeting the Panzers with an armoured counterattack were three Divisions Légères Mécaniques, which contained all the available S-35s, and four Divisions Cuirassées. The latter had heavy tanks but had been reorganized in a manner that reduced their offensive power even if they had not been wedded to slow-moving infantry tactics.

Most of the French units in the path of the Panzer offensive were equipped with Renault R-35s. While difficult to knock out, these had limited combat potential. Some units still used FT-17s, which by now were totally outdated. There were also some British armoured formations in France, but these were incomplete and most of their tanks were in light reconnaissance units. Very

A Panzer 38(t) demonstrating its excellent cross-country performance.

HEAD TO HEAD: *Somua S-35 Medium Tank* VERSUS

The French Souma S-35 was the best tank the French army possessed at the outbreak of World War Two. It had a cast turret and hull, and a useful 47mm (1.85in) gun. It was hampered mainly by small numbers and tactical doctrine. Tied to infantry formations, the S-35s were not free to make a rapid counterattack, which was the best response to an armoured thrust. Instead they were overwhelmed piecemeal.

Somua S-35

Crew: 3
Weight: 19,500kg (42,900lb)
Dimensions: length 5.38m (17ft 7.8in); width 2.12m (6ft 11.5in); height 2.62 (8ft 7in)
Range: 230km (143 miles)
Armour: 20–55mm (0.8–2.2in)
Armament: one 47mm (1.85in) gun; one coaxial 7.5mm machine gun
Powerplant: one SOMUA V-8 petrol engine develpoing 19hp (141.7kW)
Performance: maximum road speed 40km/h (24.85mph); fording 1.9m (3ft 3in); vertical obstacle 0.76m (2ft 6in); trench 2.13m (7ft)

STRENGTHS

- Electrically traversed turret
- Good armament
- Good armour

WEAKNESSES

- Commander also worked the gun and radio
- Poor visibility for the crew
- Engine difficult to maintain

PzKpfw 38(t)

The PzKpfw 38 (t) was offered for sale to the British, among others, by its Czechoslovakian designers. It was rejected, but when Germany annexed Czechoslovakia the tank was evaluated for Wehrmacht service and was found to be very suitable. More or less equivalent to the PzKpfw III and similarly armed, PzKpfw 38s were used in some formations instead of German tanks and gave good service until they became obsolete in the mid-war years.

PzKpfw 38(t)

Crew: 4
Weight: 9700kg (21,340lb)
Dimensions: length 4.546m (14ft 11in); width 2.133m (7ft); height 2.311m (7ft 7in)
Range: 200km (125 miles)
Armour: 10–25mm (0.4–1in); later increased from Ausf E version onwards to 50mm (2.28in)
Armament: one 37.2mm Skoda A7 gun; two 7.92mm (0.312in) machine-guns
Powerplant: one Praga EPA six-cylinder water-colled inline petrol engine developing 150hp (112kW)
Performance: maximum road speed 42km/h (26mph); fording 0.9m (3ft); vertical obstacle 0.787m (2ft 7in); trench 1.879m (6ft 2in)

STRENGTHS

- Good mobility
- Chassis easily adapted to other roles
- Good armament by 1939 standards

WEAKNESSES

- Light armour on early versions
- Obsolescent by 1943
- Turret too small for upgunning

few battle-capable tanks were available, and these played a critical role.

Blitzkreig in France

The offensive against France opened on 10 May 1940, with massed armoured thrusts across the border accompanied by heavy tactical air support and deeper strikes by the *Luftwaffe.* Initial resistance was brushed aside. The first real obstacle for the Germans was the River Meuse, and it was here that the offensive capability of the German Army was really tested. It is one thing to build tanks that can fight, and learn how to use them in open terrain, but there is more to tank warfare than this. All the elements have to be in place: mobility, logistics, support and, as demonstrated at the Meuse, the ability to get across obstacles and continue the advance.

Keeping the French on the defensive with artillery and air attacks, the Panzer divisions were able to cross the Meuse quickly and without undue difficulty, showing that the German Army truly did understand armoured warfare and not just how to operate tank formations in favourable conditions. Indeed, the offensive broke through the opposition and penetrating so deeply and so fast that the advancing Panzers caught many units totally unprepared. Here and there, stiff opposition was encountered, and the heavily armoured Char 1s proved to be a real problem. Even the 75mm (2.95in) gun of the PzKpfw IV struggled to do much damage to the heavy French tanks. It threw a relatively heavy shell, but velocity was not high – the PzKpfw IV was intended for fire support rather than engaging enemy tanks. Later, it would gain better armour and a longer, high-velocity gun that could destroy even heavily armoured tanks. Nevertheless, the French tanks were not concentrated nor operating as part of a coherent plan. In many cases they could be contained, bypassed and eliminated by follow-up forces.

France, 1940. The rapid advance of the panzer divisions achieved what had been impossible in 1914, covering large distances and shoving aside all opposition.

At the time of the invasion of France, it was not intended that the PzKpfw IV would become so important to the Panzer divisions, but by the end of the war it had proved so capable, reliable and versatile that over 10,500 were built. During the French campaign, Panzer IVs handled whatever tasks they were given – even those for which they were never intended to deal.

When engaging the heavy French tanks, German gunners learned that the Char 1 had vulnerable points. The tracks and radiator louvres could be successfully targeted, rendering the tank immobile. The heavy hull-mounted gun could fire only forwards, so an outflanked Char 1 had to depend on its turret gun. This was still an effective weapon, even against tanks, but it was limited by the fact that the vehicle commander operated the weapon along with his other tasks, reducing effectiveness in combat.

The French response was hamstrung by doctrine from the start, and the speed and aggression of the Panzers would have made an effective defence difficult even if the situation had not been further complicated by heavy air attacks. Here, again, it was shown that the French had not learned the right lessons from World War I. They wanted to fight from well-prepared positions and repel assaults by infantry firepower supported by tanks. The German Army, on the other hand, had learned not to batter itself to pieces against strongpoints, and now the Panzers supplied the means to quickly switch the axis of attack and either bypass areas where the enemy was strong or hit them from an unexpected direction.

With the armoured spearhead advancing at up to 80km (50 miles) per day, there were fears that the Panzers were becoming dangerously overextended. Among them were the staff at German high command, who tried to rein in the advance somewhat. A brief halt was ordered to give the supporting infantry a chance to catch up.

This concern for flank security had some basis in reality. A wide hole had been punched in the defensive lines and then widened further by supporting troops. There was a danger that French units coming up from other sectors might be able to exploit the open flank of the advance and cut off the Panzers from their supports. However, the units that did arrive tended to attack in a piecemeal fashion and achieved little.

After the brief pause, the spearhead of five armoured divisions resumed its onslaught. The speed of the assault caused a journalist to refer to this kind of warfare as *Blitzkreig*, and the name has stuck ever since. Yet the Panzers ran into trouble for the first time near Arras when they had their first taste of the only real counter to an aggressive tank advance – an armoured counterattack.

British Tanks at Arras

The Panzer divisions were only about 80km (50 miles) from the English Channel when they ran into stiff opposition from British forces that had been able to put some kind of a defence in order. General Erwin Rommel, commanding the 7th Armoured Division, attacked Arras but was unable to break the position. However, other Panzer forces were still pushing rapidly forward.

Two British infantry divisions did what they could to halt the advance but were overrun. Arras was more or less surrounded and the situation looked bleak. A broad wedge had been thrust through the British forces, cutting some units off from their lines of communications.

The German advance was halted again by high command. The Dunkirk region had a grim reputation from World War I, which may have contributed to German caution as much as the Allies' increasingly desperate resistance. On 22 May the order to advance once more arrived. Two days later, the divisions were halted again even though some of the Panzer units were only about16km (10 miles) from Dunkirk. Meanwhile, British tanks had arrived at Arras on the 21st to try to prevent

General Rommel

General Erwin Rommel made his name as a junior officer in the World War I, leading breakneck advances with light troops. Given command of a Panzer force, he repeated the feat in France and North Africa. Rommel was eventually defeated in the desert by a combination of supply problems, lack of focus from his superiors and overwhelming British strength. Even vastly overmatched, he remained a dangerous and aggressive opponent.

Thick-skinned Matildas

The Mk I Matilda was armed only with a machinegun and the Mk II, pictured here, was hardly overgunned, but these extremely tough tanks were able to shrug off most antitank weapons without coming to harm. In North Africa, Italian antitank gunners found that even at point-blank range their weapons were ineffectual against Matildas.

MATILDA MK I

Crew: 2
Weight: 11,160kg (24,604lb)
Dimensions: length 4.85m (15ft 11in); width 2.29m (7ft 6in); height 1.87m (6ft 1in)
Range: 129km (80 miles
Armour: 10–60mm (0.39–2.36in)
Armament: one 7.7mm (0.3in) MG or 12.7mm (0.5in) Vickers MG
Powerplant: Ford 70bhp (52kW) V-8 petrol engine
Performance: maximum speed 12.8km/h (7.95mph)

the headquarters from being overrun. There were now two tank regiments at Arras, supported by two Territorial Infantry battalions. The inevitable wear of warfare took many tanks out of service, with the result that the British counterattack was made with just 76 tanks. These tanks were Mk I and II Infantry Tanks – Matildas. Fifty-eight were Mk Is, with good protection but only machine guns with which to fight. The remaining 16 were Mk IIs with 2-pounder (40mm/1.57in) main guns. A reshuffle assigned a few Mk IIs to each of the two combined-arms columns put together for the attack.

In the event, the tanks initially went forward without infantry support. The infantry were worn out already and slow to get started. They followed as quickly as they could and were able to contribute to the fight, though at considerable cost in casualties. The British counterattack hit just one hour before the Panzers were due to attack Arras, catching the enemy troops in the middle of final preparations and thoroughly unprepared to defend themselves.

The counterattack struck the motorized component of the 7th Armoured Division and also the elite SS Totenkopf (Death's Head) Division, causing a panic. Many troops simply fled, and the initial response was confused and ineffective. Morale plummeted still lower as the antitank gunners opened up on the advancing Matildas, only to see their 37mm (1.45in) rounds bounce harmlessly off. Particularly disconcerting was the tendency of external stowage bins on the Matildas, containing the crew's extra gear, to catch fire. This created the appearance that the tank itself was on fire, and elation upon seeing an enemy vehicle burst into flames quickly turned to fear as it trundled onwards apparently unconcerned.

Although most of the Matildas had only machine guns, these were effective against the antitank gunners, and many crews were chased off or mown down after scoring one or more ineffectual hits. One Matilda came back from the battle with dents from fourteen 37mm (1.45in) antitank gun rounds, but no significant damage.

Rommel himself tried to remedy the situation, rallying the crews of nearby 88mm (3.46in) anti-aircraft guns and field artillery pieces. He ran among the crews, personally directing them to fire at the oncoming tanks, and the counterattack was brought to a halt. Losses were heavy: about 40 British tanks, which represented most of the available strength. However, the Totenkopf Division's panicked retreat had affected other nearby units and the 7th Armoured Division was also thrown into chaos. The attack on Arras was forestalled.

More serious was the effect at German high command. The attack had frightened Hitler's senior commanders, who were very aware that their Panzers could not be quickly replaced. Another pause in operations was ordered, and it was not until the 26th that the Panzers were authorized to resume their advance. By then, the British forces around Dunkirk had managed to firm up their positions and the ground was becoming waterlogged, reducing Panzer mobility.

The 'miracle of Dunkirk' whereby British forces were rescued from France largely intact, though without most of their heavy equipment, was made possible in part by the daring attack of just a handful of tanks. Once more, AFVs had achieved results out of all proportion to their theoretical fighting power – most of the British tanks at Arras were capable only of anti-personnel operations.

The counterattack at Arras, undertaken by just a handful of tanks, helped buy time to evacuate the defeated British Expeditionary Force from Dunkirk.

Lessons Learned in France

The crushing German victory in France validated the concept of fast-moving armoured warfare. For the German Army there was little that needed to be changed about the Panzer divisions, but a reorganization was undertaken anyway. This measure was mainly to create more armoured units by spreading the tanks more thinly.

Such a dilution of fighting power was partially offset by the increasing availability of heavier tanks. The PzKpfw I was phased out of combat duties and the PzKpfw II was able to stop pretending it was a battle tank and went over to its designed role as a reconnaissance vehicle. The heavier tanks received upgraded weaponry and armour, with PzKpfw IIIs eventually getting 50mm (2.28in) guns that were more effective against well-armoured targets.

The Panzer battalions now comprised two light companies with PzKpfw IIIs or Panzer 38(t)s (sometimes a mix of both), plus a medium company equipped with PzKpfw IVs. A Panzer regiment had either two or three such battalions, and a division now had one Panzer regiment instead of two, plus an armoured reconnaissance formation equipped with PzKpfw IIs. Supporting forces comprised two motorized infantry regiments, each of two battalions, and a motorcycle battalion. Artillery support was increased from two to three regiments, and an anti-aircraft regiment armed with 88mm (3.46in) Flak guns (deadly in the antitank role) was also assigned.

Although diluted somewhat, the Panzer divisions remained a potent all-arms force. Perhaps more potent than previously, since they now had better and heavier tanks even if there were less of them. The all-arms division spearheaded by tanks was accepted as the ideal model in other nations too.

In Britain, the armoured division now comprised two tank brigades, each with three battalions of cruiser tanks supported by an infantry battalion, plus an armoured car regiment for reconnaissance. The supports included another infantry battalion plus antitank, anti-aircraft and artillery regiments.

It was in the United States that the most radical changes were made. The US military had for a long time thought of tanks as infantry weapons, and overlooked the fact the cavalry also had them by calling them 'combat cars'. Now the distinction was scrapped and tanks (whatever they might have been called before) were amalgamated in armoured battalions.

The 88mm (3.46in) anti-aircraft gun was found to be a formidable tank-killer in the Spanish Civil War. As World War II progressed, batteries of '88s' became the standard heavy antitank weapon of the German army.

A US armoured division was extremely tank-heavy. It comprised an armoured brigade of two light tank regiments with three battalions each and one medium tank regiment with two battalions. The armoured brigade also contained a two-battalion regiment of self-propelled artillery. This formation was supported by an armoured reconnaissance battalion, a regiment of infantry and battalions of engineers and artillery. Two such divisions were initially formed.

The British Empire was extremely powerful, but it was also dispersed. If communications between parts of the Empire were severed, the British capability to fight the war would therefore be severely reduced. One of the critical elements in the chain of communications was the Suez Canal.

Suez was vital to both military and commercial shipping, and the region was of strategic importance for other reasons. As well as protecting the canal, the fleet base at Alexandria enabled the Royal Navy to project power in the Mediterranean Sea and the Indian Ocean. On top of all that, the British were present in Egypt. Dislodging themwould give the Axis powers easier access to the oilfields of the Middle East.

Defending North Africa

And thus, even as France was falling and preparations were being made to defend the British Isles from invasion, it was obvious that North Africa would also have to be defended. Sending armoured reinforcements to Africa when the survival of Britain itself was in doubt was something of a gamble, but the war could just as easily be lost in Egypt even if Britain itself were successfully defended. Arriving in September 1940, the reinforcements included one infantry tank regiment equipped with Matilda IIs, one cruiser tank regiment mostly equipped with A13s but also smaller numbers of A9 and A10 cruiser tanks, and one light regiment with Mk VI light tanks. These joined the 7th Armoured Division, which had been reorganized for the coming campaign. Originally the division had possessed a heavy and a light brigade, each of two regiments. After the reorganization, each brigade consisted of a heavy and a light regiment. The new arrivals were integrated into this formation, which necessitated a certain amount of swapping-around of vehicles between units.

The division's final configuration retained two mixed brigades, with the 7th Royal Tank Regiment (RTR) under the direct control of the commander-in-chief. Within the division, 4th Armoured Brigade was more powerful than 7th Armoured Brigade, having two heavy regiments. Divisional troops included the light tanks of the 11th Hussars.The threat facing the British armoured force and its infantry compatriots was Italian, and comprised some 1500 tanks and armoured vehicles. However, most of the strength of the Italian force was composed of vehicles bearing the designation of L3-35 light tanks. These were simply upgraded and redesignated tankettes developed from the Carden-Loyd Mk 6. They were extremely thinly armoured and armed only with machine guns.

The North African campaign was fought over vast distances, making mobility a critical asset.

M11/39 MEDIUM TANK

Crew: 3
Weight: 11,175kg (24,637lb)
Dimensions: length 4.73m (15ft 6in); width 2.18m (7ft 2in); height 2.30m (7ft 7in)
Range: 200km (124 miles)
Armour: 6–30mm (0.24–1.18m)
Armament: one 37mm (1.45in) gun; two 8mm (0.315in) Breda MGs
Powerplant: One 105bhp (78kW) SPA 8 T diesel
Performance: maximum speed 33.3km/h (20.7mph)

Actual tank numbers were far lower, and the tanks themselves were very poor. These were M11/39 medium tanks, each armed with a 37mm (1.45in) gun mounted in the hull and two machine guns in the turret. They were of very recent design and just coming into service, but they were not up to the job. Their armour was not much better than that of the tankettes, and in any case there were less than 100 of them.

There were also small numbers of the more capable M13/40 medium tank available to the Italians. This was a better version of the M11/39, with a new turret that enabled it to carry a 47mm (1.85in) gun. It also had a coaxial machine gun and two more on the hull front, with a fourth mounted on top of the turret as an anti-aircraft weapon.

The M13/40 was better than its predecessor, but was still poorly armoured. It was also unreliable, underpowered and tended to catch fire easily. Even the gun failed to meet expectations. The M13/40 was the best tank available to the Italian Army, but it was simply outclassed by its opponents.

With such an armoured force, backed up by large numbers of infantry, the Italians began pushing eastward across the coastal region of North Africa. There was little of *Blitzkreig* in the cautious advance, and after four days the Italian force began to fortify itself in new positions, most notably around Sidi Barrani and Maktila, where it remained for some weeks.

General Wavell, commanding the British forces, had about 30,000 men and 275 tanks available, whereas the Italian army in the region around Sidi Barrani at that time consisted of over 80,000 men with 120 tanks. There was another Italian force in the Sudan that could also threaten Egypt. Wavell decided to launch a spoiling attack against Sidi Barrani in the hope of preventing an Italian advance (which must come sooner or later) by keeping the enemy off balance. If successful, he planned to transfer part of his force under his subordinate Lieutenant-General Richard O'Connor to attack the Italians in the Sudan.

It fell to O'Connor to plan the attack and implement it. He intended to use some of his armoured forces as a spearhead for the 4th Indian Division, an infantry formation, while the remainder acted as a screen to keep enemy reinforcements from interfering. O'Connor's assault achieved surprise, and the enemy was late in opening fire. When they did, they found that the Matildas of the 7th RTR were extremely hard to damage. The assault overran 23 M11/39 tanks, whose crews were still trying to get them ready for action. This success represented about a quarter of the Italian medium tank strength destroyed without firing a shot.

The sudden and devastating attack caused a panic among the Italian infantry, though some of the

Italian M13/40 medium tanks. Although better than previous Italian designs, these tanks were badly flawed.

artillery and antitank gunners made a fight of it until they were overrun. Thousands of prisoners were taken as the assault rolled over the demoralized Italians. Those that did not scatter were killed or captured. The 7th RTR lost seven men killed.

As usual, combat damage and operational wear reduced the available tank strength for subsequent days' fighting. The 7th RTR had only 10 tanks available for the second day of the battle, but these were instrumental in helping the infantry maintain their advance by overrunning several artillery batteries that were holding the infantry up. The assault on the main enemy camp at Sidi Barrani went similarly well, and the defence quickly collapsed. O'Connor sent the 7th Armoured Brigade racing off westwards to establish a blocking position in the path of the retreating enemy. The eventual 'bag' was another 14,000 prisoners and 68 artillery pieces captured.

In early January 1941, the British attacked again, using as many Matildas as could be repaired and put back into service. They lived up to their name as infantry tanks; the infantry brigade given their support was successful. The brigade commander was so impressed that he claimed that each Matilda was worth a battalion of infantry. Another infantry brigade, with no armoured support available, suffered heavy casualties and did not achieve its objectives.

With armoured forces blocking the line of retreat, Italian morale crumbled in the face of this renewed attack. Some 462 artillery pieces, 127 tanks and 40,000 prisoners were captured. This feat was impressive enough, but O'Connor thought he could achieve more. Advancing the 110km (70 miles) to Tobruk, O'Connor again used some of his armour to isolate the garrison from relief or retreat, and the remainder to spearhead an attack. There were only 16 tanks available, plus the infantry of the 6th Australian Division, but they captured Tobruk and with it some 87 tanks, 209 artillery pieces and 25,000 more prisoners.

Hardly pausing for breath, O'Connor sent the 4th Armoured Brigade off 160km (100 miles) towards Mechili. An attack was put in, but this time the Italians put up a stiff fight and were able to hold their ground. Among their forces were some of their remaining M11/39 medium tanks which, poor as they may have been, were better than nothing. An attempt was made to stop this force from escaping, but by now the British forces were operating at the end of a long supply line and were running into fuel difficulties.

O'Connor's force was down to 95 light tanks and 50 cruiser tanks by this time. Many of those 'lost' were strung out all the way back to Egypt with

HEAD TO HEAD: *Matilda II* VERSUS

Britain began developing a serious battle tank only during the run-up to World War II, and was constrained by visions of trench warfare. Thus, during the development of the Matilda, the emphasis was on protection. The specification called for armour that could defeat any known antitank weapon. At the start of the war, only the German '88' could penetrate a Matilda's armour. This could be utterly demoralizing for an enemy facing apparently invincible tanks.

Matilda II

Crew: 4
Weight: 26,925kg (59,359lb)
Dimensions: length 5.613m (18ft 5in); width 2.58m (8ft 6in); height 2.515m (8ft 3in)
Range: 257km (160 miles)
Armour: 13–78mm (0.51–3in)
Armament: one 2-pounder (40mm/1.57in) gun; one 7.92mm (0.312in) Besa MG
Powerplant: two 87bhp (65kW) petrol 6-cylinder AEC engines
Performance: maximum speed 24km/h (15mph)

STRENGTHS

- Excellent armour
- Small target
- Good radius of action

WEAKNESSES

- Slow speed
- Light armament
- Expensive and slow to produce

Panzer III

The somewhat lighter Panzer III was designed with a more modern vision of armoured warfare in mind. Intended to move fast and hit hard, it started out with a 37mm (1.45in) gun and gradually gained better armour as the war went on. Later versions mounted a 75mm (2.95in) gun that could penetrate most targets without difficulty. The Panzer III eventually reached the limit of its upgradability, but its chassis remained useful as the basis for other vehicles.

Panzer III

Crew: 5
Weight: 22,300kg (49,060lb)
Dimensions: length 6.41m (21ft); width 2.95m (9ft 8in); height 2.5m (8ft 2.5in)
Range: 175km (110 miles)
Armour: 30mm (1.18in)
Armament: one 75mm (2.95in) L-24 gun; one 7.92mm (0.312in) machine gun
Powerplant: one Maybach HL 120 TRM 12-cylinder petril engine developing 300hp (224kW)
Performance: maximum road speed 40km/h (25mph); fording 0.8m (2ft 8in); vertical obstacle 0.6m; trench 2.59m (8ft 6in)

STRENGTHS

- Easy to upgrade
- Powerful armament on later versions
- Easy to create variants

WEAKNESSES

- Poor suspension on early models
- Obsolescent by 1943
- Limited combat range

repairable damage or, more commonly, mechanical problems. In time these tanks could be recovered and repaired, but they were out of the picture for the immediate future.

The advance westwards had slowed from its breakneck pace, but in early February 1941 reconnaissance indicated that the Italians were intending to retreat from Benghazi and abandon everything east of it. This decision meant funnelling a lot of troops along the coast road; there was no other suitable route. O'Connor decided to strike another decisive blow by exploiting the situation.

The 7th Armoured Division was sent off across very difficult terrain with scanty supplies of fuel and food. Armoured cars, able to travel more quickly than tanks in most terrain, were sent on ahead to establish a blocking position. They were accompanied by some infantry and artillery, but this was a recklessly small force for the task at hand. Nonetheless, they succeeded in setting up a defensive position and halted the first Italian units to reach them. The light tanks and A13s, being the fastest available, also rushed ahead and hit the flank of the traffic jam that was developing on the coast road, doing considerable damage.

A fierce action developed around Beda Fomm, where Italian forces spearheaded by M11/39 tanks tried repeatedly to break out of the trap. The British were outnumbered and hard-pressed, but were able to shoot from hull-down protected positions against an enemy that arrived in small numbers and had to attack across open ground. The action at Beda Fomm crippled what remained of the Italian army in North Africa, and by the time it was over British losses in the campaign came to somewhat under 2000 men. In return, more than 400 tanks had been captured or destroyed plus 850 artillery pieces and 130,000 prisoners taken.

From the attack at Sidi Barrani to the entrapment and annihilation of the retreating Italian forces at Beda Fomm, the campaign owed everything to armoured strength. Artillery and infantry played a big part, but it was the tank that enabled the enemy positions to be broken, and armoured exploitation that turned a tactical defeat into a general retreat. It was the ability of tanks to

General Wavell

General Wavell, who led the British forces to their first spectacular victories in the desert. 'Wavell's Thirty Thousand' routed 200,000 Italian troops, chased them along the north coast of Africa and finally cornered them at Beda Fomm after a daring flank march through almost uncharted terrain.

move fast to reach new positions, and to both fight hard and survive there, that completed the destruction of the Italian army.

Once again, a relatively small force of tanks, handled with an aggression that bordered upon the reckless, had shattered a much larger enemy force. There was nothing now to stop what had begun as a spoiling attack from going all the way to Tripoli in Libya, and O'Connor sent his light tanks westwards as soon as possible after the action at Beda Fomm.

In fact, there was no enemy force in position to prevent the advance, but there was one thing that could halt it – orders from London. The vanguard managed to reach Agheila before it was ordered to cease operations. Had O'Connor been allowed to forge ahead, he might well have taken Tripoli in time to prevent the German Afrika Korps from using the port, shortening the desert war immensely.

There were, however, other considerations. Greece was at that time under heavy pressure, and it was politically necessary to send British troops to join the defence. Meanwhile, in an effort to turn things round in North Africa, German troops were being deployed to assist the Italians. General Erwin Rommel was assigned to command the Afrika Korps, which at that time consisted of two armoured divisions. North Africa was ideal country for tank warfare, and Rommel was a master. Things were about to change.

The Desert Fox Arrives

Rommel, who reached North Africa in February 1941, had been assigned a force comprising the 15th Panzer and 5th Light divisions. By this time, the light divisions had evolved to the point where

Matilda Mk II tanks played an important part in the battles for Tobruk, where their toughness helped offset the Axis forces.

they were identical to a Panzer division; the only distinction was the unit's origin and hence its designation. Both divisions were short of their establishment; each contained two Panzer battalions supported by three motorized infantry battalions and supporting troops.

In addition, the Italian armoured division Ariete was also assigned to Rommel's force, and it was this unit that first came ashore in Tripoli. The 5th Light followed it and while the 15th Panzer was still unloading from its transports, Rommel led the two ready divisions eastwards to attack the British positions around Mersa Brega, near Agheila.

The defenders held a good position between the sea and a salt marsh, but they were not in good shape. Many tanks were still out of action awaiting repair and others had been left behind in Egypt, their crews being assigned captured Italian tanks upon their arrival. These were inadequate M13/40s and M11/39s. Rommel's attack penetrated the British positions, forcing some units to withdraw. This opened a gap for the Panzers, and they exploited it aggressively. The retreating units were harried mercilessly and given no opportunity to turn and fight. The British needed time to organize a defence, and they were not given any. It was necessary to evacuate units ahead of the enemy advance and scurry back eastwards, trying to find somewhere to establish a credible resistance.

Rommel's attack had opened on 31 March, and by 3 April his advanced elements had reached Benghazi. Confusion amongst British units stemmed partly from confusing and conflicting orders, and partially from wireless problems. Many radio-equipped tanks used the same battery for the radio as all other functions, which meant that after a lengthy halt the battery might be too run down to start the engine. The lack of a separate radio battery took many units out of service at a time when good communications were vital.

Hitler did not want to become embroiled in a campaign in North Africa. The deployment of the Afrika Korps was necessitated by the total defeat of Italian forces there.

Amidst the confusion, British troops destroyed fuel dumps to prevent them falling into enemy hands, only to find that the Panzers were elsewhere. This action further limited operations for the British armoured forces. With no diesel available, many serviceable M13/40s were destroyed by their crews, while the petrol-engined British tanks struggled to maintain combat capability. The confused situation also led to counterattacks being launched against an enemy that was not present, wasting already scant resources.

The disaster continued to get worse for the British, while a combination of aggression and opportunism allowed Rommel's forces to exploit every mistake they encountered. On 8 April a small force of Panzers attacked the British headquarters, and on the 11th Tobruk was cut off. Within a couple more days, the British had been chased out of Cyrenaica, other than the garrison of Tobruk.

The defence of Tobruk was mainly an infantry affair but some tanks were available, including a dozen Matildas, some of which had been under repair in the city. Although the perimeter was penetrated, a combination of minefields and the intervention of hull-down British cruiser tanks was able to restore the situation. Tobruk continued to hold out and Rommel decided that his best option for the near future was to contain the defenders, whose offensive striking power was very limited, and go after more important targets.

The deteriorating situation in North Africa was sufficiently alarming to the British government that the decision was taken to send a large reinforcement of over 300 tanks as quickly as possible. This meant a hazardous passage along the entire length of the Mediterranean, but the need was sufficiently great that the risk had to be taken.

The Crusader

The Crusader was fast but unreliable, undergunned and too lightly protected. It was not kept in front-line service for long after more suitable vehicles became available.

Instead of waiting for these reinforcements, which might not arrive at all, Wavell appointed Major-General W.H.E. Gott to head what forces could be gathered (O'Connor having been captured in Cyrenaica) and use these to launch a counterattack on 15 May 1941. This failed, as did another attempt launched when the reinforcements arrived.

In fact, the force opposing the assault was smaller than British intelligence had indicated, but Rommel not only knew how to attack with tanks, he also understood how to defend against them. As the British advanced, they ran into well-sited antitank guns whose fire supported one another. Attacking across undulating ground, the

M3 STUART

Crew: 4
Weight: 12,927kg (28,499lb)
Dimensions: length 4.54m (14ft 10in); width 2.22m (7ft 4in); height 2.3m (7ft 7in)
Range: 113km (70 miles)
Armour: 51mm (2in)
Armament: one 37mm (1.45in) M6 gun; three 7.62mm (0.3in) MGs
Powerplant: Continental 7-cylinder 2250bhp (186.6kW) radial petrol engine
Performance: maximum speed 58km/h (36mph)

British tanks exposed their weaker undersides to enemy fire as they crested each obstacle, and many were disabled. As the attack lost momentum, the Panzers counterattacked and inflicted serious losses.

This action was the combat debut of the Mk VI cruiser tank, built to specification A15, which had been issued just before the war. Known as the Crusader, this tank was fast and had good suspension, but was initially prone to breakdowns. It was armed with two machine guns (one on later models) in addition to its 6-pounder (57mm/2.24in) gun, but the latter did not meet expectations. The armour was not as robust as had been hoped, and could be penetrated by the 50mm (2.28in) gun of a Panzer III or a 55mm (2.16in) antitank gun of the sort in common use at the time.

The Crusaders were not the battle-winning weapon that the British had hoped, and by the end of a day of battle about half the British tanks were disabled or destroyed. The following day the Panzers attacked, intending to complete the defeat. However, they ran into hull-down British tanks that stood their ground and fought the enemy to a standstill. It was necessary for the British to withdraw, and although they were able to break off the action the withdrawal was very costly in that it left the field of battle to the enemy. All but 12 of the disabled German tanks were recovered and eventually returned to service, while the 91 lost by the British, including many that could have been salvaged, were now beyond recovery.

These battles demonstrated the dangers of attacking a strong position head-on. Antitank guns or hull-down tanks made difficult targets and could pick their shots where an advancing tank force was at a major disadvantage in even spotting its targets. The importance of armoured recovery and the value of possessing the battlefield with its wealth of salvage were both amply demonstrated.

Changes on the British Side

Taking over command in the North African theatre, General Claude Auchinleck decided that to defeat Rommel he needed both a powerful armoured striking force and also plenty more tanks in reserve to replace losses. To make real strategic gains, his tanks needed to be able to maintain an offensive rather than exhausting themselves to achieve a tactical success.

As already noted, the Crusader tank that now made up much of the British armoured strength was unreliable and had a relatively poor gun. The slow Matildas were no longer unstoppable, as the Germans now had access to large numbers of 50mm (2.28in) and 88mm (3.46in) antitank guns that could penetrate a Matilda. The British had replaced their ineffective machine-gun-armed tanks with American-built M3 Stuarts. The Stuart was an updated version of the M2 medium tank, an obsolete design even at the time when it was built. The M2 did serve its purpose, however, as a training vehicle and a means to explore concepts used in the rather better M3. The Stuart did away with five of the M2's eight machine guns, but carried the same 37mm (1.45in) gun.

M3 Light

An early-model M3 Light Tank, named Stuart in British service. Too light for the main-battle role, these fine little tanks gave excellent service in the Far East and as a reconnaissance unit in the Western theatres of war.

Fast, reliable and well-liked by its crews, the Stuart was the first tank to use a gyro-stabilized main armament, although the gun was too light for serious tank-killing.

The Stuart was designated a light tank even though it carried more armour than the M2, which was designated a medium. It had the world's first gyro-stabilized gun, enabling it to fire on the move with far greater accuracy. The Stuart was, nevertheless, outclassed by many of its opponents in the same way that the British cruiser tanks were not quite up to the standard of the equivalent Panzers.

Despite this, the Stuart was a success. It gained the nickname 'Honey' with British troops, who liked it a lot. Fast, reliable and armed with a decent gun, it was outmatched tank-for-tank but still a capable combat vehicle.

War in the East

North Africa was in some ways the key to Axis victory in World War II. The capture of Egypt would have deprived Britain of the Suez Canal, with significant consequences, and more importantly it would have given Germany easy access to the Middle Eastern oilfields. Yet as far as Hitler was concerned, it was a mere sideshow. He was fixated upon the destruction of the Soviet Union and its replacement with a Nazi state.

Despite treaties and agreements to the contrary, Hitler ordered Operation *Barbarossa*, the invasion of Russia, and preparations were made. Stalin, the Soviet premier, was warned by various sources that the invasion was planned, and then imminent, but at first refused to believe it. When Soviet preparations were made, they were too little, too late, and at first the assault enjoyed overwhelming success. Beginning on 22 June 1941, 183 divisions of Axis troops (about 3.5 million men) with about 3350 tanks advanced rapidly against their enemies, who could muster about 2.5 million troops. The latter were out of position and deprived of clear orders, greatly reducing the effectiveness of their response.

The German tanks taking part in this offensive were the PzKpfw II, III and IV discussed elsewhere, as well as Panzer 35(t)s, 38(t)s and some captured vehicles. Up-gunned Panzer IIIs became more prevalent during this period. The PzKpfw III Ausf G, with a 50mm (2.28in) gun replacing the 37mm (1.45in) version, had entered service in mid-1940, but it was not until the end of the year that extensive retrofitting of 50mm (2.28in) guns took place. The up-gunned Panzer IIIs took time to reach the combat formations, but were available for use during the battles of 1942.

The need for fast-moving mobile artillery support had been identified in earlier operations, and self-propelled artillery was beginning to become available. This included the sIG33 self-propelled howitzer. Very much an interim measure, it was little more than an infantry-support howitzer (complete with wheels and trail) perched atop a PzKpfw I chassis, with a three-sided light armoured shield for the crew. The sIG33 was a big target and very clumsy, but it was a lot better than a towed gun unable to keep up with the advance.

Half-tracked vehicles were also important, giving infantry and support elements sufficient rough-

HEAD TO HEAD: MK IV *Churchill tank* VERSUS

The Churchill was an 'Infantry tank' – in other words, one designed to support infantry operations in the manner of World War I breakthrough tanks. Its obstacle-crossing capability was prodigious, which proved useful in terrain where the enemy thought tanks could not function. The German commander on Longstop Hill, a steep and rugged feature in North Africa, dismissed reports that the British were attacking with tanks as impossible – to his cost.

MKIV Churchill

Crew: 5
Weight: 40,642kg (89,412lb)
Dimensions: length 7.442 (24ft 5in); width 2.438m (8ft); height 3.45m (11ft 4in)
Range: 144.8km (90 miles)
Armour: 16–102mm (0.6–4in)
Armament: one 6-pounder (57mm/2.24in) gun; one coaxial 7.62mm machine gun
Powerplant: one Bedford twin-six petrol engine developing 35hp (261kW)
Performance: maximum speed 29km/h (12.5mph); fording 1.016m (3ft 4 in); verticle obstacle 0.76m (2ft 6in); trench 3.048m (10ft)

STRENGTHS

- Excellent rough-ground performance
- Good armour protection
- Very adaptable to specialist roles

WEAKNESSES

- Mechanically unreliable
- Under-armed by 1941 standards
- Difficult to up-gun due to narrow turret ring

Cruiser Tank MK VI Crusader

The Crusader, on the other hand, was a 'Cruiser' tank designed for mobility and speed. Although it was extremely fast, it was very lightly protected and could be penetrated by almost any antitank weapon. Casualties from enemy action and breakdowns were heavy, and many Crusaders ended their days as artillery tractors or as the basis for other vehicles, such as AA mounts.

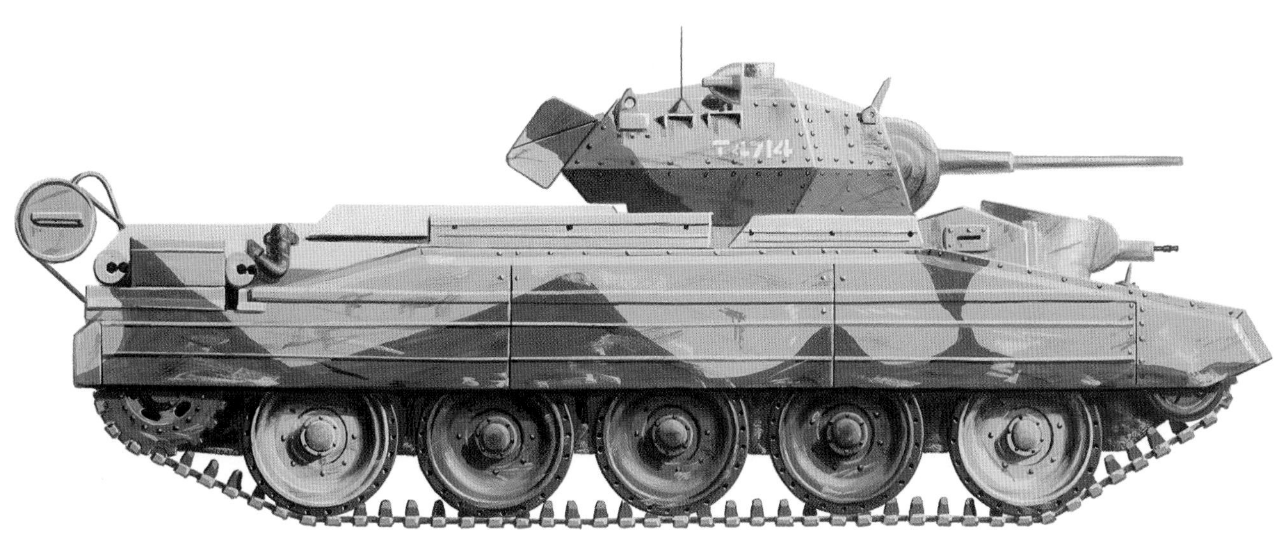

MK VI Crusader

Crew: 3
Weight: 20,067kg (44,147lb)
Dimensions: length 5.994m (19ft 8in); width 2.64m (8ft 8in); height 2.235m (7ft 4in)
Range: 204km (127 miles)
Armour: 40mm (1.57in)
Armament: one 2-pounder (40mm/1.57in) gun; one coaxial 7.62 machine gun
Powerplant: one Nuffield Liberty MK III petrol engine developing 340hp (254kW)
Performance: maximum road speed 43.4km/h (27mph); fording 0.99m (3ft 3in); vertical obstacle 0.686m (2ft 3in); trench 2.59 (8ft 6in)

STRENGTHS

- High speed
- Good suspension
- Adaptable to other roles

WEAKNESSES

- Under-armed
- Poorly protected
- Prone to breakdowns

German tanks in the Ukraine during Operation *Barbarossa*.

country mobility to keep up with the Panzers. All-arms cooperation was a hallmark of successful armoured operations, despite the role of the tank as the main striking arm, so all troop types had to be able to keep up with the armoured spearhead.

To oppose the German attack, the Soviets had 22,000 or more tanks. On paper this was a fearsome strength, but the majority were wholly inadequate designs. One such was the T-27 tankette, a two-man machine-gun carrier armoured only against small arms. It had proved useful in security operations but was no use on the battlefield. Likewise the multi-turreted T-28 was a slow and easy target with inadequate armour. Those that were thrown into action against the Panzer divisions were massacred.

The T-26 light tank had already seen action in the Winter War against the Finns. Equipped either for infantry support with two machine guns or as an 'artillery tank' with a 27mm (1.06in) or 37mm (1.45in) gun and a machine gun, it was reliable, though modest in performance even after gaining a 45mm (1.77in) gun. Large numbers – about 12,500 – were built and included a version with a 76mm (2.99in) gun, command tanks, engineering vehicles and even a glider tank. The T-26 was outclassed at the time of the invasion, but its crews did their best.

The BT-5 light/medium tank was one of the best designs available to the Soviets at the start of the war. It had already performed well in the Spanish Civil War and its 45mm (1.77in) gun was more capable than most tank armament of the time. In many ways, the BT-5 shows where Soviet tank design was going in the 1930s – a step along the path that led to the excellent T-34.

Another influence on the T-34 was the BT-7 light tank. Designed for the 'light cavalry' role, it was optimized for reconnaissance, exploitation and pursuit rather than heavy combat. Mobility was excellent and armament very good, with a 45mm (1.77in) gun and two machine guns. The BT-7 was too lightly armoured for a standup fight with other tanks, though it made the best use of its protection with sloped armour. A close support variant with a 76mm (2.99in) gun was built, as well as a diesel-engined version that influenced later tank power units. The BT-7 had proved itself in action against the Japanese and against what limited resistance the Poles could muster. Although tricky to maintain, it was available in large numbers to resist the German advance in 1941. It was, however, thrust into a role for which it was not well suited and few remained in service by the end of the year.

Despite the large quantities of tanks available to the Soviets, it was smaller numbers of much better tanks that caused the most problems for the invaders. These were the KV-1 heavy tank and the

T-34. Both designs had a number of flaws. They were cramped and uncomfortable for the crews. Vision was not good and they were hard work to drive. On top of this, mechanical problems were common. But despite their drawbacks, these two tanks were extremely good fighting machines, with powerful armament and very good protection afforded by both the thickness and shape of their armour.

The KV-1 was the first Soviet heavy tank design not to feature multiple turrets. Its 76mm (2.99in) gun could penetrate and disable any enemy tank while its own armour was impervious to most weapons. Unless an 88mm (3.46in) antitank gun or an artillery piece was available for direct fire, the only real hope for its opponents was to try to sever its tracks. During the defensive fighting of 1941–42, the KV-1 was invaluable. One tank was hit 70 times during the battle for Leningrad without being disabled, and this sort of resilience enabled the heavy tanks to contribute greatly to a battle. However, there were never enough of them to provide a decisive advantage. Furthermore, once the Soviets took the offensive, the KV-1 was found to be too slow and too unreliable and was phased out. By this time it was obsolete anyway, as new German Tiger and Panther tanks could destroy it at ranges where its own gun was ineffective. By then, though, the KV-1 had done its job. It had helped prevent defeat long enough for other designs to be available for the counteroffensive.

The other critical Soviet design was the T-34. This tank was developed in response to lessons learned from the Spanish Civil War and came as a shock to the German invaders just like the KV-1 – and for much the same reasons.

Armed with a 76mm (2.99in) gun in a well-rounded turret atop a sloped and heavily armoured hull, the T-34 was well protected and capable of taking on any contemporary tank. Just as importantly, it was mobile and easy to build in large numbers. It had its flaws, but overall it did exactly what was needed at the time – it enabled the Soviet Union to get tanks that were good enough to get the job done to the battlefield in large enough numbers to make a difference.

At the time of Operation *Barbarossa*, the T-34/76 (so designated to distinguish it from the up-gunned version that appeared later) was not

sIG 33

Fast-moving armoured formations needed self-propelled artillery weapons to support them. The sIG 33 was a clumsy first attempt to create one by mounting a 150mm (5.9in) infantry howitzer – trail, wheels and all – on a tank chassis with a light armoured shield. Initially Panzer I chassis were used, but as Panzer II and III chassis became available these were found to be more suitable and were used instead.

available in numbers. Nevertheless, those that saw action stunned the enemy with their capabilities. One T-34 is credited with over 40 kills in a single action despite every effort made by the Germans to stop it. The T-34/76 remained in production until late 1943, by which time it was outclassed. Existing vehicles continued to serve throughout the war and afterward, but by then the up-gunned T-34/85 (with an 85mm/3.35in gun) had become the standard production model.

A Soviet KV-I heavy tank in the wreckage of Stalingrad. Hard to stop, the KV-I was an unpleasant surprise.

At the time of the invasion, the Soviet Union had recently reorganized its armoured forces. As in other nations, the armoured division was the standard unit, in this case composed of two tank regiments supported by a motorized infantry regiment and an artillery regiment. An armoured division had a paper strength of about 400 tanks. Tanks were also incorporated into the motorized

Under Siege

Soviet tanks were designed for mass-production, and during the course of the war tens of thousands were produced by lines like this one.

During the great sieges of Stalingrad and Leningrad, tank production went on in the cities, at least for a time. Some vehicles were literally rolled off the line, loaded with ammunition, and taken out to fight by volunteers from among the factory workers.

infantry divisions at the rate of one armoured regiment to two motorized infantry regiments, plus artillery. An armoured corps was composed of two tank divisions and one motorized infantry division.

Early German Successes in Russia

Despite fuel shortages and a lack of motorized transport for infantry and logistics, the German Army was massively successful in the first weeks of Operation *Barbarossa*. The goal was to smash through the Soviet forces, inflicting crippling losses, and then to exploit rapidly eastwards as far as the River Volga. Much of the Soviet Union's industry and urban population lay within reach of the attack. It was not necessary to drive right across Soviet territory to render the Soviet Union impotent; the occupation of 'European' Russia would shatter its industrial capability and create a buffer zone that would prevent what was left of the Soviet Army and Air Force from harming the German heartlands.

The invasion was carried out by three Army Groups. Army Group North was to attack towards Leningrad, while Army Group Centre would undertake the main thrust into Byelorussia and smash the Soviet forces there. Once Leningrad had fallen, the next objective for the two northern army groups was Moscow. Army Group South was to attack towards Kiev, then eliminate Soviet forces on the River Dneiper before capturing the economically important Donetz Basin.

The Soviets had no defensive plan and no reserves in place, and although they were alerted just before the attack they were not permitted to take up defensive positions – as a result, many units were caught trying to establish positions or on the move. They were further hampered by the recent purges of senior officers carried out by Stalin. Competent but politically suspect officers had been replaced by more reliable but inexperienced or just plain incompetent men.

Once again, as in other theatres, speed of advance served the German Army well. Army Group Centre was opposed by the Soviet Byelorussian Group, composed of 50 infantry divisions and two armoured brigades. The Soviet commander, Marshal Semyon Timoshenko, was unable to prevent his force from being surrounded by an armoured penetration 322km (200 miles) deep. By 3 July, Timoshenko's force had been smashed with the loss of nearly 300,000 prisoners, over 2500 tanks and almost 1500 artillery pieces. By the same time, Army Group North had crossed

Assault guns like this StuG III were cheaper to build than true tanks. They were frequently pushed into a tank role.

The Soviets pursued a 'scorched earth' policy in the early years of the war. What was not destroyed by the fighting was deliberately burned or blown up.

the Dvina and Army Group South was across the River Bug.

The huge rivers of the western Soviet Union should have been major obstacles to the German advance, but as the combat engineers' adage has it 'an obstacle not covered by fire is not an obstacle'. The rapid advance brushed aside opposition and gave the enemy no chance to prepare a defence. Speed and aggression were once again the main allies of the Panzers.

The runaway success continued with the fall of Smolensk, and despite a counterattack at Elnya a second deep encirclement was accomplished – this one netted 185,000 prisoners, over 2000 more tanks and nearly the same number of artillery pieces. At this point, even though Marshal Timoshenko was collecting a defence for Moscow, there was a real chance for *Barbarossa* to achieve what no offensive in history had ever managed and put Russia out of the war.

It was not the Panzers that failed but political decisions that robbed them of victory. Hitler decided to redeploy the armoured forces of Army Group Centre from the drive on Moscow, sending some of them north to assist the attack on Leningrad and other units south to assist with the reduction of the Kiev region. In the south, the Soviet Ukrainian Group was struggling to hold a 483km (300 mile) salient against frontal attacks. The resulting encirclement from the north was a political and strategic mistake, since it gave Moscow the chance to survive, but it was a huge tactical victory. In a month-long battle, the Ukrainian Group was cut off and battered into surrender. The massive haul included more than 650,000 prisoners, 3700 artillery pieces and another 900 tanks. Leningrad, however, was not taken by Army Group North despite the assistance of armoured forces from Army Group Centre and Hitler decided that Moscow must be taken after all. This meant breaking through a Soviet force that had spent a month preparing to resist the inevitable assault.

The German battle plan was to break through with armoured thrusts and encircle the divided enemy forces. Again the Panzers achieved great things, assisted by surprise and air power. A pincer attack resulted in the usual massive numbers of prisoners – over 650,000 of them – plus yet more

Freezing Temperatures

Soviet tank crews and their equipment were much better prepared for operations in the Russian winter, where temperatures fell so low that oil froze in the sump.

tanks and guns. More than 1200 Russian tanks were captured along with an unbelievable 5400 artillery pieces. Yet it was too late. Although the Panzers were only 105km (65 miles) from Moscow and the defence was in tatters, Hitler's interference in the battle plans made victory impossible. Russia has always had three great strengths in resisting invaders. The huge numbers and dogged courage of her people are one, the massive distances that must be crossed make another. And the third is the weather, which now joined the fight.

Twice a year, western Russia was subjected to heavy rainfall that turned the countryside and more importantly the roads to mud. Known as the *rasputiza* ('season of mud'), the foul weather brought everything, most importantly the Panzer advance in the northern regions, to a standstill. Operations were still possible in the south, and successes were made, but it was not until early November that falling temperatures froze the mud and made movement once more possible. However, the freeze brought with it new problems. Hitler had decreed that Russia would be destroyed in the summer, and few preparations had been made for either an extended campaign nor winter fighting.

The attack on Moscow resumed, even though the troops and their vehicles were suffering terribly with the cold. After intense fighting, some German troops actually penetrated the suburbs of Moscow, but increasing malfunctions of equipment and deaths from frostbite and hypothermia, coupled with determined resistance from the Soviet troops and civilians, forced a retreat.

As 1941 came to a close, the Soviets counterattacked under the command of Marshal Georgi Zhukov. He had under his hand additional forces from Siberia, freed for operations in the west

HEAD TO HEAD: *KV-1 Heavy Tank* VERSUS

After a run of very poor vehicles, Soviet designers got it right with the KV-1. Not without its faults, it was nevertheless a powerful and robust vehicle whose armour could defeat most antitank weapons with ease. Only an '88' could penetrate the KV-1 while its own 76mm (2.99in) gun was more than a match for any German tank of the early war years.

KV-1

Crew: 5
Weight: 43,000kg (94,600lb)
Dimensions: length 6.68m (21ft 11in); width 3.32m (10ft 10.7in); height 2.71m (8ft 10.7in)
Range: 150km (93.2 miles)
Armour: 100mm (3.94in)
Armament: one 76.2mm gun; four 7.62mm machine guns
Powerplant: one V-2K V-12 diesel engine developing 600hp (448kW)
Performance: maximum road speed 35km/h (21.75mph); fording not known; verticle obstacle 1.20m (3ft 8in); trench 2.59m (8ft 6in)

STRENGTHS

- Extremely good armour
- Wide tracks gave good mobility in soft ground
- Good armament by 1941 standards

WEAKNESSES

- Hard work to drive
- Commander also acted as loader
- Somewhat underpowered

Panzer IV Medium Tank

The Panzer IV was much lighter than the KV-1 but fulfilled a similar role in some ways by supporting the Panzer IIIs as KV-1s supported T-34 units. Its original short 75mm (2.95in) gun had limited antitank performance, but the addition of a long gun (still of 75mm/2.95in calibre) turned the Panzer IV into a serious battle tank that became the mainstay of the Panzer formations for most of the war.

Panzer IV

Crew: 5
Weight: 25,000kg (55,000lb)
Dimensions: length 7.02m (23ft); width 3.29m (10ft 9.5in); height 2.68m (8ft 9.5in)
Range: 200km (125 miles)
Armour: 50–60mm (1.97–2.4in)
Armament: one 75mm (2.95in) gun; two 7.92mm (0.312in) MG 34 machine guns
Powerplant: one Maybach HL 120 TRM 12-cylinder etrol engine developing 300hp (224kW)
Performance: maximum road speed 38km/h (24mph); fording 1.0m (3ft 3in); vertical obstacle 0.6m (2ft); trench 2.20m (7ft 3in)

STRENGTHS

- Good armament on later models
- Well protected
- Good power-to-weight ratio

WEAKNESSES

- Early models had many design flaws
- Short gun on early models gave poor anti-armour performance
- Outdated by last years of the war

by an agreement with Japan. The Germans had to pull back to their forward supply bases, where the troops could gain some protection from the cold.

Zhukov understood armoured warfare as well as anyone else, and forbade frontal attacks in favour of flanking movements and envelopments. He stated that a frontal attack allowed a defeated enemy to retreat in good order, but a successful flanking operation could trap and annihilate an enemy force. Zhukov's tactics, coupled with new equipment, resulted in a number of Soviet successes and pushed the German forces further back.

Operation *Barbarossa* initially had a real chance for success, but that was now gone. True, some 35 divisions of armoured troops had been lost by the Soviets, but these were largely composed of obsolete vehicles while hundreds of new T-34s were becoming available to outfit replacement formations. The other Allies were sending tanks to the Soviet Union, allowing new tank brigades to be quickly created.

A late-1941 Soviet tank brigade officially consisted of three tank battalions with a mix of vehicles, supported by a machine-gun battalion, an antitank company and a mortar company. In practice, establishment varied according to what was available, and it was not uncommon for brigades to be formed with only two battalions, each with less than 25 tanks each.

Armoured brigades were formed into tank corps. These varied in composition according to what was available, but were nominally composed of three tank brigades supported by a motorized infantry brigade and a variable amount of artillery. A Soviet tank corps was thus roughly equivalent to a Panzer division. Mechanized corps also existed, comprising three motorized infantry brigades with a tank brigade in support. It was with these forces that the first Soviet counterattacks were made.

Operation Crusader

During a short lull in the war in North Africa, the British undertook a period of training and preparation for renewed operations. This included a reorganization of forces that created the famous Eighth Army. With this re-equipped and reorganized force, the British opened a new offensive named Operation Crusader on 11 November 1941.

Their opponents included the German Afrika Korps, which had also been reorganized. Its two original Panzer units were still present, though the 5th Light Division was now named the 21st Panzer Division. To this had been added an amalgamation of previously independent formations now grouped

A British Mk IV Cruiser Tank. This was an improved version of the Mk III, with thicker and better-shaped armour.

into the 90th Light Division – this contained no armour, but there was one Italian armoured division (Ariete) and five infantry divisions available. The Italian forces were largely employed in the ongoing siege of Tobruk, with three divisions involved and another in reserve. The remainder of Rommel's forces were available for mobile operations if needed.

What Auchinleck wanted was to destroy the Panzer formations, and he reasoned that the best way to do this was to provoke them to attack. Tactical command was in the hands of Lieutenant-General Alan Cunningham, who was unfortunately an adherent of the flawed naval-fleet-on-land concept of armoured warfare. Naval warfare does not take place in terrain dominated by well-emplaced artillery, nor can warships hide hull-down behind the waves and shoot at their enemies with only their turrets exposed, and this is what happened to Cunningham's command. Some of the advancing units ran into antitank guns and suffered heavily, and the 4th Armoured Brigade was battered in an engagement with the 21st Panzer Division. Even where successes were gained, heavy losses were taken from artillery and antitank guns.

By the end of the first day, 19 November 1941, the British armour had become dispersed despite a plan that called for it to concentrate. One reason for this scattering was bad communications; great emphasis had been placed upon obtaining enough tanks and not enough on controlling them. Rommel ordered a counterattack for the following day, the 20th, using all his armour in a concentrated counterthrust that inflicted heavy losses. On the 21st, the Panzers lunged against a different target. This close control and flexible handling of his forces was one of the great strengths

Cruiser tanks

Also designated A13 Mk II, the Mk IV Cruiser tank was typical of British cruiser tank designs. Its 2-pounder (40mm/1.57in) gun was somewhat light for a combat tank and armour protection was not good on the basic model.

The A13 was the first British cruiser tank to adopt Christie suspension and was very fast – so fast that it could damage itself. Its engine was sufficiently powerful that the version with extra armour was not much slower.

of Rommel's command style, allowing him to bring his force to bear as a giant hammer wielded by a single mind.

Poor communications hamstrung the British effort throughout the battle, and the situation was made worse by ill fortune. The 15th Panzer Division collided with the rear echelon of 4th Armoured Brigade Group while both formations were on the move. The Panzers could bring more firepower to bear faster and more flexibly than their opponents, and captured the entire headquarters. This German success deprived an entire British armoured brigade of orders and communications, rendering its relatively large surviving tank force impotent to affect the course of the battle. By the 23rd, 4th Armoured Brigade was out of the picture.

Communications elsewhere were a shambles and plans to launch a counterattack were abandoned by the British, as most units had no idea where they, the enemy or their allies were.

Only a handful of operational tanks remained in other British formations, but the British armour was no longer capable of affecting the outcome of the battle. The New Zealand Division, an infantry force, managed to capture the headquarters of the Afrika Korps, though this did not badly disrupt the Axis forces. General Ludwig Cruewell, commanding the Afrika Korps, had been away from HQ at a tactical command post and retained sufficiently good communications to put together a joint German and Italian counterattack. This ran into British tanks by accident and was slowed, and then hit a barrier of antitank guns that put almost half of the 150 tanks committed out of action. A second attack was scraped together, showing the value of good communications down to the tactical level, and this forced the British to fall back. Rather than drawing out the Panzers and shattering them, the offensive had cost the British most of their tank strength and heavy casualties among the infantry.

A Panzer III in North Africa, December 1941. The main problem for forces operating in the desert was getting sufficient quantities of fuel and ammunition to the fighting units over great distances.

Gathering the remaining strength of his two Panzer divisions and the Italian Ariete armoured division, Rommel took advantage of the situation to launch an offensive against the British line of communications. His aim was twofold: prevent an attack on his forward positions and threaten the enemy supply line to force a withdrawal. Retreating units were very vulnerable to armoured pursuit, and it was possible that a withdrawal could be harried into rout.

On 24 November, Rommel set out on his offensive, hoping to trap and destroy the British XIII Corps. More or less by chance, there were several British unit headquarters in his path, and these were forced to scatter into the desert. This effect added to the confusion facing the British forces, and after just five hours the Panzers had covered 95km (60 miles). Rommel fell foul of mischance himself, and was almost captured when his command vehicle broke down.

The deep penetration by German armour did not cause a panic on this occasion, and harassing attacks slowed down the advance of some Panzer units. Once again, the tanks ran into trouble from emplaced antitank guns and artillery pieces firing over open sights. Rommel's plan was over-ambitious and ended in costly failure, with British forces even pushing forward in places. Some units got through to Tobruk. As a result, Rommel had to call his Panzers back to deal with the situation in his rear area, wasting fuel and wearing down the tank force by mechanical attrition. Now the large British reserve of tanks really began to show its worth, as armoured units were brought back up to strength by replacement vehicles, while others were recovered from the battlefield and send back for repair. The revitalized British armoured brigades attacked the 15th Panzer Division, but were beaten off by antitank guns.

After some to-and-fro operations, Rommel pulled back to Agheila. An attempt to cut off the retreat failed, and attacks on the rear of the Axis force were beaten off by mobile and aggressive counterattacks. The mobility of the Panzers allowed them to lunge against pursuing forces, hit hard and escape before they could be cut off and destroyed.

Both sides learned from the campaign. The ability of mutually supporting antitank guns to break up a tank attack was clearly demonstrated, and anti-armour tactics became highly refined. Rommel reorganized his forces to deal with this, implementing closer cooperation between motorized infantry, artillery and armoured forces.

Rommel also came back from defeat with impressive speed. Within weeks, he was able to launch an operation that recaptured some of the lost territory. By late January 1942, the Panzers were just 103km (64 miles) from Tobruk. The main obstacle they faced was the British defensive line at Gazala.

Events on the Russian Front were far more important to Hitler and the Nazi leadership than the desert war, and Rommel struggled to obtain fuel and replacement vehicles. His opponents were equally hard-pressed, especially since their supply lines were long and subject to naval and air attack. A lull, characterized by probing and harassment attacks rather than major operations, descended on the desert war from February to May 1942.

The Eastern Front 1942

The Soviet Army had taken a tremendous battering in 1941 and had not yet fully recovered. Nevertheless, a series of Soviet offensives made some progress at driving back the invaders, who at times took needlessly heavy losses after being refused permission to make tactical withdrawals. The fighting was characterized on both sides by enveloping movements that aimed to trap and utterly destroy enemy formations.

Eastern Delights

German tanks advancing on the Eastern Front. The vast distances and appalling roads in Russia took their toll on the Panzers, rendering many unserviceable without any need for enemy action.

Soviet infantry advance past a T-70 light tank, for which the Red Army retained a liking, despite its inadequacies.

The German goal for 1942 was to shatter Soviet forces in the south and drive into the Caucasus to capture the oilfields there. This push would be the northern half of a grand strategic pincer movement. The southern half would be an offensive eastwards by Rommel and the Afrika Korps. The Soviets were also active. Although they made large gains in some sectors, inexperience in fast-moving armoured warfare was a problem, with some formations disintegrating under the 'friction' of high-tempo operations without enemy interference. Local superiority of equipment, and a generally higher standard of tactics and command procedures allowed the Germans to gain the upper hand.

The German summer offensive of 1942, codenamed *Fall Blau* (Operation Blue), was the last real chance for the German Army to win the war in Eastern Europe. It opened promisingly, with the Panzers smashing the nearest enemy units and blasting through the gaps in a classic *Blitzkrieg* assault. Soviet command-and-control broke down as the pace of the assault overwhelmed the Red Army commanders' ability to determine what was happening and give useful orders to deal with it. Supplies became an increasing problem, and Soviet mobile counterattacks caused some serious setbacks. At one point, six German divisions became cut off by a counterattack. They were kept supplied by the *Luftwaffe*, creating a false impression of the capabilities of large-scale air supply. Nonetheless, the previously effective German tactic of using captured fuel supplies to power further advances was often thwarted by an efficient 'scorched earth' policy on the part of the Red Army.

By the end of August 1942, the German forces had made large gains and were in the process of encircling Stalingrad. Soviet counterattacks in the north, near Moscow and Leningrad, achieved limited results. On the face of it, it seemed that the Germans were winning. This was not the case.

At this point in the war, the Germans had to win, while all the Soviet Union had to do was to avoid defeat long enough for its huge manpower reserves to wear down the invaders. As winter began to close in, the Germans had not achieved victory and their chance was slipping away. Fighting bogged down, gains became more limited, and the opportunities for massive Panzer victories became ever fewer. Towards the very end of the year, a Soviet armoured offensive at Stalingrad overran the Romanian units covering the flanks of the German Sixth Army and Fourth Panzer Army. The situation was partially stabilized by the rapid intervention of mobile forces, but after heavy fighting the German forces were surrounded.

A massive three-day tank battle resulted from an attempt by 13 German divisions, including three Panzer divisions, to punch through and rescue their surrounded compatriots at Stalingrad. General Friedrich Paulus, commanding the encircled troops, asked for permission to break out of the pocket, but this was refused by Hitler, who was still standing by his 'not one step back' doctrine. With Paulus bottled up in Stalingrad, the Red Army pushed on with its offensive as the year came to a close.

The Eastern Front in 1942 spawned a number of innovations and new vehicle designs. Among them was the Marder 'tank destroyer'. Large numbers of antitank guns were needed to deal with Soviet T-34 and KV-1 tanks, and the standard towed gun was not mobile enough to fit the need. Tanks with a big enough gun could get the job done, but tanks took a lot of time and resources to build. Something cheaper than a tank but more mobile than a towed gun was necessary.

The Marder I was the first of these tank destroyers. The idea came from a German artillery officer named Alfred Becker, who had served with an artillery battery. He had experimented with using captured motor vehicles to pull horse-drawn artillery during the 1940 campaign in Western Europe, and during the occupation of France he created several improvised self-propelled guns from captured equipment.

From these experiments came the idea of mounting an antitank gun on the chassis of a tracked vehicle. The Marder I used a German 75mm (2.95in) antitank gun on the chassis of various captured French vehicles. It could only be lightly armoured and the gun was capable of limited traverse, but it created a mobile antitank capability where none had existed before. The Marder II made use of what amounted to windfalls

MARDER II

Crew: 3 or 4
Weight: 11,000kg (24,200lb)
Dimensions: length 6.36m (20ft 10.4in); width 2.28m (7ft 5.8in); height 2.20m (7ft 2.6in)
Range: 190km (118 miles)
Armour: 10mm (0.39in)
Armament: one 7.5cm Pak 40/2 gun; one 7.92mm MG34 machine gun
Powerplant: one Maybach HL 62 petrol engine developing 140hp (104kW)
Performance: maximum road speed 40km/h (24.8mph); fording 0.9m (2ft 11in); vertical obstacle 0.42m (1ft 4in); trench 1.8m (5ft 11in)

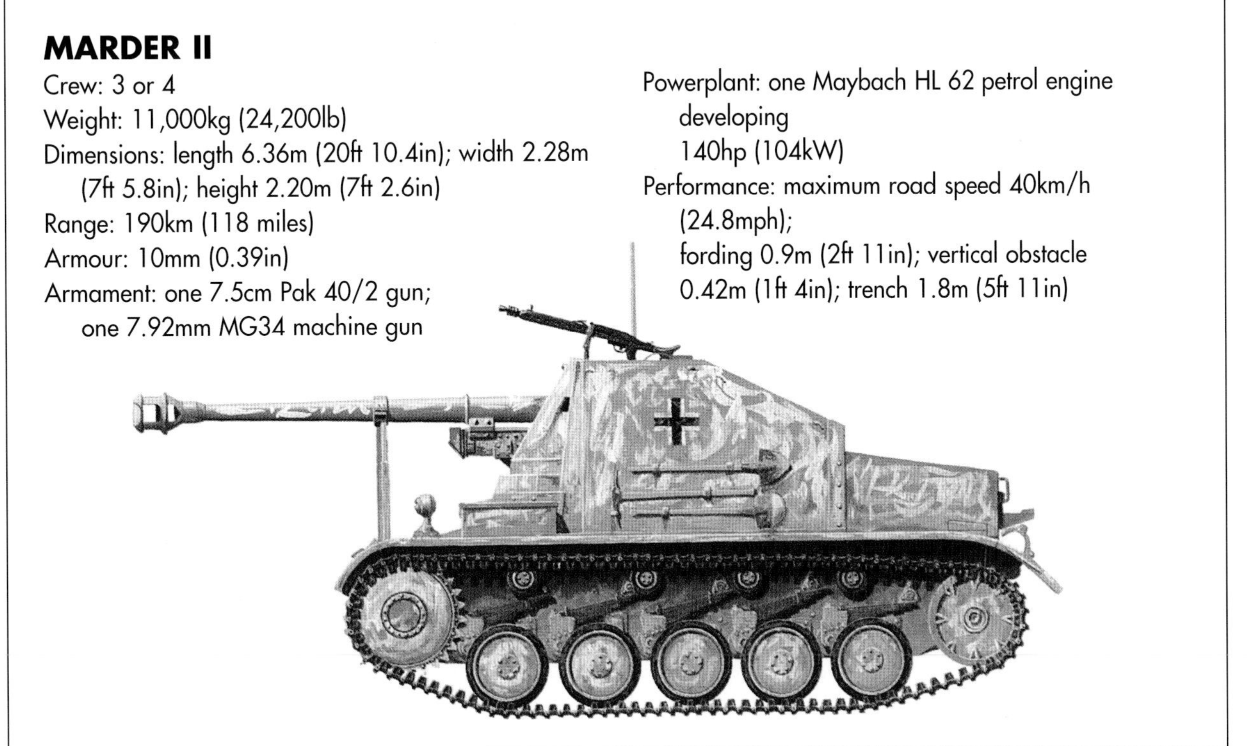

HEAD TO HEAD: *M3 Lee (Grant)* VERSUS

US tank designers needed to get a bigger gun into action as quickly as possible to counter improvements in German armour that could defeat the standard 37mm (1.45in) tank weapon. The M3's turret ring was too small for a 75mm (2.95in) weapon so the M3 Grant was created; a stop-gap measure that carried its big gun in a hull mount and a 37mm (1.45in) in the turret. It was fairly successful but was replaced by the M4 Sherman as soon as practicable.

M3 Lee Mk I

Crew: 6
Weight: 27,216kg (60,001lb)
Dimensions: length 5.64m (18ft 6in); width 2.72m (8ft 11in); height 3.12m (10ft 3in)
Range: 193km (120 miles)
Armour: 57mm (2.24in)
Armament: One 75mm (2.95in) M2 or M3 cannon; one 37mm (1.45in) M5 or M6 cannon; four 7.62mm (0.3in) MGs
Powerplant: Continental radial 340hp (254kW) petrol engine
Performance: maximum speed 42mk/h (26mph)

STRENGTHS

- 75mm (2.95in) gun could penetrate German tanks
- British experience incorporated into design
- Cast rather than riveted hull

WEAKNESSES

- Main gun had very limited traverse
- Could not engage from hull-down defensive position
- Easy to convert to other roles, e.g. self-propelled gun

Type 97 Chi-Ha

The Japanese army resisted attempts to give it medium tanks, feeling that the light vehicles it was already using were entirely adequate. This was true until they encountered European and US designs, which were entirely superior. The Type 97 would not have been considered a medium tank in Europe, though it did carry a useful 57mm (2.24in) gun. It was under-protected and very vulnerable to antitank weapons.

Type 97 Chi-Ha

Crew: 4
Weight: 15,000kg (33,069lb)
Dimensions: length 5.5m (18ft); width 2.33m (7ft 8in); height 2.23m (7ft 4in)
Range: Unknown
Armour: 25mm (0.98in)
Armament: One 6-pounder (57mm/2.24in) gun; two 7.7mm (0.3in) MGs
Powerplant: Mitsubishi Type 97 V-12 diesel 170bhp (127kW) engine
Performance: maximum speed 39km/h (24mph)

STRENGTHS

- Respectable 57mm (2.24in) gun
- Heaviest common Japanese tank
- Better armoured than lighter designs

WEAKNESSES

- Difficult to produce in large numbers
- Underarmoured by Western standards
- Basically an overgrown light tank

Marder II
The Marder II was a clever adaptation of the Panzer II chassis. Mating a 75mm (2.95in) antitank gun to an obsolete light tank chassis created an effective tank destroyer.

to create an effective combat vehicle. The PzKpfw II was by this time totally outmatched, and by converting the chassis to mount an antitank gun the resource could be re-used. Large numbers of captured Soviet 76mm (2.99in) antitank guns were available, so these were used at first. They were replaced by German 75mm (2.95in) guns when the captured examples were finally used up.

The Soviets also worked to produce new tank designs. Not all of these were as successful as the T-34. The T-60 light tank was supposed to support and scout for the battle tanks, but was too underpowered to keep pace with the T-34s, let alone advance ahead of them to conduct armoured reconnaissance. It was also very lightly armoured and armed with an inadequate 20mm (0.78in) gun. About 6000 were built and served in 1941–42 before a better armoured version replaced them. The T-70 that followed was built on the same chassis and used a complicated and unreliable two-engine system. It was still incapable of more than infantry support and some reconnaissance, but was kept in production to make use of factories that could not build heavier tanks.

Meanwhile, the T-34 was still giving excellent performance, but towards the end of 1942 large numbers of 75mm (2.95in) guns appeared on enemy tanks and tank destroyers. T-34 casualties rose rapidly, and it became desirable to create a more survivable version. Development work began on the T-43, which was to be essentially an up-armoured T-34. By the time the prototypes were ready, it was apparent that what was really needed was a T-34 with a bigger gun, and hence a longer effective range. The T-34/85 was created to meet this need and the T-43 forgotten.

Gazala and the Fall of Tobruk

New shipments of tanks and equipment reached the Axis forces at much the same time as the most experienced of their British opponents were being pulled back to refit prior to a renewal of operations. This situation meant that many of the units opposing Rommel's new offensive had little experience of operating in the desert, and in many cases little combat experience at all.

The PzKpfw IV Ausf F1 had appeared in February 1941. It had increased armour protection as a result of lessons learned in France and wider tracks to accommodate the greater weight. Its combat debut came in mid-1941. About a year later, in March 1942, the more capable F2 variant appeared. This tank was fitted with a long 75mm (2.95in) gun rather than the short one of previous models. The PzKpfw was successful in the desert as well as on the Russian steppe, and was updated later in the year to the model G, which included a slightly longer gun and a number of technical refinements. Over 1700 Panzer IV model F and G tanks were produced in 1942, while earlier models were upgraded to the same standard.

Another advantage enjoyed by the Axis forces was the availability of large numbers of half-tracked vehicles, which made mobility in the desert less of a problem. Rapid mobility was a huge asset in the campaign, as armoured forces fell on one British unit after another and inflicted sharp defeats. A new German tactic was tried that worked well:

T-70

Crew: 2
Weight: 9200kg (20,282lb)
Dimensions: length 4.29m (14ft 1in); width 2.32m (7ft 7in); height 2.04m (6ft 8in)
Range: unknown
Armour: 10–45mm (0.39–1.77in)
Armament: one 45mm (1.77in) L/46 gun; one 7.62mm (0.3in) DT MG
Powerplant: Two 85bhp (104kW) GAZ 202 6-cylinder petrol engines
Performance: maximum speed 45km/h (28mph)

antitank gun batteries advanced by 'leapfrogging' from one position to another in conjunction with the tanks. This was essentially a fire-and-manoeuvre operation carried out with tanks and guns rather than infantry squads.

Success was rapid and extensive, with the Axis forces demolishing many units and capturing large quantities of supplies. Not everything was captured intact, however, and as the supply line got longer the German forces that could be supported reduced. The forces were thus too small to break through the Allied defensive positions at Gazala, even though these were relatively weak and not held in any great depth. In fact, the Gazala line was intended as little more than a protective screen behind which to muster a new offensive. It was composed of several self-contained 'brigade boxes' protected by minefields. Some way behind it was a large logistics base for the coming campaign, and British thinking in the battle that followed centred around not allowing the enemy to capture these supplies.

As well as establishing brigade units as defensive formations, the British were again experimenting with other formations. The 'brigade group' was one such. It had been tried before, with mixed results, but again divisions were broken down into three brigade groups, with artillery and other supports shared equally between them rather than being concentrated under a central commander. Armoured forces had likewise been dispersed, despite Auchinleck's orders to the contrary. Some brigades were scattered about and others actually broken down into their components to support the infantry. This was thinking straight out of World War I, and was accompanied by the arrival of the M3 (Lee or Grant) medium tank with its hull-mounted 75mm (2.95in) gun in addition to a turret-mounted 37mm (1.45in). The Lee was an interim measure. Its designers had wanted to get a 75mm (2.95in) gun onto the battlefield, but there was no turret that would take the gun and still fit on an existing hull. There was insufficient time to develop a new tank, so the 75mm (2.95in) gun went into the right side of the hull of what was effectively an M2A1 medium tank – the same vehicle from which the 'other' M3, the Stuart, was developed. The turret, with its 37mm (1.45in) gun and coaxial machine gun, was identical.

The basic US model was designated the Lee, but in British service the tank was given a new turret and known as the Grant. Because of the way it mounted its armament, the Grant could not fight from a hull-down position. Despite this failing, it was successful in action, though it was soon supplanted by the M4 Sherman, designed from the outset to carry a 75mm (2.95in) gun.

Rommel's plan was to 'grip' the northern sector of the British front by attacking with Italian infantry divisions, hopefully pulling in reserves to that sector. The Panzers would then throw a right hook around the southern end of the line and roll it up, driving the British northwards. Pinned against the sea and surrounded, the British forces would be annihilated.

The attack opened as planned with the Italians attacking in the afternoon of 26 May 1942, and the armoured right hook was launched the following morning. Initially things went well, and some British units were scattered or smashed. The appearance of the Grant tanks, however, came as an unpleasant shock. At ranges of about 1000m (3280ft), the only vehicles that could kill an opposing tank were, on the Axis side, the PzKpfw III with its 50mm (2.28in) gun and the Grant on the British side. There were a lot more Grants than Panzer IIIs, however. The German problem was solved by the redeployment of several 88mm (3.46in) antitank batteries and the advance resumed. A fluid attack-and-counterattack battle then developed between the armoured forces on both sides, and while the British were hard pressed they were not broken.

Heavy fighting went on all through the 27th, and by next morning the 21st Panzer Division was close to the coast road – the vital supply line for the British forces. Yet its own supply situation was desperate. Almost out of fuel and short of ammunition, it was able to threaten the British supply route, but the Panzers' own position was not good. They were was short of supplies, cut off by two infantry brigade boxes and a huge minefield.

Meanwhile, the British had begun to move and were determined to smash the trapped divisions with an armoured counterstroke. They were not quick enough, however, and a gap was opened in the minefield. Ever aggressive, Rommel decided that rather than escape through the gap he would smash the nearest British brigade and widen the gap enough to supply his force – then take the offensive.

At this point, Rommel was stuck in an exposed forward position, nearly surrounded and supplied only through a gap in the British line. He chose to view the situation differently, believing that he was in a position to attack anywhere he wanted. It is more surprising that the British chose to see it that way too. It was not until 5 June that an attack on Rommel's exposed position was launched.

A Cossack officer and Soviet soldiers pose around a captured Panzer IV. The tank is an F1 variant.

An M4 Sherman rumbles through the ruins of a city while GIs take shelter in a doorway.

It went wrong from the start. The artillery support was off target and the leading units hit unshaken enemy troops. Breaking through the first enemy line, they ran headlong into the fire of emplaced artillery and antitank guns and were shot up badly. Other units became lost in their own covering smokescreen and wandered into a minefield that was covered by antitank guns and tanks.

As the wheels came off the British attack, the Panzers launched their own counterattack. This mobile offensive chased some British units off and bypassed others to hit unprepared formations, rolling up two divisional headquarters. By nightfall, the British were in chaos. A planned attack for the next morning collapsed before it began.

The results of this attack were appalling. The British had started with about 400 tanks and had lost more than half of them. The Axis force started with 230 and lost no more than 10 per cent of its numbers. Further ineffectual attacks bounced off the defensive Axis position as Rommel increased the pressure of his own attacks. He was assisted by sloppy British radio discipline, which allowed him to obtain an accurate picture of his opponents' plans, positions and strength from their own reports.

Things continued to go downhill for the British from there, and it became obvious that the battle was totally lost. The British began to retreat from 14 June onwards. Perhaps taking a leaf from Rommel's own book, the British formed an armoured covering force that provided mobile support to units that came under attack.

With the British in retreat, Tobruk was once again isolated. An initial attack broke though the perimeter and was halted only by the intervention of a mobile force of tanks. Such resistance was not enough, and subsequent attacks penetrated the city, forcing a surrender.

One factor in the loss of Tobruk, which was a terrible shock to the British, was the unavailability of good antitank guns. The available 2-pounders (40mm/1.57in guns) were increasingly outdated and found it difficult to penetrate the heavier armour of German tanks at this stage of the war. The minefields also had large gaps. To a great extent, Tobruk fell because of a lack of preparation. Nobody seriously thought that Rommel could break through the line at Gazala, chase off the forces in front of him so that they could not interfere, and then assault the city, all in a very short time period. Once again, aggressive armoured warfare, going up against an opponent who did not realize just how quickly things could change, had achieved sudden and massive results.

LATE WORLD WAR II TANKS

By the middle of World War II, the combatants were engaged in a see-saw battle of capability and countermeasure. As tanks with improved armour appeared, they were matched by tanks fitted with bigger guns. Vehicles considered adequate in 1939 were obsolete by 1943.

The United States was initially too focused on the Pacific naval war to contain Japanese expansion. Wars are won on land, however, and it was inevitable that US forces would become involved in ground combat in the Pacific and also the European theatre of war. For much of the Pacific war, US forces struggled to defend and later capture islands. The terrain they fought over was unsuitable for large-scale armoured combat, but tanks played an important role as mobile artillery that could be used to suppress strongpoints.

American armour entered the European war in November 1942, as part of an Anglo-American force landing in Morocco and Algeria. These landings, named Operation *Torch*, brought the inexperienced US tank corps into contact with their German counterparts, who had a massive advantage in combat experience. The US learning curve was cruelly steep, and the capability to fight the Panzers on equal terms was won in blood.

Left: Soviet T-34/85 tanks with turrets reversed. The T-34/85 was an upgunned, better-armoured version of the T-34/76, created in response to improved German tanks.

US tank design was heavily influenced by British experiences, and it was decided to build a tank with a 75mm (2.95in) gun, as lesser weapons were proving inadequate in action. The M3 Lee/Grant was constructed as an interim measure while a suitable battle tank was under development. After examining several designs, the US Army decided on the simplest of them, which became the M4 Sherman. The emphasis on simplicity was a good choice – the US and its allies needed a lot of tanks, fast, and as events elsewhere would show it was better to build a good tank in vast numbers than to produce handfuls of an excellent one.

The M4 Sherman used a modified version of the M3 body with a new cast, rounded turret mounting a powerful 75mm (2.95in) gun. Delivery began in January 1942, with large numbers being produced at several sites. The Sherman was good, but not great. It had a tendency to burn, which earned it the unfortunate nickname 'Ronson' after an advertising slogan for a brand of lighter that would light 'first time, every time'. In addition, its armour was somewhat weak and not well sloped. Despite these drawbacks, the Sherman was a good fighting tank that served the Allies well in many roles.

Shermans were adapted in all manner of ways. In the field they were given additional armour or sandbags for protection, and some Shermans in British service were adapted to the 'Firefly' configuration with a 17-pounder (76mm/2.99in) gun. More radical variants included the 'Crab' with its mine clearance flails and the 'DD', or Duplex Drive Sherman, developed for the amphibious invasion of Normandy.

Other projects were not so successful. The M6 heavy tank started out as an enlarged M3 with hull-mounted and turret guns, then developed into a version with co-axial 76mm (2.99in) and 37mm (1.45in) guns in its turret. The project was eventually abandoned after a number of prototypes were built. It would have been the world's most powerful tank had it entered service, but the

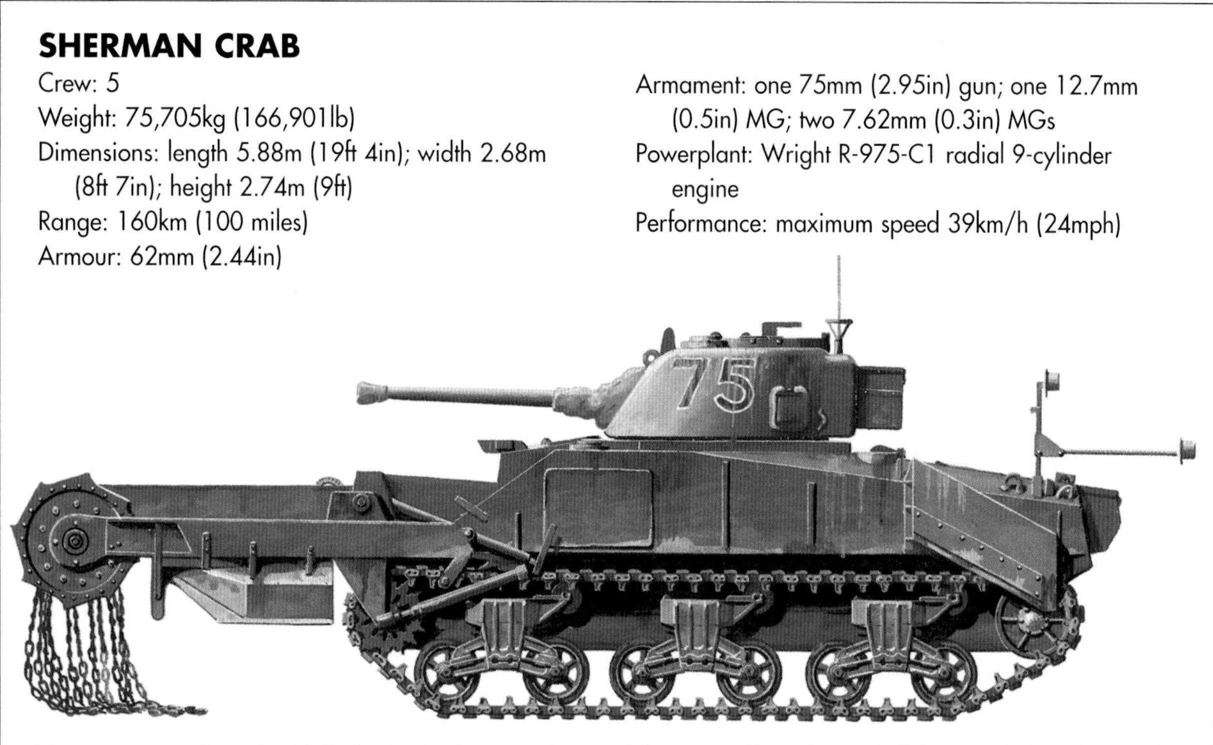

SHERMAN CRAB

Crew: 5
Weight: 75,705kg (166,901lb)
Dimensions: length 5.88m (19ft 4in); width 2.68m (8ft 7in); height 2.74m (9ft)
Range: 160km (100 miles)
Armour: 62mm (2.44in)
Armament: one 75mm (2.95in) gun; one 12.7mm (0.5in) MG; two 7.62mm (0.3in) MGs
Powerplant: Wright R-975-C1 radial 9-cylinder engine
Performance: maximum speed 39km/h (24mph)

decision was made to build more of fewer designs, and this was undoubtedly correct.

Experiments were also carried out with upgunned replacements for the M4 Sherman, even before it had begun its combat career. This was nothing unusual; the development cycle would take time to produce a new tank. Various designs were tried out, including the T25 medium tank, which was originally designed to carry a 90mm (3.54in) gun. This was downgraded to a 76mm (2.99in) gun before the project was abandoned.

Another project that began well enough was the T14, an Anglo-American project to build an infantry or 'assault' tank using components from the Sherman and M6. It was too heavy and slow, and its cost and bulk were not justified by the 75mm (2.95in) gun it would have carried.

Attempts were also made to build a new light tank. The M22 was intended to be air-mobile. However, the United States did not have the air transport assets to make use of it. The British adopted it under the name Locust, and some examples saw action in 1945.

The Tiger I – A Hamstrung Giant

The PzKpfw VI Tiger followed on from a long period of on-and-off experimentation with heavy tanks, which was given sudden importance by the need to beat KV-1s and T-34s on the Eastern Front. The designers proposed an advanced squeeze-bore 70mm (2.75in) or 60mm (2.36in) gun for the new tank, but Hitler wanted a vehicle armed with the proven 88mm (3.46in) antitank gun.

In this case, Hitler had the right idea – the squeeze-bore gun needed tungsten steel, which was hard to obtain in wartime Germany, while the 88mm was a known quantity. It could also share ammunition with existing antitank guns, simplifying logistics. After some wrangling over whether to use the design put forward by Porsche or Henschel, the two competing contractors, the Henschel design was put into production. However, a contract had already been awarded to Porsche to build their design and the chassis already built were converted into Elefant tank destroyers.

The Tiger (designated the Tiger I after the Tiger II appeared) was complex and slow to build. It was also mechanically unreliable and fuel-hungry. Yet its massive armour made it hard to kill and its gun could penetrate anything on the battlefield. To facilitate strategic mobility, the Tiger had two sets of tracks: a narrow track to allow it to be carried on railway wagons and a wide battle track. The overlapped road wheels necessary to spread out the tank's weight proved a problem in Russia, where they became clogged with frozen mud.

Despite its problems the Tiger was formidable in combat. Just a handful could inflict considerable losses on the Allies. Had they been held back until they could be committed in reasonable numbers, the Tiger companies might have achieved some decisive results, at least in the short term. However, this was not to be.

The Tiger I became available for operational service in August 1942, and despite the protests of

his advisors Hitler insisted that the first machines be sent into action almost immediately. Thus rather than being committed *en masse,* the Tigers went to the front in tiny numbers and were quickly sent into action, sometimes in unsuitable terrain.

The Tiger's resilience was a nasty fright for the antitank gunners that opposed it, but they soon discovered that it was possible to shoot the tracks off. The early commitment also allowed the Soviets to develop a countermeasure.

Some Tigers went to Tunisia to fight in the desert, but these too were committed in small numbers. The Afrika Korps developed a tactic of

The Elefant tank destroyer was an adaptation of an unsuccessful heavy tank design.

deploying Tigers in the middle-rear of a formation as fire-support tanks rather than the spearhead. This worked well, providing covering fire under which the more rapid, lighter tanks could advance. As in the East, there were too few Tigers to make a strategic difference, and the Allies were able to capture intact examples. They found that most of their weapons could not penetrate a Tiger, but the new 17-pounder (76mm/2.99in) gun had a reasonable chance. The main problem with operating the Tiger in North Africa was logistical. Its massive fuel consumption limited its utility, and in addition there were many areas where the Tigers were simply too heavy to operate.

Despite all these problems, the Tiger made a deep impression on Allied troops, acquiring something of a bogeyman reputation. Reports of a Tiger sighting in a combat zone were enough to make Allied troops nervous, even though many of these reports were groundless.

Endgame in the Desert

After the fall of Tobruk, the British forces in North Africa were in chaos. Rommel was able to exploit his advantage by pressing his pursuit. Captured fuel and tanks were put to use in harrying the retreating British, who were so badly off balance that they could not find the will or the means to make a stand, even though by the time the Axis forces reached the Egyptian border they had just 58 tanks in service.

Yet even as the disasters came thick and fast, things were changing. The Axis advance was slowed by a number of rearguard actions that individually achieved little, but collectively bought the time necessary to prepare a defence and counterstroke. Auchinleck took personal command and began putting a defence together at El Alamein. In fact, preparations had been underway, albeit as a precaution only, for a year: Auchinleck had selected this position as a backstop in case of an Axis threat to Alexandria and the Nile.

The position at Alamein was naturally strong, with its flanks covered by the sea to the north and the impassable Qattara Depression to the south. There were three slight ridges, offering emplaced troops a defensive advantage; and the position lay

HEAD TO HEAD: *T34/85* VERSUS

The T-34 was an excellent tank, and more than a match for the German designs it met early in the war. However, as better armoured panzers appeared, the T-34's 76mm (2.99in) gun was of increasingly marginal effectiveness. The result was an upgunned version capable of taking on the best German tanks, including the Panther. The new T-34/85's bigger turret held an 85mm (3.34in) gun, though otherwise the tank was little changed from the basic design.

T34/85

Crew: 5
Weight: 32,000kg (70,548lb)
Dimensions: length 8.15m (26ft 7in); width 2.99m (9ft 7in); height 2.74m (9ft)
Range: 300km (190 miles)
Armour: 90mm (3.54in)
Armament: one 85mm (3.35in) Zis-S-53 gun; two 7.62mm (0.3in) DT MGs
Powerplant: V-2-34 12-cylinder diesel, 500bhp (373kW) engine
Performance: maximum speed 55km/h (34mph); fording 1.37m (4ft 6in); vertical obstacle 0.71m (2ft 4in); trench 2.95m (9ft 8in)

STRENGTHS

- Proven and reliable basic design
- Big, powerful gun
- Existing T-34 production lined could be used without retooling

WEAKNESSES

- Inaccurate anti-armour rounds
- Prone to transmission problems
- Often very crudely built

Panther

The Panther was introduced to defeat the original T-34/76 and borrowed a number of concepts, such as sloped armour, from it. It was extremely successful, and is generally regarded as the best tank of the war. The Panther's improved characteristics were one of the reasons the upgunned T-34 was created. The Panther still had the edge, but there were a lot more T-34/85s than Panthers.

Panther

Crew: 4
Weight: 45,500kg (100,100lb)
Dimensions: length 8.86m (29ft) 0.75in); width 3.43m (11ft 3in); height 3.10m (10ft 2in)
Range: 177km (110miles)
Armour: 30–110mm (1.2–4.3in)
Armament: one 75mm (2.95in) gun; three 7.92mm (0.31 in) MG34 machine guns (one coaxxial, one ani-aircraft, one on hull front)
Powerplant: one Maybach HL 230 12-cylinder diesel developing 700hp (522kW)
Performance: maximum road speed 46km/h (29mph); fording 1.70m (5ft 7in); vertical obstacle 0.91m (3ft); trench 1.91m (6ft 3in)

STRENGTHS

- Powerful 75mm (2.95in) gun
- Excellent armour protection
- Very good mobility

WEAKNESSES

- Prone to mechanical troubles
- Complex and slow to build
- Not available in sufficient numbers

at the end of a short supply line, with a railway running 3.2km (2 miles) south of the sea. The defence was similar to that used at Gazala – four self-contained 'boxes' of infantry and artillery, with mobile forces and a few tanks available.

There was no way around the El Alamein position, so the only option available to Rommel was a frontal assault with whatever tactical manoeuvring proved necessary. The attack began on 30 June 1942 with a feint to the south by the Panzer divisions of the Afrika Korps, intended to draw the British armour in that direction.

On the following day the attack opened, though later than planned in some sectors due to sandstorms and the attentions of the Royal Air Force (RAF). Rommel hoped to punch between the 'boxes' using his mobile armoured and motorized infantry formations, attacking the rear wherever possible. This was entirely feasible, as the defence was not a 1917-style solid line but a series of strongpoints that could be used as pivots for mobile forces.

The attack was hampered by two of the main dangers in desert warfare: bad ground conditions and the lack of landmarks. As a result, the 90th Light Division was slowed by soft sand, became lost and ran right into the defences it was trying to bypass. Its movement was brought to a stop and it began to take a beating. The Panzers of the Afrika Korps, however, were doing better. Encountering the 18th Indian Infantry Brigade in hasty positions and lacking ammunition, the 55 or so tanks that comprised the entire available Panzer strength overran the positions, despite a determined defence assisted by a handful of Matilda tanks. The Afrika Korps lost about 40 per cent of its remaining tanks breaking this position.

Communications issues again dogged the British. An armoured counterattack to relieve the embattled Indians was delayed by misunderstandings, but the chance for a decisive breakthrough by Rommel's Panzers was lost. Too much time and too many tanks had been lost, and even though Rommel himself wanted to press ahead, weariness and the RAF made this impractical for a time.

One characteristic of Rommel's campaigns up to this point was that he had always held the initiative and forced his enemies to respond to what he was doing. Now Auchinleck turned the tables. His plan was to attack with tanks against the enemy infantry

DESERT WARFARE

The open terrain of the desert made armour protection even more important. With little to hide behind, lightly armoured vehicles were prone to be disabled at long range by enemy tank and antitank guns.

MK III VALENTINE INFANTRY TANK

Crew: 3
Weight: 17,272kg (38,078lb)
Dimensions: length 5.89m (19ft 4in); width 2.63m (8ft 8in); height 2.27m (7ft 6in)
Range: 145km (90 miles)
Armour: 8–65mm (0.32–2.56in)
Armament: One 2-pounder (40mm/1.57in) gun; one 7.92mm (0.31in) Besa MG
Powerplant: AEC 6-cylinder diesel 131bhp (97.7kW), or AEC 6-cylinder petrol 135bhp (181kW) or GMS
Performance: maximum speed 24km/h (14.9mph)

formations and force the Panzers to react. Along with inflicting losses on the Italian infantry, Auchinleck hoped that by forcing the small number of Panzers available to rush from one crisis to the next he would prevent them from attacking and perhaps cause them to break down or run out of fuel. It was a workable plan, but communications problems again derailed the operation.

At this point, the British had over 100 tanks available to the 1st Armoured Division alone, of which 38 were Grants. The Afrika Korps had only 26 of all types, and some of those were Panzer IIs of limited combat value. While Axis infantry forces were attacking El Alamein on 3 July, an armoured attack by the 1st Armoured Division overran the Italian Armoured Division Ariete, effectively taking it out of the battle and capturing all its artillery. On the 4th, the British plan was to continue in the same vein, using mobile striking forces against the Axis flanks and lines of communications. However, a combination of successful wireless intercepts that gave Rommel the details of the plan, coupled with lethargy on the British part, prevented the operation from succeeding.

The battle went on over the next few days, with reinforcements arriving to assist the British defenders. These brought the available tank strength up to over 200, and at the same time Auchinleck came up with a plan to achieve a decisive victory. Pulling some of his infantry back, he tried to give Rommel the impression that a general withdrawal was underway. Ever the opportunist, Rommel took the bait and pushed Italian infantry into the vacated British positions while what little remained of his Panzer divisions began to advance. This sort of aggressive pursuit had served Rommel well in the past, but this time it set him up for defeat.

On 10 July, as the Panzers turned northwards to exploit the situation that Rommel thought was developing there, Auchinleck attacked in the south. The assault succeeded on a local level, although it was prevented from being more significant by a mobile force thrown together in Rommel's absence by the staff at his main headquarters. On 11 July another counterattack, this time by the 15th Panzer Division, only just managed to prevent what was supposed to be a diversionary attack in the north from breaking right through the Axis forces. The Panzers then lunged this way and that, trying to achieve the breakthrough they needed for a victory, but succeeding only in wearing down their remaining strength.

The main British blow came at midnight of 14/15 July, and succeeded in its initial goals. Then, yet again, the attack deteriorated due to poor communications. Armoured and infantry forces became separated with the result that the German armoured counterattack hit infantry with no tank support and not even antitank guns.

The British operation had been intended to win the battle, and it had failed in that. However, the enemy was being worn down and a Panzer attack on the 16th was defeated with the loss of yet more tanks. Auchinleck now launched another attack. His goal was first to deal with the remaining Axis tank strength and then, once there was nothing to effectively oppose his advance, smash through and exploit with his own armour. Auchinleck had more than 170 tanks of the 1st Armoured Division at his disposal plus, in theory, about 150 Valentines of the newly arrived 23rd Armoured Brigade, but this force had spent two months at sea and was not in good shape. Its radio equipment had not been adapted to the local conditions and suffered severe problems as a result.

The Valentine was an infantry tank design developed as a private venture by Vickers. After a long period of consideration by the government, it was adopted and produced in large numbers as a combat tank armed with a 2-pounder (40mm/1.57in) gun and in other variants too. These included bridgelayers, self-propelled artillery and an amphibious version. Less successful was an experiment to determine if a tank could be 'hopped' over a minefield using rockets. The predictable result was that it was possible, but not if you wanted the tank the right way up afterwards.

The staff at British Eighth Army HQ had worked hard to offset their own massive advantage in armour, creating a plan with some startling defects. Deciding that tanks could not move at night, British tank forces that were supposed to be supporting infantry and protecting them from armoured counterattack were out of position when the attack began. Meanwhile the Afrika Korps, whose tanks had ironically moved into position at night, launched an effective attack of its own that then became a mobile counterattack against those units that did manage to get going.

The out-of-position armoured forces now came racing up to try to help the infantry. Many tanks were lost charging headlong into minefields covered by antitank guns. The 23rd Armoured Brigade lost 93 of its 104 tanks trying to push through before reluctantly admitting defeat. A second attempt on the night of 24/25 July met similar results. Again, the infantry did well enough at first, but were caught without armoured support and cut up by small numbers of tanks. This contrasted with the tank-destroying capabilities of dug-in infantry formations backed by antitank guns and protected by mines.

Amphibious tanks allowed an armoured covering force to be quickly pushed across a river while a crossing was prepared, or islands to be assaulted directly from the sea.

In August, there were some important changes. Lieutenant-General Bernard Montgomery took over from Auchinleck on the British side, and some of the experienced units were pulled out for refit. They were replaced by less-experienced formations, but overall the available tank strength grew to 935. Meanwhile, Rommel received infantry and tank reinforcements. These included some 200 tanks, and added to repaired units, brought his strength to 440 vehicles. Only 100 of the newly arrived Panzers were equipped with long guns, which offered greater range and armour-penetrating capability. Most were upgunned PzKpfw IIIs with long 50mm (2.28in) guns, but 23 were Panzer IVs with long 75mm (2.95in) weapons.

The next phase of the battle was an attempt by the Afrika Korps to break through the British positions in the south, where they were weak, and sweep northwards. The target sector was protected by mines and mobile forces, but there was no deep infantry and antitank gun defence in place. Auchinleck had envisaged enticing Rommel into making this attempt, and Montgomery inherited this plan. The most important component, finally beginning to be understood on the British side, was all-arms cooperation.

From the outset, the German operation was beset with difficulties. The mines proved to be a serious barrier and the RAF imposed delays and attrition. Soft sand also slowed down the attack. This forced Rommel to swing north sooner than planned, leading to a head-on attack against British tanks and guns that stood ready on the defensive.

The Grant tanks on the British side could not use their main 75mm (2.95in) armament when hull-down, and the new long guns of the Panzers made for an unwelcome surprise. Indeed, the Panzers were initially able to break into the British positions. They took heavy casulties, however, and were driven off by an armoured counterattack. The British, having sucked in Rommel's Panzers and mauled them, now went over to the offensive. As usual, success was limited by aggressive counterattacks and the Afrika Korps managed to escape – though it was forced to leave a lot of

Montgomery

Bernard Montgomery was an exponent of using massive, overwhelming force to achieve his objectives. In the later war years, with sufficient resources available, he was very successful against Rommel's depleted Afrika Korps.

Some of the weapons used against tanks were so powerful that they could blast a turret right off.

recoverable tanks on the battlefield, which now lay firmly in British hands.

The balance was shifting further in the British favour, with Rommel having virtually no reserves of armour and the British able to call upon large numbers of replacement tanks from the depots. Supplies were also a problem; the Axis forces were at the end of a long supply line and short of fuel. This necessitated breaking up armoured units so that they could operate locally without making long drives to a threatened area. Concentration had always given Rommel an advantage and now he was forced to give it up for logistical reasons.

Meanwhile, the British armoured formations were being reorganized along distinctly German lines. The new armoured divisions were now composed of a single armoured brigade, with three regiments. In the standard organizational model a motorized infantry brigade replaced the second armoured brigade, but there were so many tanks available that some divisions retained the second armoured brigade. Supporting forces now comprised an armoured car regiment, two artillery regiments, an antitank regiment and an anti-aircraft regiment.

The M4 Sherman tank also now appeared in the British order of battle. It had its flaws, including a tendency for stowed ammunition to catch fire far too readily. This was later countered by 'wet stowage' for ammunition – the shells were stored in a mix of water, anti-freeze and an anti-corrosion agent – but by then the M4 had gained an unfortunate reputation for burning its crews to death. Despite this, the Sherman was a good tank that served for many years; later models were still in service in 1990 in some nations. The initial version had a long 75mm (2.95in) gun as its main

In an effort to reduce the effects of 'tank terror', infantry officers and men were familiarized with them on special courses.

armament, enabling it to take on just about any other tank in the world at a respectable range.

The Churchill, or Mk IV infantry tank, also showed its worth in this campaign. A big, boxy vehicle, the Churchill was well armoured and hard to kill but mounted only a 2-pounder (40mm/1.57in) gun. The original design had carried a 75mm (2.95in) howitzer in a hull mount, but this was deleted in favour of a machine gun on production models. The Churchill was used as the basis for a number of vehicles, including bridgelayer tanks and the famous flamethrowing Crocodile. In Tunisia, the Churchill's main advantage was the ability to climb over almost anything – a legacy of World War I influences on its design process, perhaps – and thus to operate in areas where tank attacks had previously been considered impossible.

With these forces in hand, Montgomery opened his attack with a feint in the south while his main force struck in the north, near the coast. Cooperation between artillery, infantry and tanks enabled the Axis minefields to be breached and an armoured counterattack to be defeated at considerable cost to both sides. Another counterattack on the second day hit British troops who had time to prepare for it. Antitank guns accounted for 30 of the 50 German tanks lost in this action.

The M3 Grant's 75mm (2.95in) gun had an effective range, but could be fired only by exposing the tank's hull.

By the time the final attack opened, the Axis forces had just under 100 tanks available to meet the 800 or so ranged against them. Their excellent antitank defences, however, caused heavy casualties and held the attack up for a time. The 9th Armoured Brigade was given the critical task of breaking through this barrier and was ordered to succeed at any cost. The brigade advanced through the infantry to meet the challenge and smashed into the antitank positions, but was then savaged by Panzers from the flanks in a classic 'sword-and-shield' counterattack. There was little left of the brigade's tank regiments afterwards, but the job was done.

The 1st Armoured Division was pushed through the gap, which had been opened at such cost, and took up defensive positions to beat off the inevitable counterattack. Although assailed on both flanks, it was able to hold its positions and after this action – the largest tank-versus-tank engagement of the desert war – the Afrika Korps had only 24 tanks left.

Realizing that the situation was hopeless, Rommel began a withdrawal, but Hitler countermanded him, insisting he hold the positions. The Afrika Korps did what it could, its hull-down tanks halting two attacks at Tel el Aqqaqir. The position was then flanked by an infantry attack with tank support, which pushed its way between the Afrika Korps and the Italian divisions on its flank. The British then rushed a torrent of armour through the gap.

This time, Rommel had no choice but to retreat, whatever Hitler might have to say about it. The withdrawal was fast and as well-organized as possible despite RAF harassment which, curiously, took the form of high-level bombing. There was a half-hearted attempt to cut off the retreat with an armoured left hook to block the coast road, but it was too slow.

Some of the few remaining tanks of the Afrika Korps were abandoned for lack of fuel, leaving Rommel with only 10 tanks to oppose any armoured pursuit or rapid flanking operation. However, there was no real attempt at either; Montgomery preferred to follow cautiously, fearing that Rommel would once again turn and savage his strung-out pursuers, unaware that his enemy lacked the resources to do so. The threat, coupled with bitter previous experience, was enough to foster a cautious mindset at the time when reckless pursuit was more appropriate.

Rommel reached Agheila in mid-November and received reinforcements, including an Italian armoured division, while the pursuing British halted to bring up supplies. Seeing the Italians withdrawing, Montgomery ordered an attack. It hit empty air; Rommel was gone. After regaining contact, a force was sent around the Axis flank and succeeded in creating an 'anvil' for a frontal 'hammer' against which to smash Rommel's force. The Panzers, desperately short of fuel, managed to break through the anvil and escape westwards.

After another pause, combat resumed at the very end of the year. Rommel now had 36 German and 57 Italian tanks with which to fight. His opponents had 500. He decided to pull back his infantry, who lacked motorized transport and could not retreat quickly, and to fight a delaying action at Buerat, where several wadis would strengthen his position and allow the Panzers to inflict heavy losses before escaping. Following this action, Rommel retreated to good defensive positions on the Mareth Line in southern Tunisia. Although he had lost Tripoli, his main supply port, his position was fairly secure. His flanks were covered by the sea (in the form of the Gulf of Sidra) to the east and the Atlas Mountains to the west. He could receive supplies via Tunis, and his strong position would give him time to rebuild his forces.

Meanwhile, the British advance was suffering from supply difficulties, which hampered and delayed offensive operations. As Rommel had hoped, he was able to stand off the British without large losses. Yet American armoured units were making their presence felt, and were becoming a threat to the German supply line. These formations were inexperienced, however, while Rommel's force was extremely tough and well adapted to the unusual conditions of armoured warfare in the desert.

Rommel and General Hans von Arnim, the commander of German forces sent to help restore

American industry biased the numbers game in the Allies' favour. The M4 Sherman was inferior to the best German tanks but outnumbered them sufficiently.

the situation in North Africa, decided to dislodge the Americans and the Free French units assisting them. The speed and aggression of the German attack had the usual effect on those who had not encountered it before – it smashed deep into the Allied force and inflicted a painful defeat. The threat to his supply line had been contained, but Rommel wanted to win victories rather than reduce the risk of defeat. He thus planned a strike against the US forward supply bases.

The attack opened in mid-February 1943, and demonstrated the value of the Germans' vast experience of armoured combat. US forces put up a stiff fight all day, but their armour was clumsily handled and their commanders were simply not able to respond to the highly fluid situation quickly enough. To their credit, the Americans put in a counterattack, which was the right thing to do tactically, but they were still learning their trade while their opponents were already masters. There was nothing for the Americans to do but pull back and try to offset the Germans' superior combat capability with terrain advantages. The US force thus pulled back into the Kessarine Pass, which was only 2km (3.2 miles) wide and more defensible than their previous positions. If Rommel wanted to mount an attack now, he would have to come in head-on.

Rommel was both willing and able to do this, and personally led the 10th Panzer Division forward to the attack, smashing the forward positions and triggering a general retreat despite determined resistance in some areas. The arrival of additional Allied forces persuaded Rommel to be satisfied with what he had achieved and to pull back.

This battle was not a good start for the American armoured forces. Nonetheless, lessons were learned that would serve them well for many years. The emphasis was now placed on the concentration of force and the initiative of on-the-spot commanders. Coordination of artillery and air support was also understood to be extremely important.

Above: Infantry support was critical for tanks operating in close terrain. The tanks are well-spaced to minimize the effects of ambush or artillery strike, and the infantry will prevent close assault by enemy troops.

Early in March 1943, Rommel lunged against the British. This attack, made with 160 tanks, ran into a prepared defence comprising more than 500 antitank guns and 400 tanks. The Panzers fell back with heavy losses.

The Allies needed to break the Mareth Line, first built by the French to defend against an Italian attack – a nicely ironic parallel. The plan was to make a frontal assault coupled with a flanking movement. The latter fell to a mostly armoured force that included a contingent of Free French troops. Assisted by a diversionary attack, the flanking force was able to establish itself on the enemy's line of retreat. The German commanders realized it had to be removed, and quickly. A battle group of two infantry battalions and about 30 tanks was hastily sent in to dislodge it. The British were at a disadvantage in the ensuing battle, as their Valentine tanks were armed only with ineffective 2-pounder (40mm/1.57in) guns and suffered heavily.

The flanking force had to be withdrawn, though it achieved a partial success by keeping Panzer reinforcements away from the main battle at the Mareth Line. Meanwhile, the British 1st Armoured Division began a 322km (200 mile) redeployment that took them into position to attack – more or less straight from the march – towards El Hamma. The pinnacle of efficiency reached by the division was matched by its fighting power. Some of its tanks were armed with the new 17-pounder (76mm/2.99in) gun, and in the confused small-scale actions that followed one such blew the turret clean off a Panzer IV with a single shot.

The Axis forces fell back to another strong position at the Wadi Akarit: a 19km (12-mile) stretch between the sea on one flank and impassable rocky terrain on the other, with a huge antitank ditch in front. This position was broken by an infantry attack that captured the rocky massif which was the key to the position, and the way was opened for an armoured exploitation. However, the tank forces hesitated and the Axis troops were able to fall back again.

The final act of the desert war was played out in early March 1943, in the Medjerda valley. It opened with a night attack by infantry, who achieved surprise and broke open the Axis positions. This time the tanks were ready and poured through the gap, shattering the Axis defences and capturing the city of Tunis. Axis forces had finally been ejected from North Africa, and this victory would have major consequences for the war elsewhere.

A senior German officer speaks to a party of soldiers just before the battle of Kursk in 1943.

Last Chance in the East

The fall of Stalingrad freed up large numbers of Soviet tanks and troops, and after a string of minor Soviet advances Stalin demanded a more decisive victory. Following good initial successes, the Red Army became overextended and was driven back by a counterattack that in turn was brought to a stop by the spring *rasputiza.*

The war was obviously turning against Germany. The Battle of the Atlantic was being slowly won by the Allies, North Africa was going badly and the Eastern Front had become the scene of several defeats. Stalingrad was the worst of these, but the prestige of Germany was being dented in other sectors too. This situation in turn was affecting the morale of Germany's allies in Italy and Romania.

Something needed to be done to turn things around. It would have to be a fairly limited offensive, as the resources for anything greater were not available, and there was an attractive target available in the Kursk Salient. The Soviet Army was in a poor position that invited encirclement, which would grant a local victory. This victory could be turned into a strategic advantage, as removal of the Red Army's main force in the area would allow access to the Caucasus or even permit a renewed drive on Moscow.

Plans were drawn up for a two-pronged attack on the Kursk Salient from north and south, codenamed Operation *Citadel*, and reinforcements drafted in. The German Army also received powerful new weapons, including the Panzer V (Panther) and VI (Tiger) tanks and a range of self-propelled artillery weapons. The operation was postponed to allow these new weapons to reach the frontline, and even so only small numbers were available.

The PzKpfw V Panther was an excellent vehicle that drew on studies of Soviet T-34s. It moved away from the German system of small bogie wheels and return rollers for the tracks in favour of large wheels similar to those of the T-34. It also used well-sloped armour, whose effectiveness was demonstrated by the Soviet tanks. The package was topped off by a powerful long-barrelled 75mm (2.95in) gun.

Production of the Panther began in the summer of 1942, and many of the early vehicles suffered from mechanical problems. A lot of these issues originated in the great size and weight of the tank, which were partly offset with a more powerful engine. The Panther really needed more development time, but this was not available. Two battalions of Panthers were available in time for Operation *Citadel*.

During the great battle of Kursk, the Panthers demonstrated their strengths and their flaws. They were mobile and could hit very hard, even at long ranges, but they were also prone to breakdown and, sometimes, set themselves afire due to poor engine cooling. Developed versions appeared throughout 1943 and by February 1944 the advanced Panther Ausf G was in production. This was to be the definitive Panther and it was very good indeed.

Tank destroyers were becoming an increasingly important part of the German Army's equipment, and in that respect the Elefant was something of a windfall. During the development of the Tiger tank a contract was given to Porsche and then cancelled, with many chassis already built. These were converted into a heavy Panzerjager (Tank-Hunter) vehicle named Elefant, or sometimes Ferdinand.

The Elefant was equipped with a powerful 88mm (3.46in) gun and posed a deadly threat to

PZKPFW V

Crew: 5
Weight: 45.465kg (100,233lb)
Dimensions: length 8.87m (29ft 1in); width 3.43m (11ft 3in); height 2.97m (9ft 9in)
Range: 177km (110 miles)
Armour: 80mm (3.15in)
Armament: one 75mm (2.95in) gun; three 7.92mm (0.31in) MGs
Powerplant: Maybach V-12 petrol 700hp (522kW) petrol engine
Performance: maxium speed 54.7km/h (34mph)

HEAD TO HEAD: *Sherman M4 Firefly* VERSUS

The M4 Sherman was a fairly basic tank intended to be fielded in large numbers rather than as an individual superweapon. For all its flaws, it performed well in action and was converted in many different ways. The 'Firefly' variant was adapted to carry the British 17-pounder (76mm/2.99in) gun, whose performance against armour was superior to the M4's standard 75mm (2.95in) weapon.

M4 Firefly

Crew: 5
Weight: 30,164kg (66,500lb)
Dimensions: length 5.89m (19ft 4in); width 2.62m (8ft 7in); height 2.75m (9ft)
Range: 93km (120 miles)
Armour: 12–75mm (0.47–2.95in)
Armament: one 17-pounder (76mm/2.99in) gun; one 7.62mm (0.3in) MG
Powerplant: Continental 9-cylinder radial 400bhp (298kW) engine
Performance: maximum speed 40.2km/h (25mph)

STRENGTHS

- Available in large numbers
- Very powerful gun
- Easy to obtain spares from other Sherman models

WEAKNESSES

- Relatively weak armour
- Low rate of fire
- Enhanced capabilities made it a priority target

Tiger I

The Tiger I represented a powerful concentration of fighting force into a single package. Its big gun could kill any other tank and its armour was proof against most weapons that might be ranged against it. However, it was overcomplex and fuel-inefficient, making it difficult to field sufficient numbers to make a difference, and imposing a severe logistical problem to keep it running.

Tiger I

Crew: 5
Weight: approx 56,900kg (125,443lb)
Dimensions: length 8.45m (27ft 8.68in); width 3.56m (11ft 3.8in); height 3m (9ft 10in)
Range: 195km (121 miles)
Armour: 100mm (3.94in)
Armament: one 88mm (3.46in) gun; two or three 7.92mm (0.312in) MGs
Powerplant: Maybach V-12 petrol 700hp (514kW) engine
Performance: maximum speed 37km/h (23mph)

STRENGTHS

- Very powerful gun
- Extremely thick armour
- Reputation of invincibility

WEAKNESSES

- Available in small numbers
- Poor strategic mobility
- Needed large amounts of fuel

any enemy tank. However, it had no secondary or defensive armament and many were disabled by infantry assault. The Elefant was one reason for the delays in launching the Kursk offensive; the 90 vehicles under construction represented a significant reinforcement but needed time to get over mechanical teething troubles.

The more proven Nashorn tank destroyer, also known as the Hornisse, was also available for service at Kursk. Built on the Panzer IV chassis and armed with the big 88mm (3.46in) antitank gun, these vehicles were highly effective at long-range gunnery and were deployed in independent detachments wherever they would be most useful.

Self-propelled artillery was considered vital to the success of armoured operations by this time, and it had advanced greatly since the advent of the clumsy sIG33 in 1940. Deployed for the first time at Kursk, the Sturmpanzer IV, or Brummbar, used a shortened version of the same 150mm (5.9in) gun, but was an altogether better vehicle. Low and well armoured, it was built on the proven Panzer IV chassis. Brummbars were assault guns, intended to reduce enemy strongpoints with heavy shells from close range. They were highly effective in this role, though vulnerable to infantry assault teams if not supported properly. The only real problem with these excellent vehicles was that there were not many of them.

For indirect-fire support, the Wespe and Hummel self-propelled howitzers were coming into service. The Wespe was essentially a Marder II with the antitank gun replaced by a 105mm (4.1in) howitzer. Some vehicles were built without the gun as armoured ammunition carriers, though they retained the ability to be fitted with a weapon at need.

As with the Wespe, the Hummel self-propelled howitzer was developed from a tank destroyer. The Hummel carried a 150mm (5.9in) gun in an open-topped and lightly armoured compartment. This configuation made it somewhat vulnerable, but as an artillery piece it was supposed to stay some distance away from the enemy. There was an ammunition hauler version of this vehicle, too.

Counter-battery fire was becoming an art form by this stage of the war, and self-propelled guns allowed the German Army to pioneer what has since been known as shoot-and-scoot operations,

The Panther overcame most of its early troubles to emerge as the all-round best tank of World War II.

firing a few shots and then moving to new positions to avoid return fire. The Soviet forces had also received large numbers of self-propelled artillery pieces. These included the SU-76 assault gun. After trying to build an assault gun based on the T-60 light tank chassis, which was available in large numbers, a modified T-70 chassis was used instead. The T-70 was not a good design from the start, and its twin-engine system caused problems for SU-76 crews.

The SU-76 was envisaged as a dual-role vehicle, capable of acting as a tank destroyer or providing fire support to infantry formations. It was a merely adequate antitank weapon and an excellent support gun, so eventually all SU-76s became infantry support vehicles. A rather more effective tank killer was created in the form of the SU-152 assault gun. Mounting a fixed 152mm (5.98in) howitzer on the chassis of a KV-1 heavy tank, it was envisaged as a heavy infantry support vehicle with a secondary anti-armour role. However, it proved to be very effective at killing tanks with its massive shells. The dozen that were available in time for Kursk impressed everyone with their capabilities.

The other important Soviet self-propelled gun to make an appearance in 1943 was the SU-85. This vehicle was rushed into production as a counter to the handful of Tiger tanks encountered early in the year. An 85mm (3.3in) gun was mated to a hull adapted originally from the T-34 battle tank. Entering service in the summer of 1943, it was used mainly as a long-range fire-support vehicle.

Operation *Citadel* was originally intended to begin on 3 May 1943, but was finally launched on 4 July. The Soviets were not inactive during all this time, taking advantage of it to construct heavy defences. Their plan was first to break the German assault on their positions and then to launch a decisive counterattack.

Panzerjagers ('Tank-hunters'), self-propelled antitank guns like this Marder II, provided a valuable counter to tanks.

The Soviet defensive plan at Kursk was based on the concept of elastic defence. Rather than a hard defensive front, the 'line' was made up of strongpoints with gaps between them, limiting the effects of enemy artillery. There were three great lines of defences to a total depth of some 30–35km (19–22 miles). A typical company-strength position would contain 4–6 antitank guns protected by infantry armed with machine guns and antitank rifles, plus combat engineers equipped for close assault against enemy armour. These were backed up by a few tanks and self-propelled guns.

Operation *Citadel* was launched on 4 July 1943, against an enemy that had received warning and stood ready. Soon after the German artillery opened up, the Soviets began targeting likely concentration areas to break up units as early as possible. Counter-battery fire was also extremely effective in some sectors. A fierce air battle was

SU 76 ASSAULT GUN

Crew: 4
Weight: 10,600kg (23,320lb)
Dimensions: length 4.88m (16ft 0.1in); width 2.73m (8ft 11.5in); height 2.17m (7ft 1.4in)
Range: 450km (280 miles)
Armour: up to 25mm (0.98in)
Armament: one ZIS-3 76mm (2.99in) gun
Powerplant: two GAZ six-cylinder 70hp (52.2kW) petrol engines
Performance: maximum speed 45km/h (28mph)

fought, but the Soviet Air Force could not prevent the *Luftwaffe* from providing close support as the assault went in. The leading tanks were assisted by infantry, who suffered heavy casualties but were able to assist the tanks in closing with the enemy.

Among the attackers were small numbers of Tiger tanks, whose powerful guns were a big asset in reducing the enemy positions. They served their purpose well; enemy gunners often concentrated their fire on the Tigers, letting large numbers of lighter tanks get close to their positions. Yet there were not enough Tigers to exert a decisive influence on the battle. In some areas the heavier tanks pushed into the enemy defences, leaving lighter vehicles and infantry behind. Guns that could not harm the Panthers and Tigers were able to destroy the Panzer III and IVs that were trying to follow them, while machine guns and rifles could pin down infantry.

The perils of assaulting a deep position disabled many tanks. Some were lost to mines or ran onto unbroken positions while pursuing retreating enemy units, and artillery fire destroyed many more when they became stuck behind terrain obstacles. Despite their losses, the Germans were able to advance and continued to feed more units in, trying to wear down the defences. For their part, the Soviet defenders were able to transfer reserves quickly and the battle rapidly became an attritional struggle. Such a situation could have only one result: a Soviet victory. The Panzers needed to break through and win a decisive victory before they were ground down.

By the end of 5 July, the first day of the battle, gaps had been torn in the first Soviet line of defence. However, there were still two lines and German losses were high. About 20 per cent of the German armoured strength was out of action, including 80 per cent of the Panthers. Many of these casualties had suffered mechanical breakdowns. The Soviets were served well by their ability to transfer units to endangered areas, and on the second day of the battle they used their new-found command-and-control efficiency to set up a counterattack. Not all of the detailed units were ready on time, but the counterattack went in all the same.

On 6 July, two more Panzer divisions and another detachment of Tigers arrived. A tank-versus-tank action began around Ponryi Station and continued for four days, involving more than 1000 armoured vehicles. It started with a Soviet tank brigade running unawares into a group of Tigers, which showed what they were capable of even in small numbers. Forty-six of the 50 Soviet tanks in the brigade were put out of action and the supporting brigade was mauled as well.

The situation was extremely fluid, with some Soviet units attacked from more than one direction

and counterattacks coming from unexpected quarters. Nevertheless, the Panzers were able to push ever deeper into the Soviet positions, despite extremely stubborn resistance that cost hundreds of tanks. The advance gradually slowed as the few available Tigers and Panthers were knocked out or broke down and units lost their cohesion. By the end of the second day, the Germans had advanced deep into the Soviet defences, but had lost about 40 per cent of the tanks committed each day.

Fighting continued on 7 July, but by now the advantage was slipping away from the Germans. Some tanks were repaired and sent back into action and reinforcements were brought up, but the Soviets had greater resources. The same was happening in the air; the Soviet Air Force was slowly beginning to win the air battle and the amount of air support available to the German ground forces decreased.

On the 8th, the Germans attacked again, but their opponents were still feeding reinforcements into the line ahead of each attack. Antitank guns and hull-down T-34s took a steady toll of the armour sent against them, and every gain was made at considerable cost. In some sectors armoured counterattacks broke up the German advance, though overall the Soviet plan was not to go over to the offensive on a large scale until the Germans were unable to attack any longer.

A Soviet SU-85 assault tank. Mounting a powerful 85mm (3.3in) gun, these vehicles made efficient tank destroyers.

By 9 July, the German assault was grinding to a halt. Some Panzer formations were able to make gains, but constant counterattacks against every position the Germans captured were taking their toll. Other formations were forced to take up defensive positions to beat off such assaults, which were increasingly effective. Things had gone better in the southern sector, but there too the attack had bogged down. On 10 July the northern force, which had already suffered terribly for relatively small gains, made a valiant effort but was brought to a standstill and then shelled and strafed as it fell back. Soviet tank and infantry units pushed the northern Panzers back to their start lines and made some attacks of their own. For all the casualties on both sides, little had changed by the end of the day.

German forces were still making small local gains, but the Soviet high command could see that the balance had tipped in their favour. There was no longer any real chance of defeat, so now it was time to begin the counterattacks that would bring victory. They were aided by events elsewhere; the Allies were advancing on Sicily and reinforcements were being diverted there.

The Soviets had been making counterattacks throughout the battle, but from 12 July these became ever more powerful, with fierce close-range tank battles developing. Dust and smoke reduced visibility to virtually nothing, resulting in a confused tank brawl. At the resulting close ranges, hits were virtually guaranteed to penetrate, and large numbers of tanks were lost on both sides. Some of these attacks drove German units back, but most were indecisive. That benefited the Soviets more than their foes; the Soviets had greater reserves and, in any case, they needed only to avoid defeat, whereas the Germans needed a decisive victory to turn the war around.

Many Soviet assaults were fought to a costly standstill, while some failed to achieve more than they did for other reasons. The Soviet Eleventh Guards Army launched what was supposed to be a

Tiger

The Tiger came as a surprise to its Soviet opponents, who found that most of their antitank weapons bounced off. Had the Tigers been held back and used *en masse,* they might have achieved decisive results. But by the time they could be deployed in reasonable numbers, countermeasures were in place.

A knocked-out Panzer IV amid the wreckage of war. The PzKpfw IV was a serviceable and well-armoured tank but was outmatched in the later war years.

limited attack to reduce the pressure elsewhere, but which succeeded beyond expectations. However, a lack of preparation to exploit the advantage allowed mobile German units to restore the situation.

On the 13th, the Panzers were still grinding forward in some sectors, slowed by the deep defences and the Soviet practice of pulling battered units back into rearward positions where they could prepare defences of their own. However, on that day Hitler decided that Operation *Citadel* was costing too much and distracting attention from new problems developing elsewhere. A new operational goal of preventing a Soviet counteroffensive by eliminating their reserves was implemented, and on 17 July the order came to end the operation.

The order did not end the fighting, of course. On the 15th a Soviet attack in the region of Orel had begun, and some Panzer divisions had to be reassigned to resist this. Here, as at Kursk, the perils of attacking a prepared position were underlined. A force of powerful and well-armoured KV-1 tanks advanced without infantry support and ran into the Germans' defensive minefield. The tanks were then engaged by antitank guns and 60 were destroyed.

Tiger tanks and Elefant tank destroyers played an important part in repulsing these attacks. Their ability to engage and destroy enemy tanks at long range was more useful on the defensive than when attacking. Over the next few days, however, the German defenders were pushed back and matters became desperate.

Hitler at first refused permission for anything even resembling a retreat, but on the 22nd he relented and gave permission for an elastic defence of the sort that had served the Soviets so well. This permitted the German Army to survive and allowed the development of the flexible tactics that would stave off defeat for many months to come. It also marked the beginning of a long retreat that would end in the ruins of Berlin.

Armoured Combat in the Far East

The war in the Pacific had a number of characteristics that were very different from the European theatre. The terrain was largely jungle, which was unsuitable for large-scale tank actions, and of course much of the war was fought in island-hopping campaigns, during which tanks provided useful support rather than massive armoured breakthroughs.

For this reason, various amphibious designs were created. These included a vehicle designated Type 2

Tank Procession

Villagers wave to the crew of a passing T-34. Whether they are well-wishers, glad to be liberated or just greeting the tanks out of a sense of self-preservation is impossible to tell. The fighting in Russia wrecked large areas of countryside and caused many thousands of collateral casualties.

A column of T-34s heading towards the fighting around Kursk.

Ka-Mi. Based on the Type 95 Ha-Go, it was armed with a 37mm (1.45in) gun plus two machine guns. It was assisted by hollow pontoons and propelled in the water by a pair of propellers. The Type 2 was complemented by a heavier design designated Type 3 or Ka-Chi. It, too, used flotation pontoons and propellers. It was armed with a 47mm (1.85in) gun and two machine guns.

Also designated Type 2 was the Ho-I self-propelled gun. It was armed with a short 75mm (2.95in) gun and was intended to function as a fire-support vehicle with armoured formations. Few were built. Similarly, although development work went on throughout the war, the Japanese Army never received an improved light or medium tank design. Tanks were a low priority in a theatre of war dominated mainly by air and sea power.

There were no large-scale tank-versus-tank actions in the Pacific; the Japanese had relatively few armoured vehicles and these were scattered in small groups among the garrisons of many islands. However, tanks did exert an important influence on many actions. Usually it was US tanks that tipped the balance in this way, but not always; a handful of Japanese light tanks were used successfully against the US defence of Corregidor Island in the Philippines.

After the spectacular aggression of the advance on Singapore, Japanese armour was never again so effective. During the British retreat through Burma, light tanks were highly effective in covering the rear of the retiring forces. The Japanese armour pursuing them was less than keen to tangle with the well-handled British tanks, perhaps because they were not confident of winning a tank-versus-tank engagement.

Where armour was used offensively by the Japanese, it was often clumsily, if bravely, handled. The behaviour of tank units in the advance on Singapore was not very different to that shown later in the war – a reckless head-on charge. The difference was that the Singapore advance hit unprepared, out-of-position troops in a state of confusion. When the same sort of attacks were launched against prepared troops who knew how to fight tanks, the results were very different. For example, nearly 50 tanks made a counterattack against US troops landing on Saipan. After losing some of their strength to a bog as a result of poor reconnaissance, the attacking armoured force ran into a handful of Shermans, some tank destroyers and emplaced antitank guns. The attack was quickly broken up and the surviving tanks hunted down by infantry antitank teams.

Armour was more important for US forces assaulting Japanese-held islands, where troops in well-concealed bunkers proved very difficult to dislodge. Many of the available tanks were poorly

TYPE 2 KA-MI

Crew: 5
Weight: 11,301kg (24,862lb) (with pontoons)
Dimensions: (with pontoons) length 7.42m (24ft 4in); width 2.79m (9ft 1.8in); height 2.34m (7ft 8in)
Range: (land) 199.5km (125 miles); (water) 150km (93 miles)
Armour: 6–12mm (0.23–0.47in)
Armament: one 37mm (1.45in) antitank gun; two 7.7mm (0.3in) machine gun
Powerplant: one six-cylinder diesel 110hp (82kW) engine
Performance: maximum land speed 37km/h (23mph); maximum water speed 9.65km/h (6mph); fording amphibious

suited to this task. For example, the 37mm (1.45in) gun of the Stuart could fire only a very small high-explosive shell that was not very effective against bunkers. The armour-piercing round also caused only limited local damage to a bunker and would not harm even those personnel quite close to the impact point. Machine guns were not effective except against personnel in the open, which did not leave many options.

The problem was that heavier tanks could not operate at all in the conditions that even the Stuarts and other light tanks found difficult. Soft ground and close terrain made any sort of tank operations nightmarish, especially since concealed snipers took such a toll of tank commanders that the armour had to operate buttoned up and therefore mostly blind. This lack of visibility led to many tanks blundering into obstacles, becoming stuck in bogs, or being disabled by unseen anti-armour weapons.

Despite all this, armoured bunker-busting became an art form in some units. One tactic was to saturate the suspect area with fire from the tanks to keep the defenders suppressed while using explosive shells to remove as much foliage as possible. Once the firing slits of the bunkers could be seen by the tank gunners or their infantry liaison personnel, armour-piercing rounds could be 'posted' through them. Another trick was to put a smoke round through a vision slit and see where else the smoke emerged, thus exposing other firing slits in the same bunker complex. Once the position was mapped out in this way, infantry could advance under the cover of the tank's suppressing fire and methodically eliminate the bunkers.

Towards the end of the Pacific war, the terrain was more suitable for the deployment of tanks, and Shermans, including some adapted as flamethrower tanks, took part in the battles for Okinawa and Iwo Jima.

Developments in Antitank Warfare

As armoured vehicles became more prevalent, ways of defeating them had to be found. Obstacles such as ditches and large concrete obstructions could impose delay, as could some kinds of terrain. Unless the tanks could be disabled by weapons fire, however, they would either get through eventually or else sit outside the obstruction shooting up the defenders while infantry cleared the way.

Two important adages apply to tanks and obstructions. The first is that 'an obstacle not covered by fire is not an obstacle', and the second is that whatever the difficulties imposed by steep hills, bogs and forests as opposed to open plains, 'the best terrain for tanks is that without antitank weapons'. However hard the going, tanks can only realistically be stopped by destroying them.

The most obvious antitank method was to use gunfire. Artillery would disable a tank readily enough if a hit could be obtained, but indirect fire is somewhat random and cannot be relied upon. Artillery guns firing over open sights – i.e. in direct-fire mode – were more effective, but suffered greater losses from the tanks' return fire. Artillery weapons normally fired high-explosive rounds intended to kill personnel and smash up positions.

A big enough shell would kill a tank – there are cases of vehicles being lifted in the air or having turrets blown right off – but smaller high-explosive shells were of no real use. Thus the first high-velocity anti-armour rounds were created.

There are many variations on the theme, but essentially the intent was to use a long-barrelled gun to produce a very high muzzle velocity (which also assisted accuracy) and so to penetrate the target using kinetic energy. Even non-penetrating hits could cause hot fragments of armour, rivet heads and the like to come off the inside of the tank and kill or injure crew members.

High velocity requires a long gun barrel, and so specialized antitank guns were developed that were of limited or no use in an indirect-fire artillery role. As tank armour improved, so too antitank weapons gained a larger calibre and longer barrel. Tank guns developed the same way, and for the same reasons.

Many variants on the tank theme appeared during the war. One was the flamethrower tank, used to clear vegetation as well as to burn infantry out of their positions.

During and after the war, this method of getting through armour was developed and refined in various ways. 'Discarding sabot' rounds, consisting of a penetrator dart much smaller than the bore of the gun and launched inside a sabot ('shoe') that falls away in flight, are one way to achieve high velocity. Another is to use a tapered or squeeze-bore weapon, whose barrel diameter narrows towards the end. Squeeze-bore weapons use a composite round, with a softer metal jacket over a hard core. The tapering bore reforms the round as it passes down the barrel and increases muzzle velocity.

There are alternatives to the 'hard projectile, moving fast' approach to tank-busting. Shaped charges use an entirely different means to defeat armour. Rather than the projectile itself smashing through the armour, a shaped charge detonates on contact and creates a jet of superhot gas (plasma) that burns through. The advantage of shaped-charge munitions is that they require a lower velocity and are useful as warheads for rockets and shells to be fired from lower-velocity artillery weapons.

Armour-piercing bullets and antitank rifles had proven useful against early tanks and even some World War II designs, but by the middle of the war it was becoming apparent that any weapon an infantryman could carry would be unable to throw a round that was heavy enough and fast enough to seriously harm a tank. Thus infantry antitank weapons moved in the direction of shaped charges. A variety of shaped-charge weapons appeared, including antitank hand grenades that flew business-end first due to streamers at the rear, theoretically ensuring a decent contact with armour for the shaped charge warhead to work. Larger infantry antitank weapons included the fairly poor British PIAT (Projectile, Infantry, antitank), the marginally effective US Bazooka and the more powerful German Panzerfaust. The latter was a one-shot disposable weapon and the forerunner of modern Light antitank Weapons (LAWs).

An infantryman with a British PIAT (Projectile, Infantry, antitank) poses on the bow of a captured Marder.

Shaped-charge weapons remain the most useful way for infantry to attack tanks and other hard targets. The ubiquitous Soviet RPG-7 (RPG stands, in Western terminology, for rocket-propelled grenade) has been used in innumerable conflicts since its invention and all manner of guided and unguided anti-armour weapons are now available to the infantry. The post-war Soviet Army considered antitank capability to be so vital that every unit, even headquarters and logistics formations, was required to have at least a minimal anti-armour capability.

Mines are somewhere between a weapon and an obstruction. If they are detected in time, they can be treated as an obstruction and cleared, although

Antitank weapons

As tanks became more common, infantry antitank weapons were developed. These ranged from large-calibre rifles firing armour-piercing bullets to short-range weapons launching a shaped-charge warhead. Of the latter, some (such as the US Bazooka and British PIAT) were reusable and others (such as the German Panzerfaust) were one-shot disposable weapons.

A Panzerfaust variant with a reusable launch tube appeared near the end of the war, and formed the basis of the Soviet family of rocket-propelled grenade launchers, of which the RPG-7 is the most famous.

A US soldier aims a 'bazooka' rocket launcher. The mesh screen is to protect the user's face.

this will impose delay and expose the tanks to the fire of forces sheltering behind the minefield. If the mines are not detected, however, they can destroy tanks or at least disable them by severing the tracks.

A number of other means have been used by infantry to tackle armour. The more conventional of these include satchel charges and grenades, which suffer from the same problem as non-shaped-charge explosives; the explosive force is not concentrated and thus needs to be very large to have any useful effect. A variety of magnetic and 'sticky' mines, grenades and bombs have also been tested in combat. German tank designers considered the magnetic antitank mine to be a sufficiently serious threat that some tanks were coated with an anti-magnetic paste to prevent the mine from sticking. However, little use was made of magnetic mines by the Allies, and since they required that an infantryman run up to the tank and affix the mine by hand, all-arms cooperation or even just an alert crew on the tank's anti-personnel weapons provided an adequate defence.

Flame weapons, from flamethrowers to improvised flammable mixtures (Molotov Cocktails) have been used to attack armour from time to time. Some early tanks were quite vulnerable to this sort of attack, but it is at best a marginal method unless a tank crew are caught with their hatches open.

In 1942, Japanese troops briefly made use of glass grenades containing hydrogen cyanide gas, despite this being outlawed in warfare. The measure was not effective, however, and was dropped quickly. Other Japanese antitank measures were simply acts of desperation. Infantrymen would hide in holes with an artillery shell or bomb between their knees, waiting for a tank to pass overhead. When one did, the solider triggered the shell by striking its detonator with a rock. Other suicidal attacks were made by men who, rather than tossing satchel charges under a tank or onto the engine deck, would jump onto the tank or under it while holding the charge, ensuring that it was in the best position possible before detonating it manually.

Soldiers of all nations did occasionally manage to disable a tank by jumping onto it and dropping grenades down the hatches. There are incidents of Japanese troops trying to get into a tank with the intention of attacking the crew with firearms or even swords. Indeed, on one occasion a senior Japanese officer on a horse jumped aboard the tank with the intent of killing its commander with his sword. He was repelled with a hammer, of all things. On another occasion a Japanese officer managed to get onto a British Grant tank and kill the commander, then scrambled inside. Somehow managing to use his sword in the confines of the turret, he killed the gunner before being shot nine times by the loader. The rest of the crew were still working at their tasks, unaware of the drama playing out above their heads.

Infantry assaults of this kind were best dealt with by all-arms cooperation, with the infantry protecting the tanks from infantry assault and the tanks knocking out positions that could resist infantry assault. Other attacks were harder to deal with, such as air attacks. Aircraft had attempted to drop bombs on tanks for some time, but as the war progressed airborne tank-busting became a specialized task. Rockets and guns, sometimes of quite large calibre, were fitted to ground-attack aircraft for these operations.

Countermeasures to all these threats were developed as soon as each appeared, resulting in anti-aircraft vehicles becoming part of armoured formations and infantry cooperation being

A German soldier with a pair of Panzerfaust antitank rockets.

The Panzerfaust

The soldier in the centre foreground has a Panzerfaust over his shoulder. In use it was pointed at a tank and triggered, at which point a rocket sent the shaped-charge grenade on its way. For all its simplicity, the Panzerfaust was very effective and formed the basis of modern disposable anti-armour weapons.

standard practice. Crude field expedients led to the creation of effective spaced armour to defeat shaped charges and, later, explosive reactive armour (ERA) to disrupt the plasma jet. Of course, there were several ways to defeat these countermeasures and the advantage continues to swing between both the tank defences and antitank weapons.

Having been thoroughly defeated in North Africa and finding membership of the Axis unpalatable, Italy began seeking peace with the Allies. The catalyst for this defection was the Allied invasion of Sicily in July 1943. Although the Italians continued to pay lip service to the Axis for a time, negotiations went on regarding a peace deal and in September an armistice was signed.

The Defence Of Italy

This event did not take Italy out of the war. Although arrested and imprisoned, Benito Mussolini was rescued by his German allies and installed as the leader of an Italian republic in the north of the country. Some Italians fought for Mussolini and some for the Allies, and in the meantime opposition to the Allied advance in Italy was continued mainly by German forces.

The Allied advance into Italy was strongly contested all the way. Although Italian units were taken out of the fight by the armistice, reducing opposition to the initial landings to whatever German and hard-core Italian fascist forces happened to be nearby, they was enough to make some of the landings a hard slog indeed. At Salerno, the principal site of the invasion of mainland Italy in September 1943, the Germans had established positions in some depth and scattered tanks among them in support. While not the most efficient use of armour, this defence slowed the Allies' advance down, and concentrated German tank units made several counterattacks intended to drive the British and US forces back into the sea.

On the Allied side, tanks played an important part in holding the beachheads, often acting as mobile artillery to support the hard-pressed infantry. After a determined attempt to dislodge the

Allies, German forces retreated northwards, standing on a series of defensive lines. Breaking each took time and allowed a new line to set up in favourable terrain further north.

In between the major defensive lines, the advance was a constant struggle against the terrain, and involved fighting through many small villages where infantrymen armed with Panzerfausts could kill tanks from close range. Indeed, in the minds of some infantrymen, the emphasis had shifted from 'defending against tanks' to 'hunting tanks'. The need for all-arms cooperation was sharply underscored by losses in these small-scale but bitter actions.

After the failure of German attempts to hold further south, a defensive line was set up across the country, benefiting from the formidable Apennine mountains as an anchor. This line, codenamed the Gothic Line but later renamed the Green Line, was 16km (10 miles) deep in some areas and heavily fortified. One antitank measure was to use the turrets from disabled Panther tanks atop bunkers. Among the mobile reserves were two battalions of Tiger tanks. Getting through this fortress was a tremendous task that required close cooperation between tanks and infantry. The normal pattern was for infantry to tackle antitank positions while the armour took out machine-gun nests. More heavily armoured tanks such as the Churchill were used in the spearhead, with lighter-armoured vehicles following on to give fire support. Once a position had been taken, the tanks would remain with the infantry to protect them from an armoured counterattack, and once antitank guns had been brought up the armoured forces would be released from infantry control.

Additional support was available from artillery Forward Observation Officers (FOO), who went forward with the armour to call in artillery strikes, and sometimes from units of tank destroyers positioned to add their weight of fire to the battle when needed. Combined-arms operations of this sort were finally able to crack the defensive lines, though resistance in northern Italy went on until the very end of the war.

Return to Normandy

The amphibious invasion of France, Operation *Overlord*, was the largest operation of its kind in history, and it was a daunting task indeed. Not only

Once the Western Allies were able to establish large armoured forces ashore in Europe in 1944, the days of the Third Reich were numbered. There was still hard fighting ahead, but the balance had finally tipped.

Allied tanks and infantry advance during the fighting for Italy in 1943.

would the assault forces have to get ashore across open beaches under fire, they would have to do it in the face of antitank obstacles, barbed wire, ditches, concrete walls and other obstructions. A counterattack, especially one involving large numbers of tanks, was likely to be disastrous. There were several Panzer divisions available for such a counterattack and this eventuality, too, had to be planned for.

Tanks were obviously needed to help the infantry overcome the defences and to beat off any counterattack. US forces were primarily using the M4 Sherman; several variants existed by this time, including some with extra armour or different armament. Work was underway to create a new heavy tank for the US Army, leading to a series of fairly unsuccessful vehicles. These would, a few months into the campaign, develop into the M26 Pershing, but at the time of the landings in France the US army did not favour heavy tanks nor see the need for one.

Production had also just begun of the M24 Chaffee light tank. Armed with a 75mm (2.95in) gun, it was destined to be a world-beater, though the first examples did not arrive in Europe until close to the end of 1944. The M24 remained in service until the 1990s in some nations, and was designed from the outset to be the basis of a family of vehicles all built on the same chassis. This allowed for component standardization and eased both maintenance and logistics, improving the efficiency of the force overall.

The US Army had perceived a need for a tank destroyer since the early days of the war, but obtaining one had been slow going. By the time of the 1944 landings in France, the M10 was the standard US tank destroyer in service. It had served in Italy and went to the Pacific theatre as well. However, a lighter tank destroyer was also desirable, and so the M18 Hellcat was developed. Based on a light tank chassis, the M18 mounted a 75mm (2.95in) gun and was the fastest armoured fighting vehicle on either side. Some examples served until the 1990s in the Balkans.

There was also a need for a heavier tank destroyer to take on the most heavily armoured opponents, and this led to the development of the M36. Mounting a 90mm (3.54in) gun, the first M36s entered combat in September 1944. They gave US forces the ability to penetrate Tiger and Panther tanks at long range.

The British, meanwhile, had developed a number of new tanks, though not without going down a few blind alleys along the way. The search for a cruiser tank that could deal with the increasingly heavily armoured Panzers led to the development of the Cavalier, or Mk VII cruiser tank. The Cavalier mounted a useful 57mm (2.24in) gun, but suffered from mechanical problems. It did not go into Europe as a battle tank, but some examples, converted to artillery observation vehicles and armoured recovery tractors, did see action.

The Mk VIII cruiser tank, designated the Centaur, was also a limited success. It had a lot in common with the Cavalier and originally used the same turret, though a 75mm (2.95in) gun was later fitted. A version with a better engine and a 95mm (3.7in) howitzer replacing the main armament was used for fire support by the Royal Marines, while others served as mobile command posts, anti-aircraft tanks or even armoured personnel carriers (APCs). Most of the rest were either converted to Cromwells or used for training.

The Cromwell was an excellent tank. Essentially a Centaur with a better engine, it started out with a 57mm (2.24in) gun but gained a 75mm (2.95in) and, in some versions, a 17-pounder (76mm/2.99), gun. This final configuration created a British tank that was fast, well protected and respectably armed. A number of specialized variants were also built.

A number of other tank designs were underway, most of which arrived a little too late to play much part in the liberation of Europe. One that did arrive in time, but was not really up to the job, was the Challenger. This was essentially an enlarged Cromwell remodelled to carry a 17-pounder (76mm/2.99in) gun. Armour had to be removed to maintain decent mobility, and coupled with high

M24 CHAFFEE LIGHT TANK

Crew: 4/5
Weight: 18,371kg (723,266lb)
Dimensions: length 5.49m (18ft); width 2.95m (9ft 8in); height 2.46m (8ft 1in)
Range: 281km (175 miles)
Armour: 38mm (1.5in)
Armament: one 75mm (2.95in) M6 gun; one 12.7mm (0.5in) MG; two 8 7.62mm (0.3in) MGs
Powerplant: Two Cadillac V-8 110hp (82kW) engines
Performance: maximum speed 55km/h (34mph)

HEAD TO HEAD: *M26 Pershing* VERSUS

The Western Allies were not as keen on heavy tanks as their opponents, but late in the war some designs did emerge that could have taken them on with something like parity. The US entry was the M26 Pershing, a heavy tank fielded just in time to see action at the very end of the war. It was about as hard to kill as a Tiger and mounted a roughly equivalent gun. Pershings saw action in Korea, where they were very effective against North Korean T-34s.

M26 Pershing

Crew: 5
Weight: 41,891kg (92,354lb)
Dimensions: length 8.66m (28ft 3in); width 3.51m (11ft 6in); height 2.78m (9ft 1in)
Range: 161km (100 miles)
Armour: 102mm (4in)
Armament: one 90mm (3.54in) M3 gun; one 12.7mm (0.5in); two 7.62mm (0.3in) MGs
Powerplant: Ford 500hp (373kW) GAF engine
Performance: maximum speed 161km (100 miles)

STRENGTHS

- Powerful 90mm (3.54in) gun
- Thick armour
- Good manoeuvrability

WEAKNESSES

- Armament inferior to German 88mm (3.46in)
- Few available by the war's end
- Teething troubles with engine and transmission

Cruiser Mk VIII, Cromwell VI

Late in the war, the British fielded the Cromwell, a fast cruiser tank using Christie suspension. Despite early problems, it was a good tank by British standards, though outclassed by German designs. An upgunned version mounted a 17-pounder (76mm/2.99in) gun that could penetrate the best German tanks, while a close-support variant carried a 95mm (3.7in) howitzer. The chassis was used for other vehicles, including mine-clearance and artillery observation vehicles.

Cruiser MK VIII Cromwell VI

Crew: 5
Weight: 27,942kg (61,472lb)
Dimensions: length 6.42m (21ft 1in); width 3.05m (10ft); height 2.51m (8ft 3in)
Range: 278km (173 miles)
Armour: 8–76mm (0.3–2.99in)
Armament: one 75mm (3.03in) gun; one 7.62mm (0.31in) machine gun
Powerplant: one Rolls-Royce Meteor V-12 570bhp (425kW) engine
Performance: maximum speed 61km/h (38mph); fording 1.22m (4ft); vertical obstacle 0.9 (3ft); trench 2.29 (7ft 6in)

STRENGTHS

- Big turret allowed easy upgrading
- Very powerful engine
- Very fast cross-country

WEAKNESSES

- Relatively lightly armoured
- Development problems with weapons
- Inferior to Panther and Tiger tanks

sides this made for a very vulnerable vehicle. In the end, Challengers served as tank destroyers. As a backup in case the Challenger failed, another project had been running alongside it. This was the Sherman Firefly, also adapted to mount the 17-pounder gun. The Firefly was a huge success, though it suffered from some of the same problems as other Sherman models.

Allied tanks would have to face an impressive array of antitank defences on the beaches of Normandy. It was decided to create a specialist armoured formation to deal with them, and this task was given to the 79th Armoured Division under Major-General Hobart. The resulting vehicles became known as 'Hobart's Funnies'; some of them were quite odd indeed.

Columns of Black Prince ('Super-Churchill') and Sherman tanks pass one another.

M26 Pershing

The M26 Pershing was highly influential on post-war US tank design. Sloped armour and various suspension concepts were proven by the design and used on subsequent tanks up to the M60.

Hobart was an engineer before he was a tank man, and was known for both his genius and for being extremely difficult to work with. He created a number of specialist vehicles, but never lost sight of the fact that they were to be used in battle and that the obstacles they were to overcome would be actively defended. Thus the first requirement was to get conventional tanks ashore to act as fire support for the specialists.

The solution to that problem was an amphibious tank. Rather than attempt to design a vehicle from the ground up as the Japanese had done, Hobart used an idea originally demonstrated by a man named Straussler and converted an existing vehicle. After trials with Stuarts and Valentines, Hobart decided to use the Sherman as the basis for his 'swimming' tank, as it had better armament.

Thus was born the Sherman 'DD', or Duplex Drive. Propelled by screws in the water and made buoyant by a flotation screen, the DD Sherman could be launched offshore by a landing craft and make its own way to the beach. Once there, it would drop the flotation screen and function as a normal tank. It is a measure of Hobart's genius that he did not lose sight of his ultimate goal, which was to get a tank to the beach so that it could fight, rather than simply create a tank that could swim. The difference may appear minor, but it is, of course, critical.

Other Sherman-based 'funnies' included the Crab, which was designed to clear mines by beating the ground ahead of it with a number of chains whirled around by a rotating drum. The chains would be thrown upward rather than damaged by a mine detonation. The Crab could fight like any other Sherman when it was not engaged in its primary role. Another critical vehicle for the beach assault was based on the Cromwell tank. This was the Assault Vehicle Royal Engineers (AVRE), which could undertake battlefield demolition with its 290mm (11.4in) petard (a short-barrelled gun firing a large explosive charge). It was well armoured and had external fittings to allow a range of accessories to be mounted. Depending on what equipment was carried, the AVRE could mount a mine-clearance plough, drop fascines in a ditch or deploy remotely detonated explosive charges. It could also act as a bridgelayer or lay a carpet composed of hessian and metal tubes, creating a causeway over soft ground.

A Cromwell tank with winter camouflage – a rough coat of white paint – advances through Belgium in 1944. The Cromwell was undergunned against German heavy tanks.

DD ('Duplex Drive') amphibious Sherman tanks with their floatation screens folded and propellers clearly visible. On land, the Sherman DD functioned as a regular tank.

A rather curious vehicle, which proved itself useful nonetheless, was the Canal Defence Light (CDL). Essentially a powerful searchlight fitted in a turret with shutters on the chassis of an M3 tank, the CDL was not used until late in the campaign. It could be set to flicker rapidly, creating a disorientating effect and making it virtually impossible to shoot accurately at targets glimpsed in the bright light. The darkness between CDL beams became impenetrable to ruined night vision, while the troops advancing with their backs to the light were not affected.

The fortunes of the 'funnies' involved in the assault were mixed. Many DD Shermans were swamped by the sea and sank, but those that reached the beaches were invaluable. The troops defending the positions along the coast had no idea of their existence and were dismayed by the ease with which obstacles were breached. Such 'ease' was relative, of course: the 'funnies' worked under heavy fire and in extremely difficult conditions. Numerous vehicles were lost to mines, enemy action and the sea. However, compare the losses on the British beaches to those suffered by US troops trying to get ashore without the support of specialist vehicles, and the value of Hobart's Funnies becomes obvious.

Once ashore, it was necessary to secure the bridgehead and then push inland before an effective response materialized. The Normandy countryside was not well suited to tank warfare, being cluttered with thick hedgerows and small villages that could function as strongpoints. Fighting in the *bocage,* as the local terrain was known, required close all-arms cooperation. Without infantry to protect them, tanks were liable to be attacked at close range by infantry armed with Panzerfausts and satchel charges. Infantry without tanks would take massive casualties from concealed machine-gun positions in the hedges. It was found that a Sherman trying to ram through a hedge would usually be halted with its bow pushed up, creating an inviting target for infantry Panzerfaust teams even if heavier weapons were not available. Eventually a variety of hedge-cutters and ram bumpers were improvised that allowed brute force to reassert itself. In the meantime, other measures were used.

Some units developed a tactic for dealing with enemy infantry based on a single tank and a small infantry force. The tank would advance and fire through a hedge at enemy troops using the next hedge as cover. While the tank engaged the suspected locations of machine guns and mortars suppressed the remainder, infantry passed through the hedge and attacked the position with grenades.

Engineers then blew a hole in the hedge for the tank to pass through, allowing it to join the close assault.

Other units used tanks on a larger scale, hosing a section of hedgerow with machine-gun fire to cover the advance of infantry to eliminate the position. These tactics had a number of features in common with World War I trench-clearing operations, with some of a unit's tanks penetrating a hedge and then turning along it, to trap units using the hedgerow as cover between the tanks on either side while infantry closed in for the kill.

Deadly as infantry and antitank guns were in the *bocage* country, there were greater dangers even than a Panzerfaust ambush from close range. Among them were Tiger and Panther tanks whose powerful guns could kill any Allied tank at long range. Advanced tank destroyers were also a deadly threat. Among these were earlier designs and some lethal new designs. The Jagdpanzer IV was developed to mount a 75mm (2.95in) tank-killing gun on the proven chassis of the Panzer IV. Its low silhouette and extremely heavy frontal armour made it hard to kill. There were several variants of this vehicle, including one that used a Stug III gun and superstructure on the Panzer IV chassis as well as the definitive version armed with the same long 75mm (2.95in) gun as the Panther.

For all its faults, the Tiger I was an imposing and deadly vehicle. The Allies routinely suppressed reports of Tiger sightings, as this led to a kind of panic dubbed 'Tiger Terror'.

The 75mm (2.95in) gun was by this time more or less the industry standard for tank-killing. Another vehicle developed to carry it was the Jagdpanzer 38(t) Hertzer. This used the chassis of the Panzer 38(t), which was obsolete for duty as a combat tank, to create an effective tank-killer. It also had a remote-controlled machine gun for close-in defence.

Tank destroyers based on the Panther tank were also developed. The Jagdpanzer V Jagdpanther was created as a means to get more mobile 88mm (3.46in) antitank guns into action. Lesser chassis could not cope with the weight of this weapon and a decent amount of armour, so the Panther chassis was used. Armour was somewhat light by the standards of the time, but it was well sloped and the vehicle's low silhouette made a hard target.

The Jagdpanther possessed good mobility and decent speed, and its gun was able to kill enemy tanks at very long ranges. It was, however, available only in tiny numbers for the defence of Normandy. Those that did get into action made an impression; three Jagdpanthers were able to destroy 11 Cromwell tanks in two minutes in one action, and their opposition derailed at least one operation.

The most frightening thing lurking in the *bocage*, at least according to most Allied troops, was the Tiger I tank. Fuel consumption, mechanical reliability and speed were not major issues for a vehicle waiting in ambush in a wood or village, and even when the tank was spotted its armour gave it a good chance for survival. There were less than 100 Tiger Is in Normandy, but such was their effectiveness that their numbers tended to be greatly exaggerated. In one action in Normandy, five Tigers (with eight more giving distant fire support) were able to destroy more than 30 Allied armoured vehicles without loss. As they were withdrawing, they became embroiled in a close-range brawl with British tanks and an antitank gun, losing four tanks in the process. The eventual 'score' was the loss of 48 Allied vehicles and the advance of a brigade temporarily halted. This owed as much to the firepower and protection of the Tiger as it did to the hard-charging Panzer spirit that still burned within the aggressive German tank crews.

However one-sided the loss ratios became, those Tigers that were disabled, or broke down and had to be abandoned, could not be replaced, and gradually the Tiger strength of the German Army waned. Only 1350 Tiger Is were ever built, while the Allies fielded over 40,000 Shermans. With the numbers game so dramatically rigged in their favour, the Allies could afford to lose a lot of tanks and still maintain their advance.

Gradually the German Army was pushed eastwards towards the borders of its home country, and the Soviet Red Army was closing in from the other side. An attempt to shorten the war by taking the Arnhem bridges was fiercely resisted and local counterattacks with increasingly small battlegroups thrown together from whatever forces were available contested every advance.

Tanks could shoot up an advancing force, then reverse out of cover and escape before an effective response were made.

There was one last great Panzer drama to play out in the West, a final attempt to inflict a defeat on the Allies. This took the form of a counterattack in the Ardennes region where the assault on France had opened a few years before. Known in the West as the Battle of the Bulge, it was the last great Panzer offensive, and it was with this determined if ultimately futile charge that the name of the Tiger II, better known as the King Tiger, will be forever associated.

Tigers in the Ardennes

The Panzer VI B Tiger II, King Tiger or Royal Tiger, emerged in the last months of the war. It was influenced by the Panther, having well-sloped armour that enhanced the protection from its already impressive thickness. The King Tiger mounted the formidable 88mm (3.46in) gun used by the Tiger I. The tank was extremely tough from the front, but could be penetrated from flank or rear by a 17-pounder (76mm/2.99in) tank or antitank gun. It was even more fuel-hungry than the Tiger I, and was primarily useful on the defensive as a mobile emplacement. This was exactly what the German army needed at the time, and King Tigers played an important part in slowing down the Allied offensives of 1944–45.

King Tigers were available during the battle for the Arnhem bridge, but are mostly remembered for their involvement in the Ardennes offensive. In fact, there were only about 50 King Tigers involved in the Battle of the Bulge and they did not play such a prominent role as is generally supposed. The close terrain of the Ardennes forest was tough going for the huge 70-ton (71-tonne) monsters, so they were forced to follow a more mobile spearhead of Panzer IVs and Panthers. Once the King Tigers got into action, they proved deadly and hard to kill, but were hamstrung by lack of fuel. Many were abandoned for logistical reasons rather than being disabled by enemy action.

Despite its drawbacks, which included poor mobility, the Tiger tank was the basis of a number of other vehicles. One such was the Sturmpanzer VI Sturmtiger. This mounted a short barrelled 380mm (14.9in) petard or 'assault mortar' in a box that was heavily armoured (even by Tiger standards) atop a Tiger I chassis. The Sturmtiger's

A direct hit from an artillery round or a heavy rocket from a ground-attack aircraft could completely destroy any tank.

HEAD TO HEAD: *IS-2/3* VERSUS

The IS-2 became known in the Soviet Union as the 'Victory Tank'. Armed with a 122mm (4.8in) gun quite capable of shooting right through a Panther and out the back, it was also well protected and even looked good.

IS-2

Crew: 4
Weight: 46,000kg (101,200lb)
Dimensions: length 9.9m (32ft 5.8in); width 3.09m (10ft 2.6in); height 2.73m (8ft 11.5in)
Range: 240km (149 miles)
Armour: 132mm (5.2in)
Armament: one 122mm (4.8in) gun; one 12.7mm (0.5in) machine gun; one 7.62mm (0.31in) machine gun
Powerplant: V-12 600hp (447kW) diesel engine
Performance: maximum road speed 37km/h (23mph); fording not known; vertical obstacle 1.0m (3ft 3in); trench 2.49m (8ft 2in)

STRENGTHS

- Extremely powerful gun
- Heavy armour
- Gun can fire HE for infantry support

WEAKNESSES

- Slow to produce
- Low ammunition stowage
- Low rate of fire

Panzer VI Tiger II

The Tiger II or 'King Tiger' used a longer-barrelled version of the 88mm (3.46in) gun with awesome penetrative capability and had even thicker armour. It also used the same engine, with detrimental results in terms of mobility and fuel consumption.

Panzer VI Tiger

Crew: 5
Weight: 69,700kg (153,340lb)
Dimensions: length 10.26m (33ft 8in); width 3.75m (12ft 3.5in); height 3.09m (10ft 1.5in)
Range: 110km (68 miles)
Armour: 100–150mm (3.94–5.9in)
Armament: 88mm (3.46in) KwK 43 gun; two 7.92 MG34 machine guns (coaxial, and on hull front)
Powerplant: one Maybach HL 230 P30 12-cylinder petrol engine developing 700hp (522kW)
Performance: maximum road speed 38km/h (24mph); fording 1.60m (5ft 3 in); vertical obstacle 0.85m (2ft 10in); trench 2.5m (8ft 2in)

STRENGTHS

- Excellent gun
- Very heavy armour
- Sloped armour further increased protection

WEAKNESSES

- Low mobility
- Overcomplex
- Short operational range

role was to deliver a massive explosive charge against enemy positions. They were meant to take part in the Ardennes offensive, but could not keep up with other tanks and tended to be left too far behind to be any use.

The tank destroyer version of the Tiger II, designated Jagdpanzer VI Jagdtiger, was supposed to be armed with a 128mm (5in) gun that was so powerful its high-explosive rounds were only a little less effective at penetrating armour than the armour-piercing shot fired by a 88mm (3.46in). There were not enough guns, so many Jagdtigers were given 'mere' 88s instead.

The Jagdtiger was so massively armoured as to be invulnerable from the front. Its high sides, however, made a better target than other tank destroyers and could be penetrated by Allied guns. It was also fuel-hungry and slow, with poor mobility due to its great size and weight. Although Jagdtigers were deployed for the Ardennes Offensive, they were not included in the attack for these reasons.

The Jagdtiger was a symptom of the German fascination with gigantic, overcomplicated and all-powerful vehicles, which finally led to the Maus. This supertank project was armed with coaxial 150mm (5.9in) and 75mm (2.95in) guns in an immense turret. It weighed three times as much as a Jagdtiger and moved only at a crawl. It represented a terrible waste of effort and it is ironic that the nation that showed mobile tank warfare to be hugely effective should end up building something that could only be of use lumbering across a 1917 trench landscape.

The Ardennes offensive itself was an ambitious plan to force the Allies to negotiate peace. The aim was to break though a weak sector and advance rapidly on Antwerp, eliminating large numbers of Allied troops in a classic armoured battle of annihilation. In truth, it was too ambitious, and senior German officers wanted a more limited version. Hitler was adamant that his counteroffensive could restore the situation, however, and insisted on unrealistic goals.

The offensive opened well for the German Army

Jagdtiger

As the war progressed, it became German policy to create a tank-destroyer based on each new tank design. The Jagdtiger was such a vehicle. They were intended to be armed with a potent 128mm (5in) gun but shortages ensured that many received 88mm (3.46in) guns instead.

on 16 December 1944, and it hit a lightly held sector populated by battle-weary units busy recuperating, or new arrivals with little combat experience. For a short time the attackers were able to run wild, assisted by deception operations and the general confusion engendered by surprise. Yet resistance firmed up quickly, and although outnumbered and surrounded US troops were able to hold out in the town of Bastogne. The assault was eventually fought to a standstill and faltered for lack of supplies – especially tank fuel. Large numbers of German troops were trapped in a more or less surrounded pocket. Those that escaped left behind large quantities of equipment, including broken-down or out-of-fuel tanks.

The Ardennes counteroffensive represented the last chance for a great Panzer victory in the West, and with it the only real hope of averting total defeat. In due course, and after desperate resistance all the way, the Western Allies would be able to cross the Rhine and advance deep into Germany. Meanwhile, the shrinking Panzer battlegroups had been hopelessly trying to stave off final defeat in the east.

Retreat in the East

After the great armoured clash at Kursk, the German Army was forced to begin a retreat that ended only at Berlin. There were local successes, counterattacks and even small advances, but the tide had turned and there could be no stopping the Red Army.

The appearance of Tigers and Panthers on the Eastern Front had caused alarm among Soviet commanders, who rightly decided that their tanks needed bigger guns to stop these monsters. As an interim measure, the existing KV-1 heavy tank was redesignated KV-85 and given an 85mm (3.34in) gun, but the increase in weight that went with the new armament reduced performance to a level acceptable only until something better could be fielded. The turret developed for the KV-85 formed the basis for that of the T-34/85 (see below), while the IS-1 was developed with the intention that it would replace the KV-85 in service. (IS is sometimes translated as JS, since the tank was named for Iosef/Josef Stalin.) This new heavy tank was built on an adapted KV hull with a new transmission and worked well enough, but it

Soviet infantry hitching a ride aboard a T-34 during the push westwards through German resistance all the way to Berlin.

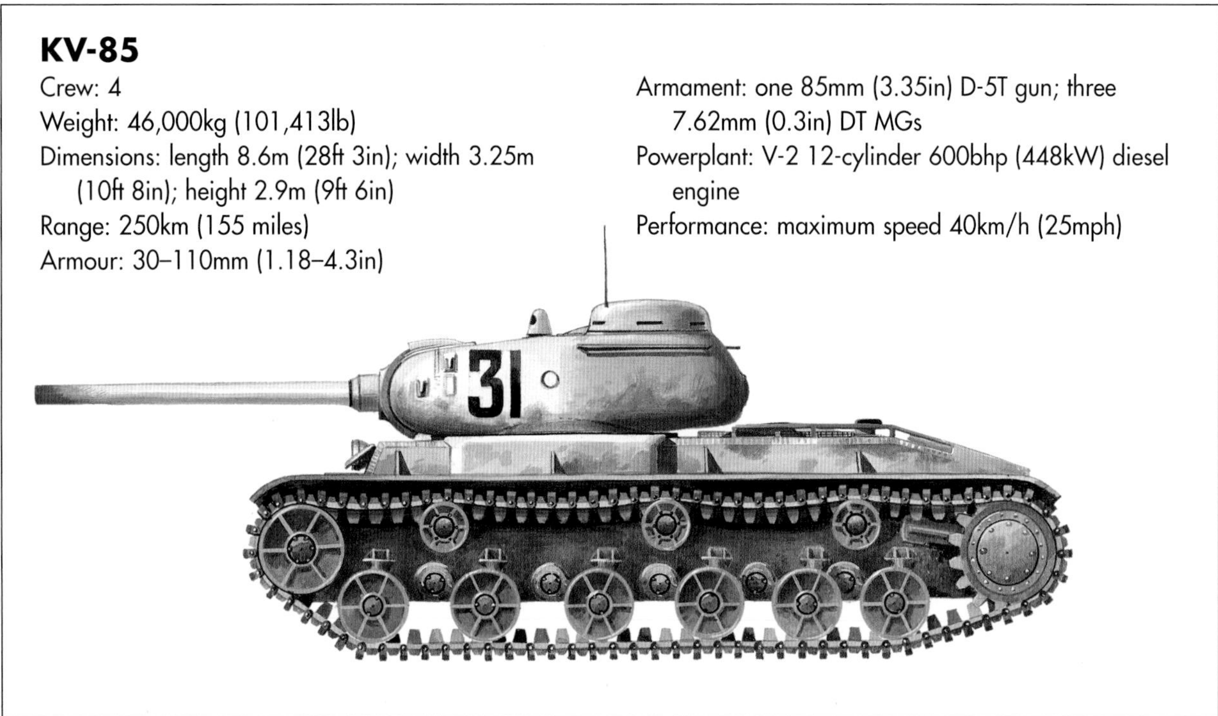

KV-85

Crew: 4
Weight: 46,000kg (101,413lb)
Dimensions: length 8.6m (28ft 3in); width 3.25m (10ft 8in); height 2.9m (9ft 6in)
Range: 250km (155 miles)
Armour: 30–110mm (1.18–4.3in)
Armament: one 85mm (3.35in) D-5T gun; three 7.62mm (0.3in) DT MGs
Powerplant: V-2 12-cylinder 600bhp (448kW) diesel engine
Performance: maximum speed 40km/h (25mph)

was supplanted quickly by the IS-2, which was much more powerful.

The IS-2 was also known as the 'Victory Tank'. It mounted an impressive 122mm (4.8in) gun on an almost identical hull to the IS-1. The gun's amour-piercing capability was good enough to knock out Panthers and Tigers, and it could also fire a useful high-explosive shell against softer targets. Appearing at much the same time, the T-34/85 was the other significant Soviet tank of the later war years; it was possibly the most important tank design of the entire period. Other than some slight improvements in armour and a better gearbox, the new model was simply an upgunned T-34. Yet the new turret needed for the bigger weapon allowed the crew to be increased to five by the addition of a loader, which enabled faster and more efficient firing. Although not quite as good, tank-for-tank, as the Panther, the T34/85 was available in far greater numbers. It was reliable and dependable in combat, and took part in the great drive westwards that ended in the ruins of Berlin. After the war, T34s were widely exported and some examples saw action in the Balkans in the 1990s.

The German principles of mobility and flexible command that had served so well during the offensives of the early war were also important during the retreat across Eastern Europe. Shattered units were combined into battlegroups with a little artillery, some infantry and a few tanks, and sent back into combat where they performed impressively well. This system was used in the West as well, and combined with a practice of always keeping a reserve in hand no matter how bad things were, allowed the battered *Wehrmacht* to respond aggressively to threats time and time again. Innumerable times during the retreat, the German Army turned and lunged at the Soviets, or created positions that had to be taken at great cost. The policy of holding ground was abandoned in favour of a mobile and flexible defence. Units would stand and fight, forcing the Soviets to halt and make preparations for an assault. More often than not, the attack arrived empty air; the defenders would pull back, let the attack exhaust itself and then make a savage counterattack before falling back again.

Thus it went on across Russia and Poland, and finally into Germany itself. As the Western Allies landed in Normandy and pushed across Europe from that direction, the Red Army ground its way towards Berlin. More than 6000 Soviet tanks were available for the final assault on Berlin.

Attempting to stop them were a number of tanks. Some were obtained from the repair shops or development laboratories, some were newly built in the factories and not yet delivered. A few belonged to units that had retreated all the way to Berlin and now made a final stand. Backing this inadequate force were antitank guns, old men and boys of the *Volksturm* armed with Panzerfaust antitank weapons, and anything else that could be scraped together and forced into the line by desperate patriotism or the bayonets of SS troopers.There could be only one ending, and finally the defence collapsed before the might of the Red Army.

Fighting went on for a while after the official surrender as pockets held out, notably in northern Italy. An uneasy peace settled across Europe as the Eastern and Western allies came face to face. Some, notably George S. Patton, advocated a continuation of the war, driving east to eliminate the Soviet Union before it could consolidate its hold on Eastern Europe. Given what had happened to everyone else who had tried this, it is as well perhaps that the Western Allies settled for what they had. The Cold War was unpleasant, but there is no guarantee that an offensive against the battle-hardened armies of the Soviet Union would not have ended in utter defeat. As the dust settled in the West, there was one final act to play out before the war could truly end.

Epilogue: Armour in the East

Three months after the end of the war in Europe, Russian forces opened an offensive against the Japanese in Manchuria. Named Operation *August Storm*, this offensive included about 5000 tanks, of which most were T-34s transferred from Europe.

The Soviet plan was to use a double envelopment supported by airborne landings and amphibious operations. Of the several hundred Japanese armoured vehicles available to oppose the attack, most were armoured cars and tankettes, and even those tanks that were deployed were of designs that were not up to fighting a first-rate army of 1939 standards. They stood no chance at all against the tanks that had beaten the Panzers of the *Wehrmacht.*

The Soviet operation was a runaway success, which slowed down only when the supply lines became too long even for airborne logistics. Opposition was overrun or brushed aside and all attempts to make a stand were crushed or scattered. Operation *August Storm* was an important factor in forcing the Japanese surrender, and it had other consequences too. Not least of these was that the northern end of the Korean peninsula came under Soviet influence, setting the stage for a new war before the decade was out.

A Soviet T-34/85 and infantry move through an otherwise peaceful suburb in 1945. Occupation duty in conquered territory was not always a safe or peaceful task.

TANKS OF THE COLD WAR

At the end of World War II, Europe was divided between Soviet and Western spheres of influence, and huge political differences existed between the former allies. On both sides of the 'Iron Curtain', as the East-West divide became known, there were huge stocks of wartime-produced weaponry and vast numbers of men under arms.

Thus the Cold War began. Essentially this represented an armed standoff between East and West and was characterized by political manoeuvring, spying and proxy conflicts in various parts of the world. Both sides were willing to sponsor allied nations and rebel groups against one another, seeking to gain small advantages each time and eventually achieve dominance.

In 1949, the North Atlantic Treaty Organization (NATO) was formed, with more nations joining in 1952. Its aim was to protect the West from the Soviet Union, and in turn those nations under Soviet influence formed the Warsaw Pact in 1955. Its aim was to protect the Soviet-bloc nations and their interests from the West. Where NATO was an alliance of equals, albeit of very different levels of military capability, the Warsaw Pact was unified under the control of the Soviet Union.

Left: The M36 tank destroyer saw action in Korea and continued to serve with the armies of foreign countries for many years after the end of World War I.

NATO nations often cooperated on joint military projects such as the creation of new ship, aircraft and tank designs (and sometimes fell out over these projects), but more often each nation used whatever equipment it preferred, subject to agreements over weapon calibres and similar logistics-related matters. On the other hand, Warsaw Pact equipment was generally standardized. Some items were built in the various Warsaw Pact member nations, and were subject to slight local variations. Others were constructed only in certain nations and supplied to satellite countries. Some equipment was reserved for the exclusive use of the forces of the Soviet Union.

The result of these political differences was that NATO equipment during the Cold War was more diverse than that of the Warsaw Pact. Nations not directly part of either faction tended to obtain their equipment from one side or the other; it was relatively rare to find a country using both Western and Soviet equipment. Eastern and Western equipment clashed in battle on many occasions, even if the troops of each side did not come into direct conflict. Soviet equipment was supplied to many communist rebel groups (and many that paid lip service to Communism to obtain equipment) and many nations aligned themselves with one side or the other for various purposes.

Warsaw Pact Tanks of the Cold War

In Europe, forces ranged on opposite sides of the Iron Curtain faced one another uneasily. The Soviets were well equipped to fight a renewed war. In addition to their vast arsenal of T-34/85s, new shipments of the powerful IS-3 heavy tank were appearing. This was a developed version of the IS-2, which had entered service in the last days of World War II. Mechanically sound, well protected and armed with a powerful 122mm (4.8in) gun, it was enough to worry the Western troops that might have to face it. Though it carried only 28 rounds for its main gun, the IS-3 was a formidable tank.

The last Soviet heavy tank was the T-10. This, too, was developed from the IS series and mounted

Aggression Deterrent

Tensions remained high enough that the Allies left large forces in Germany, their purpose more than the enforcement of the surrender: they were a deterrent to Soviet aggression in Europe.

the same 122mm (4.8in) gun. Although it was powerful and substantially armoured, it represented a major logistics drain – the resources to keep a few heavy tanks running could be better spent on larger numbers of general-purpose MBTs – so the heavy tank was phased out of the Warsaw Pact arsenal.

Another Soviet tank that entered service in the last days of the war, too late to play any major part, was the T-44. Essentially a redesigned T-34, it was easier to build and designed from the outset to carry the 85mm (3.34in) gun of the T-34/85. It was also better protected and had improved suspension. Only a few T-44s arrived in time to see action, but the design was very advanced and served as the basis of a new generation of Soviet tanks. This started with the T-54, which went into production in 1948 and was finally curtailed three decades later. Along with an improved version designated T-55, the T-54 became the backbone of Warsaw Pact armoured forces right through the Cold War, remaining in service even when more advanced tanks were available. The T-54 was supplied to communist China, whose own version was in service for many years as well as serving as the basis for other vehicles. Examples were exported to more than 30 nations and saw action all over the world. Some remain in service today; they are cheap and simple to keep running and entirely adequate for most combat operations.

The successor to the T-54/T-55 was developed from it and entered service as the T-62. It represented evolutionary rather than revolutionary development, but did have nuclear, biological, chemical (NBC) protection to enable it to function in the expected nuclear- and chemical-weapon contaminated battlefield. When the T-62 entered service in 1961, it mounted the world's first smoothbore tank gun, a 115mm (4.5in) weapon.

Next came the T-64, which was a new design and suffered from the inevitable teething problems. It used hydro-pneumatic suspension and initially mounted a 115mm (4.5in) gun. However, comparisons with the US M60 resulted in an upgunned version mounting a 125mm (4.9in) gun. This was later adapted to launch guided antitank missiles and was fed by an autoloader that reduced the burden of handling the big shells. Unfortunately, the autoloader was very bulky and had a habit of trying to load crew members into the breech along with the shell.

T-64s were not exported, but went to Soviet units only. They were, however, very unreliable and completely eclipsed by the T-72 of 1972. This had its basis in a project to develop a replacement for the T-62, and it ended up using many components in common with the T-64. It was a better tank, representing an excellent compromise between combat power, protection and mobility, while not costing an excessive amount.

The T-72's powerful 125mm (4.9in) gun was stabilized to allow shooting on the move, but its stabilization system did not work out as well as those of some contemporary tanks and halting to fire remained standard practice. Later T-72s gained steel/ceramic composite armour and the ability to fire a laser-guided round from the main gun. ERA was also introduced in the mid-1980s to help defeat shaped-charge warheads.

The T-72 never quite lived up to its promise, and suffered heavily against Western tanks deployed by Israeli forces in the 1980s and the Coalition nations in the Persian Gulf War of 1990–91. Admittedly, it was never really intended to take on these tanks one-on-one. It was a cheap and simple battle tank to fill out armoured forces, and in that context it remains a decent enough fighting vehicle.

The T-80, unlike the T-72, was intended as a frontline tank to take on the best anyone else might have. Developed from the T-64 with the worst of its faults (such as the unreliable suspension system) rectified, the T-80 was well protected and armed with the standard Soviet 125mm (4.9in) gun. It

Displays such as the May Day parades in Red Square were an important propaganda tool during the Cold War.

HEAD TO HEAD: *M60* VERSUS

The tanks of the early Cold War period were mostly developed from late-wartime models. The M60, for example, was an evolution of the M48, itself designed just after the World War II. Since its inception, the M60 has continually evolved to make use of new equipment. The A2 version, mounting the Shillelagh gun/missile system, was not a success, but the more conventional (and more advanced) A3 was a good tank. M60s are still widely in service today.

M60

Crew: 4
Weight: 48,872kg (107,520lb)
Dimensions: length 9.436m (30ft 11.5in); width 3.631m (11ft 11in); height 3.27m (10ft 8.25in)
Range: 500km (310 miles)
Armour: 25–127mm (0.98–5in)
Armament: 105mm (4.1in) gun; 12.7mm (0.5in) machine gun; 7.62mm (0.3in) coaxial machine gun
Powerplant: one Continental 12-cylinder diesel engine developing 750hp (560kW)
Performance: maximum road speed 48.28km/h (30mph); fording 1.219m (4ft); vertical obstacle 0.914m (3ft); trench 2.59m (8ft 6in)

STRENGTHS

- Adaptable design can be easily upgraded
- Good electronics on later versions
- Well-sloped armour for better protection

WEAKNESSES

- Based on a WWII-era design
- Basic M60 model lacked gun stabilization
- M60A2 variant was a total failure

T-72

The T-72 began development at about the same time as the M60. It was designed to be relatively cheap and simple, and was always intended to be used *en masse,* making up for its rather basic specification with sheer numbers. The cramped and uncomfortable conditions aboard a T-72 are tiring for the crew, which reduces combat efficiency. T-72s did not do well against Israeli tanks in the 1980s.

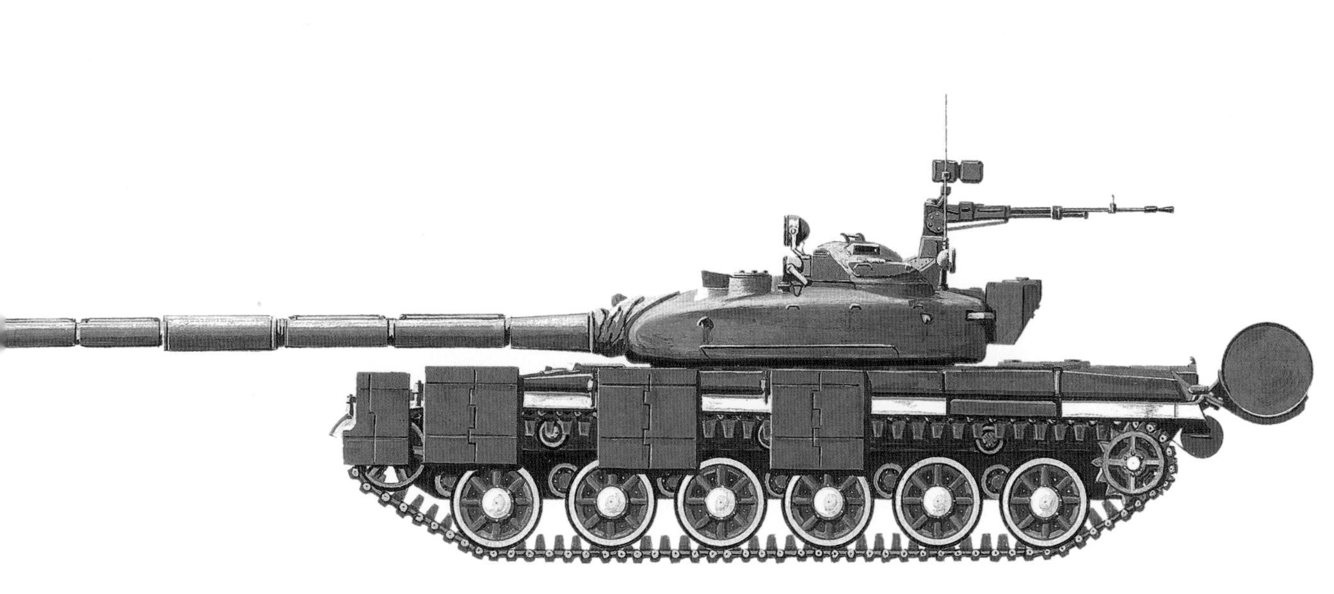

T-72

Crew: 3
Weight: 38,894kg (85,568lb)
Dimensions: length 9.24m (30ft 4in); width 4.75m (15ft 7in); height 2.37m (7ft 9in)
Range: 550km (434 miles)
Armour: classified
Armament: one 125mm (4.9in) gun; one 12.7mm (0.5in) anti-aircraft machine gun; one 7.62mm (0.3in) coaxial machine gun
Powerplant: one V-46 V-12 diesel engine developing 840hp (626kW)
Performance: maximum road speed 80km/h (50mph); fording 1.4m (4ft 7in); vertical obstacle 0.85in (2ft 9in); trench 2.8m (9ft 2in)

STRENGTHS

- Produced in enormous numbers
- Powerful 125mm (4.9in) smoothbore cannon
- Relatively cheap to build

WEAKNESSES

- Very cramped crew compartment
- Gun stabilization fairly poor
- Tendency to catch fire when penetrated

The T-72 has been widely exported to many nations worldwide. This example is in Iranian service, but was quite possibly captured from Iraqi forces during the 1980s.

was the first Soviet tank to be given a ballistic computer and laser rangefinder and could launch guided missiles from its smoothbore gun. The T-80 is still in production and has been widely exported, though today it is somewhat outdated and would fare badly in a clash with the best Western tanks.

The Soviet fascination with light tanks eventually faded in favour of an MBT, as epitomized by the T-34 and its successors. The light tank still had a part to play in Soviet armoured doctrine in the Cold War, however. The PT-76 was designed for armoured reconnaissance and in addition was amphibious to enable it to make an assault crossing of a river or to support a beach invasion. Armed with a modest 76mm (2.99in) gun, the PT-76 entered service in the early 1950s and was widely exported. Production was curtailed in 1967, but it remained in service for many years afterwards and was copied by other nations, notably China.

The Soviet Union was a great proponent of mobile armoured warfare and created 'motor rifle' units equipped with trucks and supported by tanks. A range of tank destroyers was developed to support these formations, and gradually APCs appeared. There was nothing new about this concept – an armoured personnel transport was developed from a tank design in World War I – but the Soviets took the idea of armoured transport further.

Many nations were using APCs as 'battle taxis' for troops and were fitting some with firing ports for infantry weapons or machine guns for support, but the Soviets were the first to field what today is termed a Mechanized Infantry Combat Vehicle (MICV) or Infantry Fighting Vehicle (IFV). This was the BMP-1, armed with a 73mm (2.87in) gun as well as an antitank guided missile launcher.

The low silhouette of Soviet tanks was ideal for fast-moving operations in the open, making them difficult targets.

Amphibious Manoeuvres

Soviet doctrine emphasized river crossings and amphibious outflanking manoeuvres, for which the PT-76 amphibious tank was well suited. It also found success overseas, though mainly as a conventional light tank.

BMP-1

Crew: 3 + 8
Weight: 13,900kg (30, 650lb)
Dimensions: length 6.74m (23ft); width 2.94m (9ft 8in); height 2.15m (7ft 1in)
Range: 500km (310miles)
Armour: 33mm (1.3in) max
Armament: one 73mm (2.87in) Grom low-pressure gun, one 7.62mm (0.3in) MG, one AT-3 Sagger ATGW system
Powerplant: one Model 6-cylinder 300bhp (224kW) diesel
Performance: maximum speed 80km/h (50mph); 8km/h (5mph) in water

There is a common misconception that an APC, MICV or any other vehicle with tracks and a gun is, by definition, a tank. The fact is, though, that even the best-armed MICV cannot survive in a straight fight with tanks. What it can do – and what it is designed to do – is give effective fire support to its infantry and, in some cases, destroy tanks at a distance with guided missiles. The advent of the MICV added a new dimension to the threats faced by tanks on the battlefield, putting powerful vehicle-mounted anti-armour weaponry in the hands of infantry.

US Tanks of the Cold War

The vast numbers of extremely capable Soviet tanks facing them across the Iron Curtain gave Western commanders cause for concern. A powerful counter was needed, and quickly. As with the Soviets, a range of gun- and later missile-armed tank destroyers began to appear, but the best counter to a tank is another tank, and so new designs were developed.

As a general rule, Western tanks have always had higher turrets than their Soviet equivalents, and this to a great extent reflects the respective doctrines concerning their use. Soviet tanks were low and difficult to hit, making them more survivable when in the open. This profile was a major advantage when making a massed armoured charge. Western tanks, on the other hand, tended to be better suited to hiding hull-down and firing over an obstruction while being protected by it. The high turret gave a better field of fire while the tank remained concealed.

Had East and West clashed, it was expected that vast numbers of Warsaw Pact tanks would pour westwards, while the outnumbered but technologically superior NATO armoured forces tried to stop them. The tanks of both sides were well suited to their expected role and the tactics associated with it. In the West, the big question was: could the tanks of the day halt the Warsaw Pact Juggernaut?

For a time, it seemed that heavy tanks were the way to go. The US Army received small numbers of the M26 Pershing heavy tank at the very end of the war, too late to make much difference. Heavily armoured and armed with a 90mm (3.54in) gun, it was more mobile than a Tiger and about as robust. It was followed by an enlarged version designated T32, with improved armour, and finally grew into the M46, sometimes called the 'Patton' tank. The M26 and M46 were the main US tanks in the Korean conflict and gave good service, proving capable of stopping North Korean armoured forces armed with T-34s and other Soviet hardware.

The heavy tank was dying out by the early 1950s, but the United States had one last go at producing one. This was the M103, an ostensibly powerful vehicle with a 120mm (4.7in) gun. It was underpowered and unreliable, and quickly faded from the scene. Meanwhile, the US was more successfully looking into lighter tanks.

The M47 Patton tank was a deliberate attempt to get a powerful gun (in this case, a 90mm/3.54in weapon) into a vehicle that was reliable and easy to maintain and not too heavy. The idea was sound, but the tank was rushed into production for service in Korea and suffered from many mechanical problems. It was quickly replaced by the M48, also designated the Patton, which was similarly rushed but eventually developed into a good tank.

Updated M48s are still in service in some nations, despite the basic design being more than 50 years old. Not all the developed versions worked out well, however. The M48A3 was fitted with a 105mm (4.1in) gun in an attempt to upgrade

Guided missiles emerged as a threat to tanks in the early Cold War period. They could be carried on lighter vehicles and helicopters, and launched by infantry teams.

Camouflage

Camouflage breaks up the distinctive outline of a tank and makes the human eye less likely to identify it at a distance. It is obvious close up, but at combat distances this tank could disappear into the landscape, enabling it to strike by surprise.

firepower, and proved effective. The A4, on the other hand, was armed with the Shillelagh gun/missile system that set a new standard for failure.

The M48 continued to develop despite the flirtation with the appalling Shillelagh and evolved into the M60 MBT, armed with a 105mm (4.1in) gun. It entered service in 1960 and continued to develop for many years. In 1964, this basically good tank was given a Shillelagh gun/missile system, creating the M60A2, which spent eight years in development before entering service in 1972. Few A2s survived long; most were converted to bridgelayers or engineering vehicles. The M60A3 was the definitive version, returning to the proven 105mm (4.1in) gun. This tank was sold to many nations, and large numbers remain in service. Israel received over 1300 M60A3s and gradually upgraded them. Developed versions, renamed Magach and Sabra, were used and exported by Israel.

Watercourses are a severe obstacle to all vehicles. Bridging operations are thus a vital part of all armoured operations.

An M551 Sheridan travels across urban terrain, this tank was name after Civil War General Philip Sheridan.

The US also developed lighter tanks after World War II. The first was the M41 Walker Bulldog. Designed as a replacement for the M24 Chaffee, this was a light tank armed with a useful 76mm (2.99in) gun that could not take on the frontline Soviet tanks of the era, but was nevertheless an effective fire-support vehicle. It arrived too late to do much in Korea and was replaced before the Vietnam conflict, but did achieve export success. Next was the M551 Sheridan. It was intended as an air-portable light tank capable of destroying heavier armoured vehicles. Unfortunately, the means chosen to undertake this task was the Shillelagh gun/missile system. Problems with the weapon delayed entry to service for some years, and when it was deployed the Sheridan was found to be extremely vulnerable to enemy fire. The gun/missile system was an interesting idea that unfortunately did not live up to its promise. The basic idea was to be able to fire shells of various sorts from the gun for most uses, and to switch to guided missiles when precision at long ranges was required. The problem with the Shillelagh was that the missile system weakened the gun barrel while the residue from firing shells impaired the missile launching system. Thus a weapon system designed to provide two capabilities in the end did neither very well. After a lengthy period spent trying to get the concept to work, the idea was dropped and US tanks returned to a straight gun armament.

British Tanks of the Cold War

British tanks of the early Cold War period had their basis in wartime designs. The A34 Comet was a cruiser tank design that arrived too late to achieve much in the last months of the war. Fast across country, it used an electrical system to traverse the turret. The Comet served with the British Army into the 1960s and was exported overseas.

Where the Comet looked like a World War II tank, the A41 Centurion that was developed at much the same time had a more modern appearance. Originally armed with a 17-pounder (76mm/2.99in) gun, sometimes with a co-axial 20mm (0.78in) cannon, the Centurion was gradually upgraded with bigger guns and additional equipment. Late-production Centurions were armed with a 105mm (4.1in) gun and served with distinction in a number of conflicts worldwide. In addition to considerable export success as a gun tank, the chassis was adapted to a variety of roles. As late as the 1990s, the Centurion-based AVRE was still serving in combat zones around the world.

The Comet and Centurion were the British tanks that would have faced a Warsaw Pact advance in the 1950s. Concerns about the ability of British forces to stop the big Soviet tanks, led to the development of the Conqueror heavy tank. Armed with a 120mm (4.7in) gun in a big single-piece cast turret, the Conqueror was notoriously unreliable. Within a few years of its introduction in 1956, it was supplanted by the upgunned Centurion, which did the same job better, cheaper and more reliably.

The Centurion dates from the end of World War II. It was an excellent tank that spawned upgrades and variants.

In 1963, the classic Cold War British tank appeared: the Chieftain. With a 120mm (4.7in) gun and protected by good armour, it was widely exported. It never served with British forces, but saw action in the Iran-Iraq War, proving more than a match for the Soviet-designed Iraqi tanks.

Another concept to emerge from the Cold War was the Combat Vehicle, Reconnaissance, Tracked (CVRT). A light tank by any other name, the Scorpion CVRT entered service in the mid-1970s and was initially armed with a 76mm (2.99in) gun. A 90mm (3.54in) version followed and was exported to several nations. Built on the same chassis but with a different turret mounting a 30mm (1.18in) Rarden cannon, the Scimitar was very similar to the Scorpion. Fast, agile and with a ground pressure so low it could cross ground where a man on skis would get stuck, both vehicles served in the Falklands War, albeit in very small numbers (three of each). An updated Scimitar, named Sabre, entered British Army service in the 1990s.

The Chieftain

This was a contemporary tank of the Soviet T-62 that served in the British army until the mid-1990s. It emphasized firepower and protection over speed.

European Tanks of the Cold War

Germany was divided into two states after the end of World War II. East Germany was part of the Warsaw Pact and equipped accordingly. West Germany became part of NATO and was permitted to re-arm to help defend the West against the Warsaw Pact.

Where Britain and the United States followed a similar doctrine of building heavily armoured tanks, the German philosophy was that mobility was more important than protection. The first post-war German tank was the Leopard I, which entered production in the mid-1960s. The project started out as a collaboration between Germany, France and Italy and eventually produced a relatively lightly armoured but fast MBT armed with a British-designed 105mm (4.1in) gun.

The Leopard I was developed through several versions and widely exported. Examples remain in service in several countries and in many roles. The Leopard I was designed to be fitted with a range of accessories such as bulldozer blades as standard, and has been adapted to many roles.

Italy, which was part of the consortium that created the Leopard I's specifications, built the Leopard under licence for many years and created a design based upon it for export. This was designated the OF-40 MBT and initially attracted considerable interest. A few sales were made to the

HEAD TO HEAD: *Centurion* VERSUS

The British Centurion was developed from a specification laid down in 1943 and evolved through several variants. It started out with a 17-pounder (76mm/2.99in) gun and eventually gained a 105mm (4.1in) weapon. In the 1960s, the Centurion gained infra-red driving lights and the ability to take a range of accessories, including bulldozer blades and deep-wading kits.

Centurion

Crew: 4
Weight: 43,182kg (95,200lb)
Dimensions: length 7.82m (24ft 6in); width 3.39m (11ft 2in); height 5m (9ft 11in)
Range: 192km (120 miles)
Armour: 17–127mm (0.75–4in)
Armament: one 17-pounder (76mm/2.99in); one coaxial 7.92mm (0.3in) Besa MG or one 20mm (0.79in) Polsten cannon
Powerplant: Meteor V-12 650bhp (485kW) petrol
Performance: maximum speed 35km/h (22mph); fording 1.45m (4ft 9in); vertical obstacle 0.91m (3ft); trench 3.35m (11ft)

STRENGTHS

- Well protected
- Powerful main gun
- Easily upgradable

WEAKNESSES

- Based on a wartime design
- No NBC protection
- Short operational range

T-55

The T54 and its derivative, designated T-55, were designed in the late 1940s. Like the Centurion, they proved to be extremely long-lived designs. Armed with a 100mm (3.94in) gun, T-55s served in Soviet and Warsaw pact forces right to the end of the Cold War period. It was also widely exported and found a home with Egypt and Syria, among others. Upgraded versions, some of them with Western powerplants, have appeared from time to time.

T-55

Crew: 4
Weight: 36,000kg (79,366lb)
Dimensions: length 6.45m (21dt 2in); width 3.27m (10ft 9in); height 2.4m (7ft 10in)
Range: 400km (250 miles)
Armour: 203mm (8in) max
Armament: one 100mm (3.94in) gun, two 7.62mm (0.3in) MGs, one 12.7mm (0.5in) AA MG
Powerplant: 12-cylinder 520bhp (388kW) diesel
Performance: maximum speed 48km/h (30 miles); fording 1.4m (4ft 7in); vertical obstacle 0.8m (2ft 8in); trench 2.7m (8ft 10in)

STRENGTHS

- Good armament
- Built in huge numbers
- Upgraded throughout its career

WEAKNESSES

- 'Shell traps' on original models
- Unstabilized gun
- No NBC protection on early models

An Italian design, the OF-40 was developed from the Leopard I for the export market.

United Arab Emirates, where it proved not to be a success, despite the fact that it was a Leopard by any other name.

French tank design also came to a more or less complete halt, though this was due to the German occupation rather than armistice conditions. Some design work went on in secret, resulting in the Char ARL-44 heavy tank, a throwback to the Char 1 in many ways, with similar tracks, though it mounted a powerful 90mm (3.54in) gun in its turret. Only about 50 were built and these proved unsatisfactory, so they were withdrawn from service as soon as something better was available.

At the other end of the scale, the French also produced the AMX-13 light tank. This vehicle looked a lot more modern than its 1952 introduction date would imply. It used an oscillating turret – i.e. one in which the top half of the turret, including the autoloader and ammunition store, elevated along with the gun mounting. Designed to be air-mobile, the AMX-13 was a long-lived design that got a useful gun (75mm/2.95in initially, sometimes 90mm/3.54in or even 105mm/4.1in) into the field with good mobility if modest protection. Its low profile was a better defence than its armour, but overall the AMX-13 was a very good light armoured vehicle that could serve a wide range of purposes.

The basic AMX-13 spawned a number of possible variants, including one armed with HOT antitank guided missiles plus an APC and various self-propelled artillery weapons. However, the French still needed a battle tank. The first was

SCORPION CVRT

Crew: 3
Weight: 8073kg (17,798lb)
Dimensions: length 4.38m (14ft 5in); width 2.18m (7ft 2in); height 2.09m (6ft 10in)
Range: 644km (400 miles)
Armour: not available
Armament: one 76mm/90mm (2.99in/3.54in) gun; one 7.62mm (0.3in) MG
Powerplant: Jaguar 4.2 litre petrol 190bhp (141.6kW) engine
Performance: maximum speed 80.5km/h (50mph)

the Char AMX-50, a design heavily influenced by the wartime Panther tank. It used an oscillating turret similar to that of the AMX-13 but much larger; it needed to be to contain the 90mm (3.54in) or 100mm (3.94in) gun originally envisaged. The AMX-50 was finally armed with a 120mm (4.7in) gun when it appeared in 1951, putting it ahead of the curve in terms of Western tank armament. It was, nevertheless, high-sided and underpowered, and so after some development work the project was halted.

Replacing the AMX-50 was the much lower and more business-like AMX-30. Like the Leopard I, it had its origins in the 1950s collaboration between France, Germany and Italy to come up with a specification for a new battle tank. Entering service in the mid-1960s, the AMX-30 was armed with a

A French AMX-30 moving cross-country. The AMX-30 is very lightly protected by MBT standards but has very good mobility due to its relatively light weight.

105mm (4.1in) gun with a coaxial 20mm (0.78in) cannon. Its chassis was adapted for all manner of other vehicles and the design was a considerable export success. Many updated AMX-30s are still in service, usually with better engines and ERA to improve survivability. The latter was a problem with this design; the emphasis was always on mobility and speed, and its armour was very light for a battle tank. Despite this, the design has served well for many years and was adopted by the armies of several nations, including Spain, Greece and Saudi Arabia.

Many other nations outside the Warsaw Pact used tank designs created in Britain, the United States or Europe. These were often adapted versions to suit local needs. Spain, for example, took delivery of a number of modified American M47 tanks in the 1950s. These were always intended as an interim measure when the US Army took them on, and when they were supplanted there was plenty of life left in them. The M47s taken by Spain received a new engine and a better gun; this sort of upgrade was common on exported tanks.

Some European nations, however, went their own way. Sweden, which had remained neutral in World War II, had developed a number of tank designs during the war, and afterwards felt the need to preserve its neutrality with a good military force. Some tanks were obtained overseas, but the most definitively Swedish design of the Cold War years was the S-Tank, or Stridsvagen 103.

The S-Tank was more of a tank destroyer than a true battle tank. In fact, it could be argued that it was only a tank because the designers said it was. It was an effective combat vehicle. Designed to fight a defensive war against an invader, the S-Tank had no turret at all. Its 105mm (4.1in) gun was fixed, reducing the effectiveness of the vehicle on the offensive, but enabling it to hide in ambush very well indeed. To this end, the S-Tank had a bulldozer blade to allow itself to dig a scrape to fight from, and once it had made its attack it could be driven rapidly away from danger going backwards. A second driver, whose controls faced back, was carried for this job. The S-Tank was a unique artefact of Swedish Cold War neutrality and was not exported.

The innovative Swedish S-tank might more properly be considered a tank destroyer. Ideal for defensive warfare it made a difficult target when hiding in ambush.

New Tanks in the East

China did not begin to develop armoured vehicles of its own until the 1950s, and initially received a great deal of assistance from the Soviet Union. China's first tank was the Type 59, essentially a copy of the T-54 with a 100mm (3.94in) gun. Large numbers of this basic but serviceable tank were built and many were exported. Another design heavily influenced by the Soviets was the Type 63 light tank, an amphibious vehicle with an 85mm (3.34in) gun. (Chinese and Soviet doctrine had a lot in common, with large numbers of amphibious tanks spearheading a coastal landing or covering an assault crossing of a river.)

A lighter version of the Type 59, designated Type 62, entered service in 1962. It mounted an 85mm

Type-59

The earliest Chinese Main Battle Tank was the Type-59. Simply a copy of the Soviet T-54, these simple but effective vehicles were available in enormous numbers.

(3.34in) gun and was significantly lighter, reducing ground pressure. This capability made it attractive to overseas buyers such as Vietnam, who needed a tank that could function in close terrain. Another Type 59-derived design was the Type 69, an updated version that entered service in 1980. Although improved, there was little new about it and most of its design features dated back to the Soviet T-54. Several variants appeared, including one sometimes named Type 79. Later versions used a 105mm (4.1in) gun derived from the British L7 weapon used on the Centurion.

Chinese armour did not take any real leaps forward in the Cold War years. The basic technology was obtained overseas and gradually improved upon. The end result was a family of workman-like and relatively inexpensive armoured vehicles that were exported in considerable numbers. Although these tanks were not up to facing the best the West could field one-on-one, they were available in large numbers that could offset the disadvantage in capabilities.

In the late 1960s, as China and the Soviet Union gradually moved away from their stance of mutual friendship as fellow communists and back to the ages-old suspicion of one another, there was a point where Chinese tanks might have been tested against the Soviet ones they were derived from. Although a border clash did take place in 1969 and both sides deployed large forces, all-out conflict was averted.

The politics of the post-war years were such that while China was developing tanks based on Soviet designs, Japan's first post-war armoured vehicle was heavily influenced by US designs. It was the Type 61, which entered service in 1962. Japan's armed forces were heavily restricted by treaty, being named a 'self-defence force' and forbidden to operate other than in the defence of the homeland.

Unsurprisingly, the Japanese Type 61 was derived from the US M48 Patton tank. It lacked NBC protection and gun stabilization, but the latter might not have been critical in a tank designed primarily, like the Swedish S-Tank, to fight defensively against an invader. The Type 61 was a first attempt to create a modern tank and was sensibly conservative. A follow-up design designated Type 74 appeared soon after. This vehicle was somewhat more ambitious and mounted a 105mm (4.1in) gun instead of the Type

A Japanese Type 74 MBT. The general lines of this tank show the influence of US AFV designs.

61's 90mm (3.54in). It also had gun stabilization, a laser rangefinder and a ballistic computer. Later models gained night-vision equipment as well, creating a much more capable combat vehicle. The Type 74 largely supplanted its predecessor in service and was converted to a number of other roles, including an air defence tank and an armoured recovery vehicle.

Other Cold War Era Tanks

Elsewhere in the world, armoured vehicles were generally obtained from the major tank-building nations. Nations aligned with the Soviet Union (or those being cultivated by the Soviet Union) tended to get their equipment there, while others bought from whichever of the Western nations' designs best suited their purposes or budget.

Some countries had their own requirements and could afford to either commission a design overseas or build one themselves. Alternatively, an existing design could be modified to create a hybrid suited to local needs. One such was the Vijayanta tank adopted by India in the mid-1960s. Designed by Vickers, it took the 105mm (4.1in) gun from the Centurion and installed it in a new hull built around the motive and fire-control systems of the Chieftain. The resulting tank was lighter than a Chieftain but had good firepower and protection as well as mobility.

Israel led the way in upgrading tanks designed in other nations, sometimes creating what amounted to new designs after the upgrade process had been through a few iterations. The first was the M4 Sherman, Israel's first tank. Upgraded Shermans gained a 90mm (3.54in) gun, new fire control and better suspension and were still on active service in the 1970s.

Captured T-54 and T-55 tanks were pressed into Israeli service and received upgrades along the way, but these were phased out in favour of more 'Western' designs. Those included modified Centurions with a better engine and powertrain, and a bigger gun. M60s obtained from the United States were also upgraded and given a new designation: Magach.

The Magach appeared in several models that differed from the M60. They were heavier so had a new engine and tracks. Armament was a 105mm (4.1in) gun built in Israel, supplemented with improved fire control. A modified version of the Magach, named Sabra, was on offer for export at the end of the twentieth century.

Indigenous tank designs began to appear in various nations in the 1970s. Many had obtained surplus World War II vintage equipment from the stocks of the combatants. This equipment had soldiered on for decades but was becoming worn out, while spares were increasingly difficult to obtain. Buying in foreign tanks, some of them surplus machines of the generation currently being replaced in Europe and elsewhere, was one option. Another was to develop home-grown designs. Argentina, for example, took the route of ordering a design from overseas (in this case, from Germany) and then building it in Argentinean factories once the prototypes and licences to build the tank had been delivered. Brazil developed its own light tank design by reworking the old M3A1 Stuart of World War II vintage and developing a new turret to carry a modern 90mm (3.54in) gun.

These two somewhat different approaches represent the different routes taken by nations with developing arms industries. Experience gained with these vehicles assisted the development of later designs and related equipment such as APCs and armoured cars.

Armoured Conflict in Korea

Even before the Warsaw Pact had come into being, equipment developed on both sides of it had been committed to battle. Although NATO and the Warsaw Pact never clashed head-on, their doctrines and equipment met on several occasions.

The first clash was the Korean War (1950–53). The Korean peninsula was divided at the end of World War II; US troops held the south and Soviet forces the north. It was a situation that divided the country into communist and 'Western' halves, though the intention was not to create a permanent division. US and Soviet forces withdrew in 1949, causing severe political troubles, as well as clashes between the forces of communist North Korea and democratic South Korea.

Taking advantage of its possession of large quantities of obsolescent but effective Soviet military equipment, North Korea invaded the south in 1950, hoping to reunify the country by force. About 250 tanks took part in the initial advance, of which more than half were T-34s. Caught by surprise and lacking in equipment – especially antitank weapons – the South Korean army was roughly handled in the first days of the war and driven south in flight.

The army of South Korea had never faced armour and had none of its own, so 'tank terror' was a factor early on, and this was exacerbated by the fact that the best antitank weapons available to many units were US-made M9 antitank rocket launchers (bazookas), whose 60mm (2.34in) rockets could not harm a T-34. The only real alternative was infantry close assault, attempting to get close enough to a tank to use a satchel charge or put a grenade into an open hatch. In close or urban terrain there was a chance of success, but most attempts resulted only in brave but futile sacrifice.

The United Nations (UN) voted to support South Korea and, led by the United States, a coalition of nations began to send forces. The North Korean advance was finally halted and pushed back as increasingly large UN forces entered the fray. Tanks and antitank weapons were especially useful. The first arrivals, M24 light tanks from bases in Japan, were useful in infantry support but no match for North Korean T-34s.

US infantrymen hitch a ride on an M46 in Korea. These tanks formed the basis of US armoured forces in the Korean War.

HEAD TO HEAD: *Chieftain* VERSUS

British tank designers chose to emphasize firepower and survivability when they created the Chieftain in the 1960s. Almost 1000 examples were built for the British army, with half that number exported to foreign buyers. The Chieftain also formed the basis for the Khalid or Shir tank, a hybrid between the late-model Chieftain and the newer Challenger. The Chieftain's L11A5 120mm (4.7in) gun can penetrate any tank and was used on later designs, including the Challenger.

Chieftain Mk V

Crew: 4
Weight: 55,000kg (121,254lb)
Dimensions: length (hull) 7.52m (24ft 8in); width 3.5m (11ft 6in); height 2.9m (9ft 7in)
Range: 400–500km (249–280 miles)
Armour: not available
Armament: one 120mm (4.7in) L11A5 gun; two 7.62mm (0.3in) MGs; one 12.7mm (0.5in) MG
Powerplant: Leyland L60 multi-fuel 750bhp (559kW)
Performance: maximum speed 48km/h (30mph); fording 1.06m (3ft 6in); vertical obstacle 0.91m (3ft); trench 3.15m (10ft 4in)

STRENGTHS

- Powerful main armament
- Good fire control electronics
- Well protected

WEAKNESSES

- Slow relative to Leopard
- Unreliable multi-fuel engine
- Heavy compared to Leopard

Leopard I

The Leopard I, which entered service the same year as the Chieftain, mounts a 105mm (4.1in) gun and emphasizes mobility rather than protection. Its designers followed the maxim that 'speed is armour', creating a very fast MBT. Many variants have appeared, each tailored to the needs of a different user or incorporating advances made since the initial design work; the chassis has also been used for air defence vehicles and other specialist applications.

Leopard I

Crew: 4
Weight: 39,912kg (87,808lb)
Dimensions: length (hull) 7.09m (23ft 3in); width 3.25m (10ft 8in); height 2.61m (8ft 7in)
Range: 600km (373 miles)
Armour: classified
Armament: one 105mm (4.1in); one coaxial 7.62mm (0.3in) MG; one 7.62mm (0.3in) anti-aircraft gun; four smoke dischargers
Powerplant: one MTU 10-cylinder 830hp (619kW) diesel engine
Performance: maximum speed 65km/h (40mph); fording 2.25m (7ft 4in); vertical obstacle 1.15m (3ft 9in); trench 3m (9ft 10in)

STRENGTHS

- Very fast
- Reliable
- Easy to adapt and upgrade

WEAKNESSES

- Light armour
- Relatively light 105mm (4.1in) gun
- No definitive version – dozens of variants

Soon units equipped with M4 Shermans and M26 Pershings as well as British Centurions arrived and began to win victories. At the time, there was deep concern about a possible East-meets-West war in Europe and many observers considered Korea a useful field test that would show whether or not their equipment was up to the job.

There were no great tank battles in Korea; the terrain was not suited to massed armoured operations. Thus armoured forces were used to support infantry in fairly small units. Operations in Korea had much in common with the advance up Italy in the latter half of World War II.

Having established superiority, the UN forces were able to push the North Koreans back for a long period, until China entered the war. The Chinese contribution involved direct combat on the ground and in the air, but it was large infantry forces that threatened the UN troops, not tanks. After a long period of stalemate an armistice was agreed, which established the division of the country as permanent.

Tanks in the Jungle

In the early months of World War II, Japanese forces demonstrated that tanks could be effective in jungle terrain. There was no possibility of grand sweeping armoured charges, but armoured vehicles proved useful as mobile and well-protected fire support platforms. The jungle restricted their movement, but contrary to popular belief the entire country was not covered in dense forest.

Where the jungle was very dense, vehicles of all types were restricted to the roads, and this created a certain vulnerability to mines and barricade ambushes, which would trap vehicles in the killing zone. The presence of tanks in such a situation was useful in several ways. They could return fire with heavy weapons while shrugging off most of the incoming fire, and could also be used to bulldoze crippled vehicles aside to clear the way.

Armour-piercing antitank rounds were less useful in the jungle than high-explosive or anti-personnel ammunition. This included 'beehive' rounds filled with flechettes that could penetrate the foliage to a considerable distance (a quarter-mile, or 400m, in

Tanks in Vietnam

Tanks were used in the Vietnam war mainly to protect firebases and to provide fire support. In close terrain against an enemy without tanks, anti-armour rounds were fired less often than canister or high explosive. Seen here is a Centurion tank.

some cases), stripping away cover and suppressing or disabling enemy personnel. Canister rounds, consisting of a large number of small balls contained within a thin metal case, turned the tank gun into a giant shotgun and was highly effective.

Where the terrain was more open, tanks could make better use of their mobility, or could find a good firing position to support infantry at long range. Using a tank gun for counter-sniper fire or to take out a machine gun may seem excessive to some people, but it is certainly effective.

Tanks were used, albeit in small numbers, by French forces as they fought to prevent French Indochina from becoming an independent communist state. At the battle of Dien Bien Phu, French infantry were supported by M24 Chaffee light tanks in their long battle to defend the surrounded base. The French defeat in Indochina resulted in the creation of North and South Vietnam. Communist North Vietnam attempted to gain control of the whole country. This was opposed by the United States as part of a general policy to contain the spread of communism, and resulted in a drawn-out conflict.

Armour again played a relatively minor role, but tanks were useful in a fire support role and to help protect roads and installations such as firebases. The main US tank in the conflict was the M48 Patton, though other armoured vehicles played their role too. The unfortunate M551 Sheridan was deployed to Vietnam where its supposedly advanced gun/missile system was primarily useful to deliver anti-personnel 'beehive' rounds at close range.

Tanks in the Middle East

In the Middle East, the terrain was rather more suitable for tank action. Here Israel was surrounded by hostile Arab states. The latter obtained a lot of their military equipment from the Soviet Union, while Israel was largely supplied with Western equipment, albeit much of it adapted and upgraded to local requirements. The period just after the foundation of the State of Israel was troubled, and the declaration of Israel as an independent state in 1948 was followed by an attempt by Arab neighbours to crush Israel by force. Armoured forces played little part in the fighting that followed, as there were few tanks available on any side. Fighting broke out again in 1956, with Israeli forces advancing across the Sinai desert in support of an Anglo-French invasion of Egypt intended to secure the Suez Canal. The international political situation surrounding these operations was complex and led to a number of compromises and

The M24 Chaffee challenged its designers, who wanted to get a 75mm (2.95in) gun on a light tank.

promises, and an Anglo-British withdrawal that left the canal in Egyptian hands.

Israel continued to feel threatened, however, and in 1967 responded to perceived aggression with a pre-emptive air-land strike. Known as the Six-Day War, this operation was spectacularly successful, with armoured forces racing all the way to the Suez Canal protected by total air supremacy.

The success owed much to the body of knowledge available from studying World War II. The Israeli armoured forces used an indirect approach and good combined-arms tactics to achieve rapid and decisive victories over their stunned foes. That was another reason for the overwhelming success – the attack came as a complete surprise. The attack was similarly successful in the north, against Jordan and Syria.

A ceasefire was eventually agreed and there was no large-scale conflict until 1973, though shelling and skirmishes took place. Israel had gained a northern buffer zone in the form of the Golan Heights and, against Egypt, the depth of the Sinai Desert and the obstacle formed by the Suez Canal, giving the Israelis a sense of security.

In 1973, that sense of complacency was almost fatal. The Yom Kippur War, as it is known, began with a surprise attack by Egyptian and Syrian forces in early October. The Egyptians had developed techniques for making an assault crossing of the Suez Canal, which included using high-pressure hoses to wash away obstructions and create ramps for tanks once they were across.

Upgunned and modified Shermans served for many years with the Israeli armed forces. Shermans were also found in the inventory of other nations for several decades.

Israel's enemies used primarily Soviet equipment, such as FROG launchers and T-55 tanks as shown here.

There were other unpleasant surprises for the Israelis. Among the weaponry obtained by Egypt from the Soviet Union were quantities of anti-air missiles and antitank guided missiles (ATGMs). This time, the Israeli Air Force (IAF) suffered heavy losses from ground fire and could not achieve the sort of spectacular air supremacy it had enjoyed in 1967. Worse than this, the Israelis had become complacent and expected to win. When the attack began, Israeli tanks advanced confidently to counterattack without proper infantry support. Instead of scattering the enemy, they ran into fire from hull-down Egyptian tanks and a large number of infantry-launched guided missiles.

In the north, things went better for Israel. The Golan Heights proved their worth as a defensive buffer zone, and every one of the 180 Israeli tanks deployed there engaged the enemy. Most were able to shoot from good hull-down positions where enemy ATGMs and gunfire were less effective against them. This helped offset the fact that they were outnumbered by more than seven to one. The fighting in the north was desperate for a time, but eventually the Israelis were able to counterattack into Syria itself. The advance was halted by the intervention of Jordanian and Iraqi forces.

After a period of confusion and consternation in the south, the Israeli Defence Force (IDF) regained its composure and began to take control of the situation. Infantry and armour cooperation was relearned, and the infantry were able to deal with many Egyptian tanks using US-made M72 LAWs. The IDF launched an armoured counterattack that punched through the Egyptian line. Some forces were even able to advance across the Suez Canal, and once the surface-to-air missile (SAM) sites were overrun on the ground, the IAF was able to intervene decisively once again.

Pressure from the United Nations and the obvious shifting of the balance in favour of Israel prompted a ceasefire. After a number of incidents and fraught discussions between Moscow and Washington, this was gradually converted into peace of an uneasy sort. Israel's troubles were not over by any means, but the threat of annihilation had been averted.

The 1973 War of Atonement, or Yom Kippur War, involved a number of what were at the time new or untried technologies. Primitive night-fighting equipment had been improvised on a few Panther tanks in World War II, but in 1973 a more developed version was fitted as standard to Arab T-62s. Israeli tanks had no comparable system and keenly felt its lack during night actions. Infantry guided missiles proved to be a deadly threat to tanks for the first time, while light, disposable anti-armour weapons in the hands of infantrymen were shown to be effective at close range. Guided anti-aircraft missiles, protecting the ground forces from attack, also made a significant contribution to the course of the war.

All elements of the modern air/land battlefield were now in place and had been tried out under operational conditions. To all intents and purposes, the modern era of tank warfare had arrived.

B-43

MODERN TANKS

The three basic requirements for an armoured combat vehicle have not changed – it must be able to move and shoot, and to resist being disabled while it is doing so. Protection is not simply something bolted on after the tank is built; effective designs consider survivability from the earliest stage of development.

Defending against the many threats that are encountered in the modern battlespace is a complex business. Ideally, the enemy will be destroyed before being able to fire a single shot, or will be unable to hit the tank due to its high speed or concealment. If these measures fail, the last chance for survival is the tank's armour. Providing armour that effectively protects a tank requires an understanding of the threats it is likely to face. The most common involve shaped charges that burn through armour or high-velocity projectiles to punch holes in it. However, there are other means of attack, such as large explosive charges that rely on brute force rather than precision, or weapons such as SADARM (Sense and Destroy Armour), which drive a lump of metal at great speed into the top of the tank to crush and smash it. Flame weapons such as Molotov Cocktails are little use against modern tanks, which are designed to resist such attacks.

Left: An M1 Abrams at speed in the desert. Composite armour is difficult to cast in curved shapes, leading to a slab-sided look for tanks using it.

It is also possible that in the not too distant future tanks will be attacked by directed-energy weapons (lasers). Many tanks already carry laser detectors and countermeasures launchers to interrupt the beam. At present this is to counter laser-guided weapons, but in the future similar countermeasures may protect against laser attack. That said, the dust, smoke and generally poor visibility of a battlefield is likely to provide quite a decent defence anyway.

Various means are used to improve survivability if the armour is penetrated, such as fireproof ammunition stowage, internal bulkheads, fire suppression systems and blow-out panels to allow blast to escape rather than killing the crew. Despite all this, however, the aim of the design team is to ensure that the tank's armour is not penetrated.

Armour has come a long way since early experiments with boiler plate. The most basic form of armour is simple steel plates, but even then these can be sloped to deflect incoming weapons and to present the greatest effective thickness of armour against hits from the most likely angles. A metal plate at an angle presents more metal to an incoming round than one that is aligned at 90° to the angle of attack.

Modern tank armour is often not just simple steel, however. Composite armour such as Chobham (named after the laboratory where it was invented) contains layers of hard steel and ceramics that help dissipate the energy of an incoming round. A given amount of composite armour offers better protection than an equivalent weight of simple steel.

Shaped-charge weapons can be defeated by the use of reactive armour. This is fitted over other armour and consists of blocks of explosive material that explode when hit by a warhead. This disrupts the formation of the plasma jet, essentially defocusing the cutting effect of the shaped charge and giving the conventional armour underneath a better chance to resist it. Reactive armour is

Reactive Armour Systems

Not all tank defences are passive. The cylindrical containers at the left of the picture are smoke grenade dischargers, which can hide the tank from observation as well as defeating laser designators and rangefinders. The boxes are part of the tank's reactive armour system. Each contains an explosive charge that can disrupt a shaped-charge warhead, preventing it from forming a plasma (superheated gas) jet that can burn through the conventional armour underneath.

expended when used, which means that another hit on exactly the same spot will hit the conventional armour underneath.

Of course, for any countermeasure there will be a corresponding counter-countermeasure as the weapon designers seek to gain an advantage. Reactive armour can be countered by fitting shaped-charge weapons with a standoff probe, essentially a rod sticking out the front of the warhead, which detonates it at a short distance from the armour and allows the plasma jet to form before the reactive armour can disrupt it. Other methods include 'smart' munitions designed to attack the weaker parts of a tank. Some antitank missiles are programmed to fly just over the target and attack from above with downward-angled warheads. Tandem warheads allow two attacks on the same spot in rapid succession. Mines and similar weapons are a constant threat, too. Mines can sever a track or attack the belly armour of a tank, which is usually much thinner than the sides or front. This is necessary since weight considerations require armouring a tank to be subject to some tradeoffs. The vehicle cannot be invincible everywhere, so the most likely directions of attack are most heavily protected.

For modern tanks, survival is a matter of good tactics, cooperation with other forces such as infantry, effective use of speed, cover and concealment, and the rapid destruction of threats by accurate fire, ideally at long range. Good armour protection allows the tanks to shrug off a certain amount of incoming fire, which in turn permits very aggressive tactics designed to crush the opposition quickly. But today, just as in 1916, tanks are not invulnerable and need to be intelligently handled.

To this end, the modern tank is intended to operate in conjunction with infantry riding APCs and IFVs, self-propelled artillery and support troops as well as air support. Tanks can achieve a lot on their own, but they are at their best as part of a combat team. It took some time to establish that tanks were neither infantry weapons nor battleships on land. But today, less than a century after their first appearance, they have taken their rightful place in the pantheon of arms.

In the age of Napoleon, the most effective armies used their infantry, artillery and cavalry in close

Mines represent a serious threat to all vehicles. It is not possible for a vehicle to be impenetrable everywhere, and relatively light belly armour can be defeated by a powerful enough shaped charge.

conjunction. When improvements in firepower drove cavalry from the battlefield, it became difficult to achieve decisive results in combat. Tanks represent the return of cavalry to the battlefield, albeit wearing a suit of composite armour and riding a mechanical horse.

Modern British and American Tanks

Development of a replacement tank should always begin long before it is needed, to allow a mature design to be implemented. The results of rushing have been seen several times and are rarely good. Thus it was that while the Chieftain had plenty of service life left in it, work began on a new MBT to meet British needs. This was to become the Challenger, though along the way its components were used in a hybrid Chieftain/Challenger design named Shir.

The Shir was built for export, using the engine and powertrain being developed for the Challenger in a late-model Chieftain hull. It was ordered by the Shah of Iran, and in very large numbers. When the Shah was deposed in 1979, development was well underway and some modified Shirs went to Jordan under the new designation Khalid.

The first Challenger Is were delivered to the British Army in 1983. The tank's slab-sided appearance is due to the difficulty in casting Chobham composite armour in curved shapes. The tracks are protected by skirts that were originally made of aluminium; composite-armour skirts are now available.

Challenger is an advanced tank, with good electronics including thermal imaging, laser sighting and ballistic computers. It is armed with a 120mm (4.7in) gun capable of firing smoke in addition to several kinds of combat ammunition.

HEAD TO HEAD: *CHALLENGER II* VERSUS

The Challenger II was developed privately by Vickers, making it the first private-venture tank to be accepted by the British army since the end of World War II. It uses the same hull and running gear as Challenger I, with a new turret and electronics fit. Among its features the Challenger has the capability to 'buddy refuel' another Challenger, transferring fuel from one to the other.

CHALLENGER II

Crew: 4
Weight: 62,500kg (137,500lb)
Dimensions: length 11.55m (35ft 4in); width 3.52m (10ft 8in); height 2.49m (7ft 5in)
Range: 400km (250 miles)
Armour: classified
Armament: one 120mm (4.7in) gun; two 7.62mm (0.3in) machine guns; two smoke rocket dischargers
Powerplant: one 1200hp (895kW) liquid-cooled diesel engine
Performance: maximum road speed 57km/h (35.6mph); fording 1m (3ft 4in); vertical obstacle 0.9m (2ft 10in); trench (9ft 2in)

STRENGTHS

- Good protection
- Excellent electronics package
- Well protected ammunition stowage

WEAKNESSES

- Faulty thermal imagers on early models
- Expensive to produce
- Slower than Leclerc

LECLERC

The Leclerc is the replacement for the French AMX-30 MBT, and is much more heavily protected than its predecessor. Like the Challenger, it uses a 120mm (4.7in) main gun backed up by excellent fire control electronics. Planned upgrades will keep the Leclerc in service for many years to come.

LECLERC

Crew: 3
Weight: 53,500kg (117,700lb)
Dimensions: length 9.87m (30ft); width 3.71m (11ft 4in); height 2.46m (7ft 6in)
Range: 550km (345 miles)
Armour: classified
Armament: one 120mm (4.7in) gun, one 12.7mm (0.5in) machine gun, one 7.62mm (0.3in) gun
Powerplant: one Hyperbar 8-cylinder 1500hp (1119kW) diesel engine
Performance: maximum speed 73km/h (45.6mph); fording 1m (3ft 3in); vertical obstacle 1.25m (4ft 1in); trench 3m (9ft 10in)

STRENGTHS

- Can be retrofitted with a 140mm (5.5in) gun
- Computerized autoloading system
- Excellent electronics package

WEAKNESSES

- Expensive to produce
- Lack of export success
- Relatively low ammunition stowage

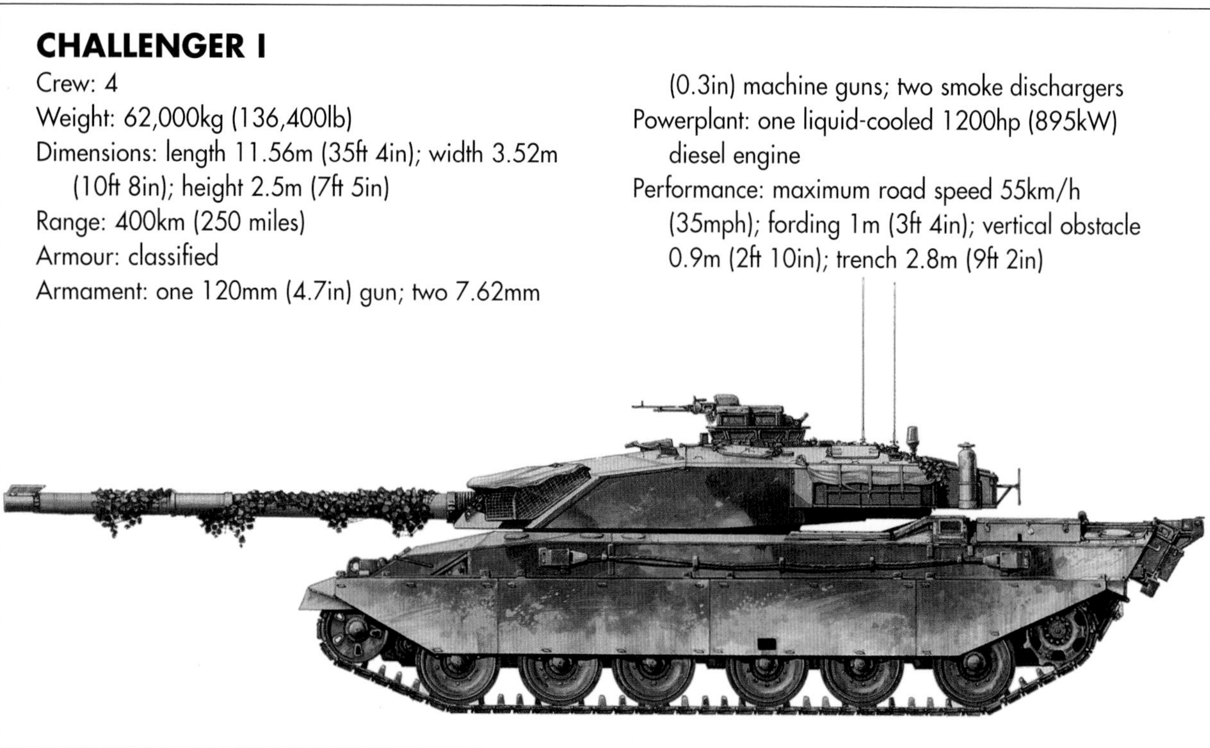

CHALLENGER I

Crew: 4
Weight: 62,000kg (136,400lb)
Dimensions: length 11.56m (35ft 4in); width 3.52m (10ft 8in); height 2.5m (7ft 5in)
Range: 400km (250 miles)
Armour: classified
Armament: one 120mm (4.7in) gun; two 7.62mm (0.3in) machine guns; two smoke dischargers
Powerplant: one liquid-cooled 1200hp (895kW) diesel engine
Performance: maximum road speed 55km/h (35mph); fording 1m (3ft 4in); vertical obstacle 0.9m (2ft 10in); trench 2.8m (9ft 2in)

These include High-Explosive Squash Head (HESH; a form of advanced shaped-charge round) and several types of Armour-Piercing Discarding Sabot (APDS) round.

The Challenger I began to be replaced from 1994 onwards by the Challenger II. This is the first British tank in 50 years to be entirely developed as a private venture by a contractor. It uses the same hull, powertrain and tracks as the Challenger I, but has an entirely redesigned turret incorporating electronics developed from those aboard the M1A1 Abrams. The Challenger II is improved in other ways. Its radar signature has been reduced by the use of a new composite armour composition, though in no way could this be called a 'stealth tank', and the armament has been upgraded. The 120mm (4.7in) gun now has a chromed bore for longer life and the co-axial 7.62mm (0.3in) weapon is a chain gun rather than a traditional machine gun. Room for development was left in the turret, including the provision for a gun of up to 140mm (5.5in) calibre.

At about the same time that the Challenger was under development, the US Army was looking for a replacement for the M60. This was intended to be the 'MBT-70', a joint US-German project based around the Shillelagh gun/missile system. However, a loss of German interest in the project, coupled with deficiencies of both Shillelagh and the engine developed to power the tank, resulted in a rethink. New designs were invited and the US Army eventually opted for Chrysler's tank, which became the M1 General Abrams. Like the Challenger, the Abrams is low and slab-sided due to its use of composite armour. It uses an advanced gas turbine engine designed for easy maintenance in the field.

Multibarrel 'vulcan' weapons have an immensely high rate of fire, making them ideal for close-in air defence.

The M1A1 has been in service since 1985. It incorporates several improvements over the basic M1. It was intended that the Abrams would have a 120mm (4.7in) gun, but this was still in development when the tank went into production, so early models were rolled out with a 105mm (4.1in) gun instead. The M1A1 can carry a range of guns, but normally uses a 120mm (4.7in) German-designed weapon with a US-made breech.

The M1A1 is also better armoured than the original model. A 1984 version designated M1 IP (for Improved Protection) was fielded, and this configuration was used on the M1A1 until 1988. A new version designated M1A1 HA (Heavy Armour) was trialled in that year and found to be very satisfactory. This variant uses composite steel/depleted uranium armour, and this became standard on the M1A1. Depleted uranium gets its name from the fact that it is no longer radioactive. It is, however, very dense and gives good protection. So good, in fact, that no M1A1s were penetrated by enemy fire during the Gulf War. Even accidental hits with state-of-the-art armour-piercing ammunition fired by other M1A1s failed to disable the victims or kill any of their crew.

Among the other features of the M1A1 are NBC protection and an advanced electronics package that includes excellent ballistic computers. These, coupled with laser rangefinders and advanced gun stabilization, allow a moving Abrams to make first-shot kills on enemy tanks at 3km (1.9 miles). The A2 version gained even greater electronics capability in the form of digital integration systems that allow information to be easily shared between combat vehicles, aircraft and command posts.

It was planned to end Abrams production in 1990, but overseas orders prolonged production until 1995. Most of the production run was M1A1s, with small numbers of A2s. Several hundred A1s have since been upgraded to A2 capabilities.

Logistics and Support

Modern tanks, like this M1 Abrams require a great deal of support to keep them combat-worthy. Armoured warfare is thus more than just massing tanks and sending them at a target; logistics and support cannot be overlooked but are essential.

Modern European Tanks

The French AMX-30 MBT was a considerable export success, but as a combat tank it was generally considered a bit light. The Leclerc, which replaced it as the mainstay of French armoured forces, is better protected and much more advanced. Armed with a 120mm (4.7in) gun (the 'industry standard' for a Western MBT) fed by an autoloader and aimed by computer, the Leclerc is designed to shoot fast and accurately, and can select between ammunition types stored in the autoloader. Its electronics package also includes a

The terrain of the Middle East is a punishing environment. Sand and dust clog air intakes and choke the engine.

battlefield management system to assist the commander and liase with higher command.

The Leclerc has found export success with a large order for the United Arab Emirates, which is a modified version that uses a German powerplant. Those in French service are due for upgrade in the imminent future and should receive improved armour, automated missile defences and better electronics.

Germany's current front-line MBT is the Leopard 2. After pulling out of the MBT-70 project, German designers were able to use some of the concepts intended for that vehicle in their new design. As with most of its contemporaries, the Leopard 2 uses Chobham composite armour and a 120mm (4.7in) gun capable of handling a range of ammunition types. The electronics package

French Military Glory

The Arc de Triomphe in Paris was commissioned 200 years ago to commemorate French military glory and contains the Tomb of the Unknown Soldier. Cavalry once paraded where their modern successor, a Leclerc Main Battle Tank, now stands.

All modern tanks possess good cross-country mobility, but the Leopard 2 surpasses its competitors for speed on and off the road.

includes the usual ballistic computers and laser rangefinders. Germany fielded what was probably the first night-fighting tank during World War II in the form of a converted Panther with an infrared searchlight fitted. The Leopard 2 is generations ahead of that primitive device, with thermal night vision equipment provided to all crewmembers.

Fast and agile, the Leopard 2 has been sold to several European countries, including the Netherlands, Austria and Denmark. Spain, Sweden and Switzerland also produce it under licence, making the Leopard 2 one of the most widely used tanks in the world. Production was in several batches, with improvements incorporated between each. By the time the A5 version was reached, the tank had been almost entirely redesigned. A version with a new gun of up to 140mm (5.5in) was considered, but the improved 120mm (4.7in) gun of the A5 is so good that no need was perceived for anything bigger. An A6 variant is available for export, incorporating even more advanced features. Some of the licenced builders incorporated their own modifications, in effect creating sub-variants.

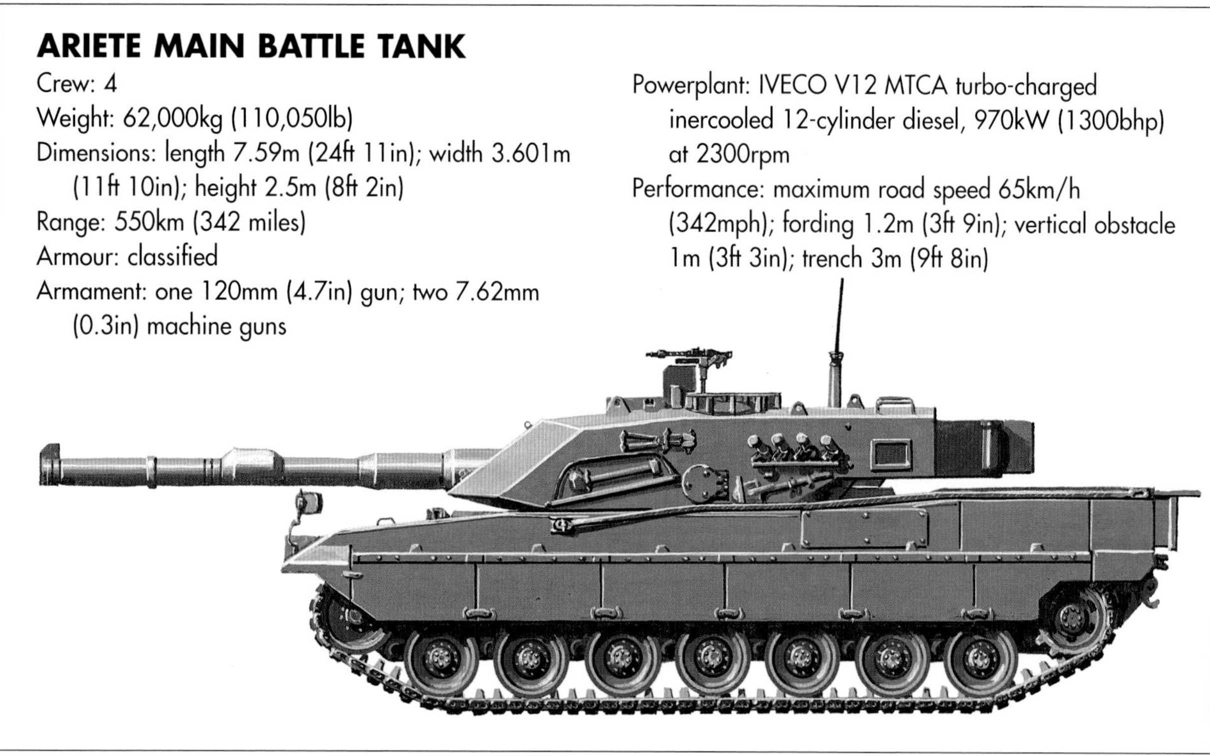

Italy built Leopard 1s under licence for a time, and created a version designated OF-40 for export. However, the Ariete MBT which went into service in 1995 is a local design. Armed with the industry-standard 120mm (4.7in) smoothbore gun and protected by slabs of composite armour, the Ariete has all the usual features of a European MBT: good speed and agility coupled with a comprehensive electronics fit and ballistic computers enabling accurate shooting on the move.

Survivability is improved by blow-out panels in the ammunition storage area, designed to allow the blast from an ammunition explosion to escape outwards rather than into the crew compartment. The tank is designed to be easy to maintain – an important feature in an environment where individual vehicles are becoming increasingly expensive. A tank down for maintenance represents a lot of dollars-worth of fighting capability standing around doing nothing.

One interesting development of recent years is the Swedish CV 90-120. This is a light tank developed from the CV-90 infantry combat vehicle (ICV) and capable of carrying four infantrymen while still functioning as a tank. It mounts a powerful 120mm (4.7in) gun, but at less than half the weight of an Abrams or Challenger it is much less well protected.

Post-Soviet Vehicles

In the 1990s, a time of great political changes in the former Soviet bloc, a new battle tank was under development. It entered service under conditions somewhat different to those prevailing when it was conceived.

The T-90, as this tank is designated, is an evolutionary development of the T-72, with good protection further enhanced by appliqué armour segments and advanced reactive armour in critical areas. It also mounts countermeasures intended to disrupt optical missile targeting and laser designators. The T-90's gun is the same as that of its predecessor, the T-80. This 125mm (4.9in) smoothbore weapon can fire a range of shells in addition to launching guided missiles. Russian tanks make considerable use of gun-launched missiles, and presumably have had better success with them than Western equivalents.

The T-90 is available for export and may appear in the order of battle of other nations. However, some former Soviet countries have chosen to develop their own battle tanks. The Ukraine uses a developed version of the T-80, named T-84. This made sense from an industrial point of view, as the Ukraine inherited factories tooled to make T-80s at the breakup of the Soviet Union. The T-84 has a welded rather than cast turret and a Ukraine-designed 125mm (4.9in) smoothbore gun. The same tank is in use with the army of Pakistan, and a variant with a NATO-standard 120mm (4.7in) gun has been developed with Turkey.

The creation of MBTs was once the province only of the largest military powers, but today it is possible to come up with a workable design on a lower budget, especially if a previous tank can be used as a starting point. Croatia has managed

Main Battle Tanks are not the exclusive province of the richest nations. The Degman is a Croatian MBT derived in turn from a Yugoslavian design.

to field a home-grown battle tank (albeit one derived from a Yugoslavian design) designated Degman. This carries a 125mm gun (4.9in) and is protected by ERA, though its capabilities are unlikely to match first-rate tanks like the Abrams or Leopard 2.

Poland's PT-91, which entered service in 1993, is a developed T-72 with many modern features such as fire control for the 125mm (4.9in) smoothbore gun and an advanced engine-management system. The basic components of the T-72 are sound. By adding some modern electronic systems, the Poles are able to get more out of their tanks without vastly increasing their cost.

The Romanian TM-800 is a more radical redesign of an existing tank. It was developed from the T-55 but changed so much along the way as to become more or less an entirely new design. This was designated TR-85 and served through the 1980s and 90s before being upgraded again. It now bears only a faint resemblance to the venerable T-55 in both appearance and performance.

Armour in the Middle East

With the deposition of the Shah of Iran in 1979, relations with the West deteriorated. An order for the Shir MBT was cancelled, and new sources of armoured vehicles had to be found. The Warsaw Pact was the obvious choice and in addition to employing tanks as supplied, Iran developed its own versions.

Despite its name, the Iranian T-72Z is a derivation of the Soviet T-55 with a 105mm (4.1in) gun and an electronics package to support it. The upgrade is relatively modest and mainly involves adding night-fighting capability and uprated fire control. The Iranians also have a tank named Zulfiqar, derived from the T-72. Zulfiqars are built using imported parts assembled in Iran, and have an NBC protection system in addition to their electronics package. Iraq also fielded an upgraded T-55, influenced by Chinese vehicles based on the same tank. Although up-armoured, these tanks proved no match for modern armour and Western tank-killing technologies in the Gulf War. Other

HEAD TO HEAD: *MERKAVA* VERSUS

The Israeli army is probably the most combat-experienced armed force in the world. After many years of using imported vehicles, the Israelis set out to build a tank specifically for their needs. The somewhat unusual Merkava series was the result. Each new model has added improved features without changing the tank's basic emphasis on protection and firepower.

MERKAVA MK I

Crew: 4
Weight: 55,898kg (122,976lb)
Dimensions: length 8.36m (27ft 5.25in); width 3.72m (12ft 2.5in); height 2.64m (8ft 8in)
Range: 500 km (310 miles)
Armour: classified
Armament: one 105mm (4.1in) rifled gun; one 7.62mm (0.3in) machine gun
Powerplant: one Teledyne Continental AVDS-1790-6A V-12 diesel engine developing 900hp (67kW)
Performance: maximum road speed 46km/h (28.6mph); vertical onstacle 1m (3ft 3.3in); trench 3m (9ft 10in)

STRENGTHS

- Extremely survivable design
- Small target
- Large ammunition capacity

WEAKNESSES

- Slow and underpowered
- Relatively light 105mm (4.1in) gun on early models
- No coaxial machinegun

LEOPARD 2

The German Leopard 2 is a better-protected successor to the Leopard 1. The design is conventional but well engineered with the best available technology integrated into the vehicle. As with its predecessor, the Leopard 2 has already produced several upgraded models and other vehicles based on its chassis, including armoured recovery vehicles and air defence platforms.

LEOPARD 2

Crew: 4
Weight: 54,981kg (120,960lb)
Dimensions: length 9.668m (31ft 8.7in); length (hull) 7.772m (25ft 6in); width 3.7m (12ft 1.7in); height (overall) 2.79m (9ft 1.75in)
Range: 550km (342 miles)
Armour: classified
Armament: one 120mm (4.7in) gun; one coaxial 7.62mm (0.3in) machine gun; one 7.62mm (0.3in) anti-aircraft machine gune; eight smoke dischargers
Powerplant: one MTU 12-cylinder mulit-fuel, developing 1500hp (1119kW)
Performance: maximum road speed 72km/h (45mph); fording 1m (3ft 3in); vertical obstacle 1.1m (3ft 7.25 in); trench 3m (9ft 10in)

STRENGTHS

- Very fast on and off road
- Excellent electronics
- Powerful 120mm (4.7in) gun

WEAKNESSES

- Armour protection still somewhat light
- Gun underperformed until lengthened
- Many different versions

An Iranian T-72Z MBT is armed with a 105mm (4.1in) gun and has improved armour plus computerized fire control.

Iraqi tanks were used as supplied, but even the more modern ones did not fare much better.

For many years, Israel used tanks bought from overseas (or captured in battle) and adapted them to local needs. The Merkava represents a departure from this policy, and also a different philosophy in tank design from the mainstream. The Merkava mounts a 120mm (4.7in) gun supported by good electronics – the need for night-fighting capability was underscored when Israeli tanks without night vision gear were forced to take on Syrian opponents in the dark. It is respectably mobile too. However, experience has shown the Israeli Army that while firepower and mobility are important, the most critical feature of a battle tank is protection. The Merkava is built to survive whatever is thrown at it.

Unusually, the Merkava's engine is at the front. Since the tank is most likely to be engaged from the front, the bulk of the engine provides the crew with a last line of defence against a penetrating hit. Another uncommon feature is the capability of the Merkava to carry infantry. The rear of the fighting compartment has a set of doors allowing for easy maintenance and loading, and in the event that some of the ammunition load is left behind, a small number of infantrymen can be carried within the hull.

The Merkava

The Israeli Merkava is unusual in that it mounts the engine at the front, providing additional protection for the crew in the event of a hit. Doors at the rear give access to a space that can be used for additional ammunition or even to carry a handful of infantrymen.

The Merkava has been upgraded in service, gaining better fire control and improved armour as well as better NBC protection. The latest version, Merkava Mk IV, has been adapted for urban combat and has better underbody armour to protect against mines. Like other first-line battle tanks, the Merkava is designed to function as part of an integrated battle group and can obtain information in real time from sources such as manned and unmanned air reconnaissance assets and other combat vehicles.

As with many emerging nations, India made the decision to start developing its own military equipment. India is unusual in that it has at times obtained its weaponry from the West and from the Soviet Union. There have even been some hybrid systems mixing components from East and West, though this is very uncommon. After years of satisfactory service, the Vijayanta MBT was getting long in the tooth and needed to be replaced. A new design was commissioned and, in due course, it appeared. India's new MBT is the Arjun, a workmanlike design built around a 120mm (4.7in) gun and the usual supporting electronics. The Arjun has NBC protection and hydro-pneumatic suspension and may eventually serve as the basis of a family of related systems, including armoured recovery vehicles and bridge-layers.

A Chinese Type 98 MBT. Chinese tanks have moved on from being merely copies of Soviet designs and matured into world-class combat vehicles.

K1A1 Main Battle Tank

Based on the American M1 tank, but with a diesel powerplant, the K1A1 is a thoroughly modern main battle tank. Its firepower, protection and mobility are as good as any fighting vehicle in the world.

China's help. Most components are built in Pakistan with some bought in from overseas, notably China. The Al-Khalid can mount ERA when necessary, but this is not fitted as standard.

For many years, China built mediocre tanks based on obsolete Soviet designs, but the experience gained with these vehicles has recently been put into new designs. These are so well regarded that some nations, notably Pakistan, have sought Chinese aid to develop their own new AFVS.

China took the first big step forward with the Type 80 MBT. Armed with a 105mm (4.1in) gun apparently derived from the British L7, the Type 80 has an air of the Soviet MBT about it, with a curved turret and low silhouette. This is not surprising; the turret comes from the Type 69, which can trace its ancestry all the way back to the Soviet T-54. The turret is surrounded by a stowage basket that may help protect the tank from shaped-charge munitions by detonating them at a distance from the turret armour.

The Type 80 successfully implemented gun stabilization, electronic fire control and advanced sensors in Chinese tanks, and found modest export success. It was followed by another new tank, the Type 85. Many of the systems for the Type 85 come from the Type 80, but the hull is different. The turret, too, has finally been changed. It is welded rather than cast and is lower than the T54-derived Type 80 turret, with a long bustle at the rear.

Working with Pakistan on a project sometimes called MBT-2000, China produced small numbers of a tank designated the Type 90 in Chinese service and Al Khalid in Pakistan. From this highly modern tank was developed the Type 98, a version optimized to meet the needs of the Chinese Army. Among its advanced features are a laser detector and a dazzler to defeat enemy optical sensors.

Japan also gained a new MBT in the early 1990s. Designated the Type 90, it has been in development since its predecessor, the Type 74, entered service. Japanese tanks tend to be very 'Western', and the Type 90 uses a 120mm (4.7in) gun produced by the German company Rheinmetall. It also bears a noticeable resemblance to the M1 Abrams, although it was designed entirely in Japan. The Type 90 uses composite armour of a type developed in Japan, with the usual slab sides that result from this armour type. It has

NBC protection and state-of-the-art electronics to improve battle efficiency. The forward hull has attachment points for a bulldozer blade.

South Korea once suffered the consequences of not being able to deal with a tank assault, and today uses a home-grown design named the K1. It is offered on the export market as the Republic of Korea Indigenous Tank (ROKIT). The basic K1 is armed with a 105mm (4.1in) gun, with the uprated K1A1 carrying a more powerful 120mm (4.7in) weapon. Work is underway on a K2 tank, even though delivery of K1A1s will not be complete until 2010. The K1A1 uses the same gun as the US M1A1 Abrams, sighted by an advanced combat computer that can handle complex fire-control tasks such as handoff targeting from the commander's position or direct control by the commander.

International And Export Tanks

Vehicles such as the Abrams and the Challenger are extremely powerful, but lie beyond the budget of all but the best-funded militaries. There is thus a market for reasonably priced tanks of lesser, but still good, capabilities on the international market.

In 1985, Vickers produced the Mark 7 MBT for the international market. This vehicle mated the the chassis of a German Leopard 2 to the turret of the Valiant, a Vickers-designed technology demonstrator (a functional tank that is meant to show what can be done rather than to actually fight). The Mk 7 can carry a range of British and European guns in its Chobham-armoured turret, and it also has a good electronics and fire-control package.

Another private venture for the international market appeared a year later. This was a joint project between Vickers and US-based FMC. The resulting Vickers VFM Mark 5 Tank is typical of what might be termed 'light export' tanks. At 19,200kg (42,240lb), it weighs a third as much as a Challenger II and is fast and agile. Protection is light compared to first-rate battle tanks, but the Mark 5 can field a 105mm (4.1in) gun in an easy-to-maintain and affordable package.

Many overseas customers need a tank that can be upgraded in service, ensuring a long life to offset the initial cost. This capability is built into the Stingray light tank from US-based Textron Marine and Land Systems. As standard, the Stingray comes with a 105mm (4.1in) gun with good stabilization, and a range of extras include night-vision and thermal imaging equipment. The Stingray has been an export success, especially in the Far East where lighter, cheaper tanks are desirable. An updated version, Stingray II, appeared in 1996 with new armour and improved fire control.

Armed with a 120mm (4.7in) gun and fully-integrated computerized fire control, the Indian Arjun MBT is a strong contender in the battlespace of the twenty-first century.

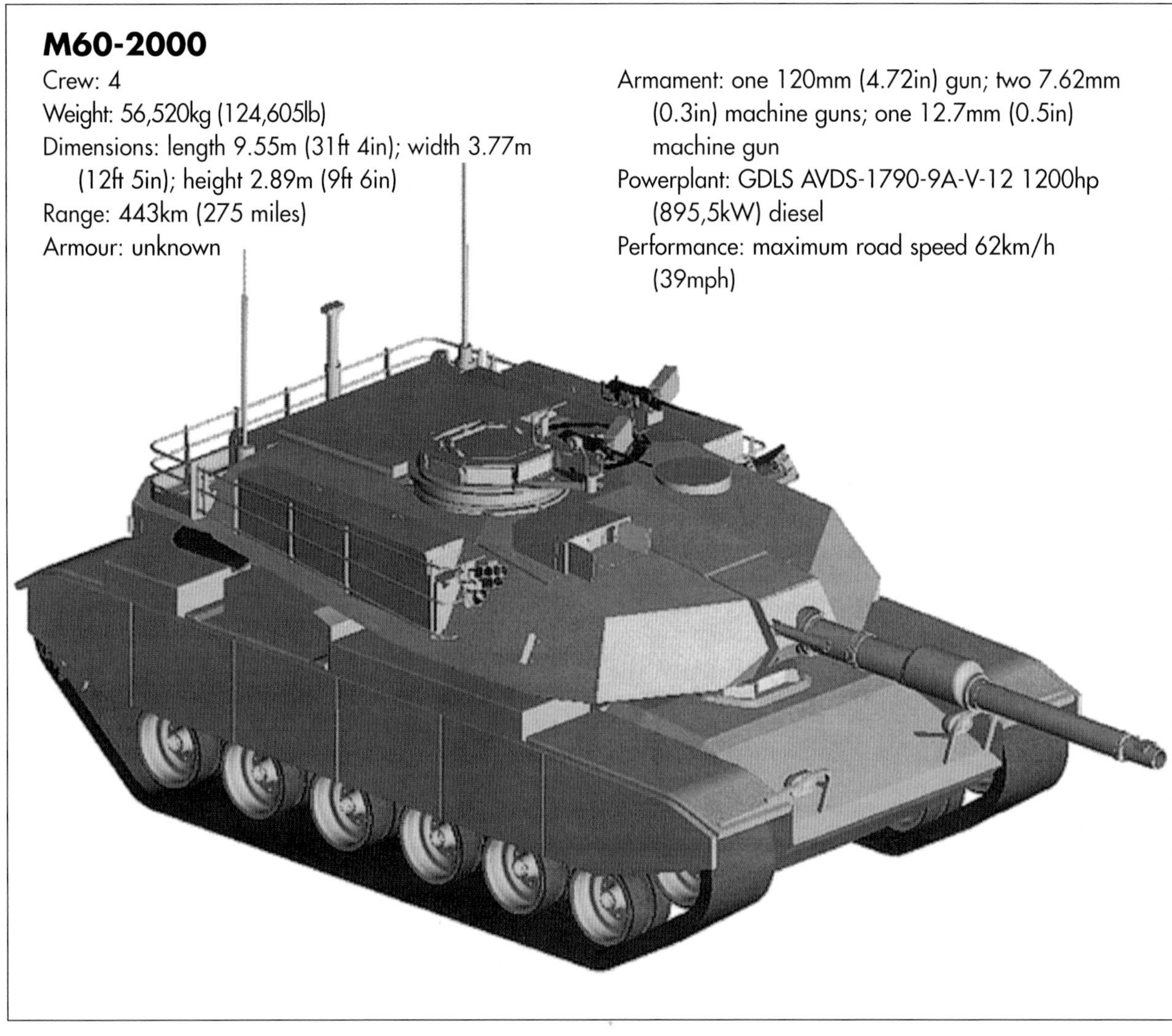

General Dynamics has taken a different route to offer a cheaper tank for the export market: the M60-2000 project. This involves supplying a conversion kit to users of ageing M60 tanks, allowing them to fit an M1A1 turret to existing hulls. Upgraded powerplants are also available. These features offer most of the capabilities of an M1 Abrams at a fraction of the cost.

Another such project is the PSP T-72 MP offered by PSP Bohemia, a Czech firm. This is a T-72 tank upgraded for the international export market. Among the refinements are ERA and new defensive countermeasures, plus vastly improved fire control for the main gun. Similarly, South Africa used British Centurions for many years, under the name Olifant. These tanks were steadily upgraded over the years, gaining 105mm (4.1in) guns and improved electronics. The latest upgrade to the Olifant allows it to carry either a 105mm (4.1in) or 120mm (4.7in) gun. This represents a considerable evolution for a tank that started out with a 17-pounder (76mm/2.99in) gun.

The practice of upgrading obsolescent models gives nations unable to afford a first-line design the ability to at least play in the same ballpark, even if they are not up to the standards of the great military powers. However, the 1991 Gulf War showed what happens when a power equipped with obsolescent and upgraded obsolete tanks takes on the best the Western armies can field.

Return to the Desert

After the deposition of the Shah of Iran in 1979, war between Iran and Iraq raged from more than eight years. By the end of the war in 1988, Saddam Hussein, dictator of Iraq, commanded an army of almost a million troops and about 5500 MBTs. Of this, the fourth-largest tank force in the world, about 1000 were T-72s and the remainder comprised older Soviet vehicles, some upgraded and some not.

In 1990, this vast army was used to invade and annex neighbouring Kuwait, triggering an international response. After a period of confrontation and build-up, the international Coalition began the work of dislodging Iraqi forces from Kuwait. The largest contingents of troops

The South African Tank Technology Demonstrator was based on the Olifant MBT (itself a locally upgraded Centurion).

among Coalition forces came from the United States and Britain, two nations that had spent half a century developing tanks and doctrines for their use, specifically geared to destroying large formations of Soviet armoured vehicles. Most other Coalition nations used Western equipment, with only Egypt and Syria using any Soviet-derived weaponry.

Coalition forces were aided by the fact that Iraqi forces did not use their tanks aggressively, but preferred to dig them in as defensive strongpoints. These, along with defensive infantry positions, could be savaged by air attack before the ground war started. Indeed, many were outflanked and destroyed with their weapons still pointed toward the expected direction of attack. When the ground offensive did begin, in early 1991, it was not sent head-on at prepared positions. Instead the spearhead of US and British troops used the time-honoured armoured warfare principle of the indirect approach, breaking through and getting behind the main defensive line, then 'rolling it up' from the flank and rear as other forces applied pressure to the front. There was a real concern that the Iraqis might respond with chemical weapons, but NBC protection and the training to use it had been in place for many years and the Coalition forces were ready to deal with the worst if it happened.

The Iraqi Army, though numerous, was technologically outmatched. Tank crews soon learned that sleeping in their vehicles was a bad idea, as they tended to mysteriously blow up during the night. This was caused by aircraft using precision-guided munitions and thermal targeting equipment to kill parked vehicles. When night actions occurred in the ground war, these too went badly for the Iraqis. Western tanks used night-vision equipment as standard and, more importantly, their crews were entirely comfortable with the gear they used. The Iraqi Army, on the other hand, lacked similar capabilities, though some T-55s equipped with infra-red searchlights were encountered.

Many of the tanks initially encountered by the advancing Coalition troops were T-55s, which stood virtually no chance. Many were destroyed before their crews could mount up, or while they were hiding in nearby bunkers. The Coalition advance was sufficiently fast that in many places the spearhead reached enemy positions before any warning of the attack. The result was a classic armoured rampage, smashing through what opposition was mounted and terrifying the unprepared troops behind the front line into panicky withdrawal or immediate surrender.

There was one attempt to launch a counteroffensive, by elements of the Republican

HEAD TO HEAD: M1 *Abrams* VERSUS

The M1 Abrams has gone through a series of upgrades, gaining ever better armour protection along the way. After early problems with the gas turbine engine, the M1's fuel-economy problems were eventually solved. As newer versions proved themselves, older M1s were upgraded to the same standard, which necessitated a rapid up-armouring project just before the 1991 Gulf War.

M1 Abrams

Crew: 4
Weight: 54,269kg (119,392lb)
Dimensions: length 9.766m (32ft 0.5in); width 3.655m (12ft); height 2.895m (9ft 6in)
Range: 450km (280 miles)
Armour: classified
Armament: one 105mm (4.1in) gun; two 7.62mm (0.3in) machine guns (one coaxial, one on loader's hatch); one 12.7mm (0.5in) machine gun
Powerplant: Avco Lycoming AGT-1500 gas turbine, developing 1500hp (1119kW)
Performance: maximum road speed 72.5km/h (45mph); fording 1.219m (4ft); vertical obstacle 1.244m (4ft 1in); trench 2.743m (9ft)

STRENGTHS

- Powerful 120mm (4.7in) gun
- Excellent electronics package
- Extremely good armour protection

WEAKNESSES

- Expensive to build and maintain
- Armour contains depleted uranium
- Very heavy even for an MBT

T-90

The T-90 is a development of the T-72, incorporating a number of evolutionary improvements. It is a lower-cost vehicle than equivalent Western MBTs and not quite up to the task of facing them one-for-one. Russian experience with gun/launcher systems has been better than that of other nations; the T-90 is the latest in a long line of tanks to be built to launch guided missiles from the gun.

T-90

Crew: 3
Weight: 46,500kg (45.76 tons)
Dimensions: length (hull) 6.86mm (22ft 6in); width 3.37m (11ft 1in); height 2.23m (7ft 4in)
Range: 650km (400 miles)
Armour: Unknown
Armament: One 125mm (4.9in) 2A46M Rapira 3 Smoothbore gun; one co-axial 7.62mm (0.30in) PKT MG; one 12.7mm (0.50in) NVST AA MG
Powerplant: V-84MS 12-cylinder multi-fuel diesel, 627kW (840bhp) at 2000rpm
Performance: speed 65km/h (40mph); fording 5m (16ft 5in); vertical obstacle 0.85m (2ft 9in); trench 2.9m (9ft 6in)

STRENGTHS

- Relatively inexpensive
- Gun can fire shells or missiles
- Good armour protection

WEAKNESSES

- Inferior electronics to M1
- Based on an obsolete design
- Ammunition stored in the turret

T-72s

T-72s formed the backbone of Iraqi tank strength during the Gulf War. Iraq had one of the largest tank concentrations in the world at the beginning of the conflict, but a combination of better technology and tactics enabled the Coalition forces to smash their opponents without taking serious losses. The Iraqi practice of digging tanks in as immobile bunkers was tried by the British in 1917, with equally dismal results. Tanks are supposed to move and fight, not wait to be attacked in static positions.

Guard. This was beaten off easily enough and elsewhere the Coalition forces had little difficulty in driving their enemies back. The extremely rapid Coalition advance resulted in large numbers of Iraqi troops, who had been deployed in Kuwait in great strength, becoming more or less cut off. The only avenue of retreat was through Basra, and retiring Iraqi forces were subjected to massive air attack along the way.

With Kuwait liberated and the remains of the Iraqi Army streaming homeward in defeat, a ceasefire was agreed. The Coalition had lost about 150 killed and a little more than twice that number wounded. Iraqi losses came to almost 4000 tanks, 2400 APCs and 3000 artillery pieces plus about 50,000 casualties and 80,000 prisoners. These figures do not include the troops who deserted and made their way home.

The actual ground offensive was only about 100 hours long from start to finish. It was preceded by a period of build-up and consolidation, then an air campaign lasting 43 days, which softened up the Iraqi troops facing the attack, sapping morale as well as destroying equipment. Despite this overwhelming defeat, Saddam Hussein remained in power and managed to salvage some of his tank strength. As a result, the Iraqi Army still represented a threat in 2003, when a rather smaller Coalition entered the country with the goal of deposing Saddam.

Rather than repeat the lengthy air bombardment that preceded the 1991 operation, this time the Coalition forces used a combination of sudden air and land attack to paralyze the Iraqi command structure. The goal was the destruction of Iraqi warfighting capability through the elimination of headquarters, communications and logistics capabilities, with the destruction of enemy units a secondary objective. Territory could be taken later; what was important was to cripple the enemy's capability to fight.

In this goal, the Coalition was highly successful. British troops fought their largest tank battle in 60 years, destroying 14 Iraqi tanks at Basra for no loss. Elsewhere, the advance was rapid and organized resistance collapsed quickly in most areas. By the time the Coalition forces reached Baghdad, the Republican Guard was preparing to make a stand. The resulting combat saw most of the remaining Iraqi armoured strength destroyed. The taking of Baghdad involved two 'Thunder Runs' launched by US forces – highly aggressive rapid advances through hostile territory. One was aimed at the airport and the other at the Presidential Palace. Both were successful despite determined resistance.

It is worth noting that British Challengers and US Abrams both encountered other tanks and were also attacked by infantry antitank weapons, improvised explosives and various other weapons. No tanks were lost, however, a fact that demonstrates beyond doubt the value of the heavy armoured vehicle.

Coalition tactics used in both Iraq campaigns would have made sense to Fuller, Guderian and other early armoured force commanders. Firepower, speed and aggression, coupled with good reconnaissance, air support and the cooperation of infantry and artillery where needed, allowed the tanks rapidly to overrun and scatter their opponents.

The destruction of the Iraqi Army in some ways represented the culmination of almost a century of preparation. It had taken many years for the equipment to be developed and the doctrines to evolve to the point where tanks could finally achieve what their inventors had meant them to do. Yet the process of attack, breakthrough and exploitation used in 2003 was little different to what was intended for Cambrai in 1917. Operations in Iraq demonstrated what tanks could do when properly handled. Even so, there are those who predict that the days of the heavy armoured vehicle are numbered; that it will soon disappear and be replaced by something that is faster, lighter and cheaper.

Tanks are not unstoppable. This T-55 has 'bellied' on a concrete road edge, depriving its tracks of sufficient grip to climb over the obstacle.

Experiments and New Directions

Quite apart from the tendency for the media to refer to anything with a turret on top as a tank, it is sometimes difficult to say where a vehicle ceases to be a tank and becomes, say, a light reconnaissance vehicle or a tank destroyer. Some designs push the boundaries of the 'tank' definition, while others explore new concepts that might – but usually do not – turn out

to be the next great revolution in armoured combat. Since the introduction of air-mobile troops, their users have wanted to be able to send artillery and armoured support with them into action. A tank light enough to be carried aboard an aircraft or even dropped by parachute can never be as powerful as a conventional MBT, but any armour is better than none, so light air-mobile tanks are considered desirable.

The M8 Armoured Gun System was not a main battle tank, even though it looked like one. It was, in fact, a tank gun.

The M8 Armoured Gun System (AGS) was intended to replace the Sheridan in US Army service. Essentially a light tank capable of being airdropped and armed with a 105mm (4.1in) gun, the M8 AGS could not stand up to even third-rate battle tanks in a straight fight, but would have been entirely capable of killing them from ambush. It could also perform in a fire-support role, cracking bunkers to assist the infantry. The M8 was designed to take a range of appliqué armour fits, the heaviest being capable of stopping 30mm (1.18in) cannon fire. It would have been a useful addition to the arsenal of air-mobile troops, but was axed as part of budget cuts.

Another interesting experiment was the SK105. This small not-quite-tank used an oscillating turret similar to that on the AMX-13 light tank, with rounds fed into the 105mm (4.1in) gun from a pair of revolver-type magazines located at the rear of the turret. Armour was very light; too light for the conventional battle tank role, but sufficient to permit the SK105 to function as a fire-support vehicle or a tank destroyer.

Armoured vehicle design tends to evolve along with the threat. Just as the first tanks were designed for a specific role – to cross trenches and break through a heavily defended enemy line – so later generations reflected the sort of combat they were expected to have to engage in. For many years, the predicted role of tanks was to fight other tanks in massive clashes where the ability to shrug off a large-calibre hit was vital. However, there is an increasing need for another kind of tank, one that is cheaper and more lightly protected than MBT yet capable of bringing heavy firepower to bear at need. Many of the likely opponents in today's world lack battle tanks and all but the lightest antitank weapons. This makes a vehicle capable of surviving in combat against 120mm (4.7in) guns somewhat overkill. Thus there is a move towards lighter tanks, though retaining a large-calibre armament. The need for powerful MBTs will not evaporate, but for the urban environment or fast-moving combat against a relatively lightly equipped foe, vehicles like the ASCOD light tank are a viable option. (ASCOD stands for Austrian-Spanish Cooperative Development.)

The ASCOD tank is built on the chassis of an ICV, an increasingly common design concept. In ICV form the ASCOD mounts a 30mm (1.18in) cannon and is used by Austria and Spain. By fitting a light turret with a 105mm (4.1in) gun, the designers created a light tank that offers good fire support and is relatively cheap to maintain since it shares a lot of components with existing vehicles.

Other moves towards a light tank with MBT firepower have been made. In the late 1970s and early 1980s, the US experimented with the High Mobility Agility (HIMAG) Test Vehicle. This was a light tank chassis with experimental suspension, to which was fitted an advanced 75mm (2.95in) hypervelocity cannon. The weapon mounting used a gun-over-hull configuration rather than a conventional turret. The gun-over-hull concept has never really caught on, though it does offer some advantages, including a very low silhouette. The weapon is exposed and unprotected but makes a very hard target, while crew survivability is improved by their being located in the low hull.

The ARES cannon (ARES is an acronym for Agile Responsive Effective Support) was also used in the High Survivability Test vehicle project, undertaken a little after HIMAG. This vehicle had a turret, albeit a very low and flat one, with the crew riding in semi-reclined positions in the hull. Although lightly protected, this vehicle was intended to be hard to hit, improving survivability. It was light enough to be air-mobile.

From the High-Survivability Test Vehicle project came the AAI Rapid Deployment Force Light Tank, which was similar in appearance. This vehicle also used the 75mm (2.95in) ARES cannon, though versions sold outside NATO were to be fitted with a more conventional 76mm (2.99in) gun. The tank was intended to arm rapid-reaction forces, but despite promising tests there was little interest and the project faded away for economic reasons rather than a lack of capability.

A more radical approach to the light armoured vehicle concept is represented by the Spitterskyddad Enhets Platform (SEP) programme in Sweden. This is a modular combat vehicle that can be driven either by wheels or tracks. Drive is electric, and uses batteries to permit the vehicle to operate for a long period without starting its engine. The hull can be fitted with a range of 'mission modules', allowing the vehicle to carry out a variety of tasks. The standard SEP hull is protected only against rifle rounds and shell fragments, but armour can be added to provide better defence. The heaviest configuration can defeat 30mm (1.18in) anti-armour rounds. At present, SEP is designed for a range of support functions, including tank destroyer, mortar carrier, forward observation vehicle and APC, but it is possible that a gun version may be developed for the light tank role.

It has been common for many years to create families of armoured vehicles based on common chassis. SEP and projects like it represent another

STEYR SK105 LIGHT TANK

Crew: 3
Weight: 17.7 tonnes
Dimensions: length 7.75m (25ft 5in); width 2.5m (8ft 2in); height 2.53m (8ft 3in)
Range: 520km (325 miles)
Armour: classified
Armament: one 105mm (4.1in) 105 G1 main gun; one 7.62mm (0.3in) Steyr machine gun 74
Powerplant: one 239kW (320hp) Steyr liquid-cooled 6-cylinder diesel
Performance: maximum road speed 65km/h (40mph); fording 1m (3ft 4in); vertical obstacle 0.8m (2ft 7in); trench 2.4m (7ft 11in)

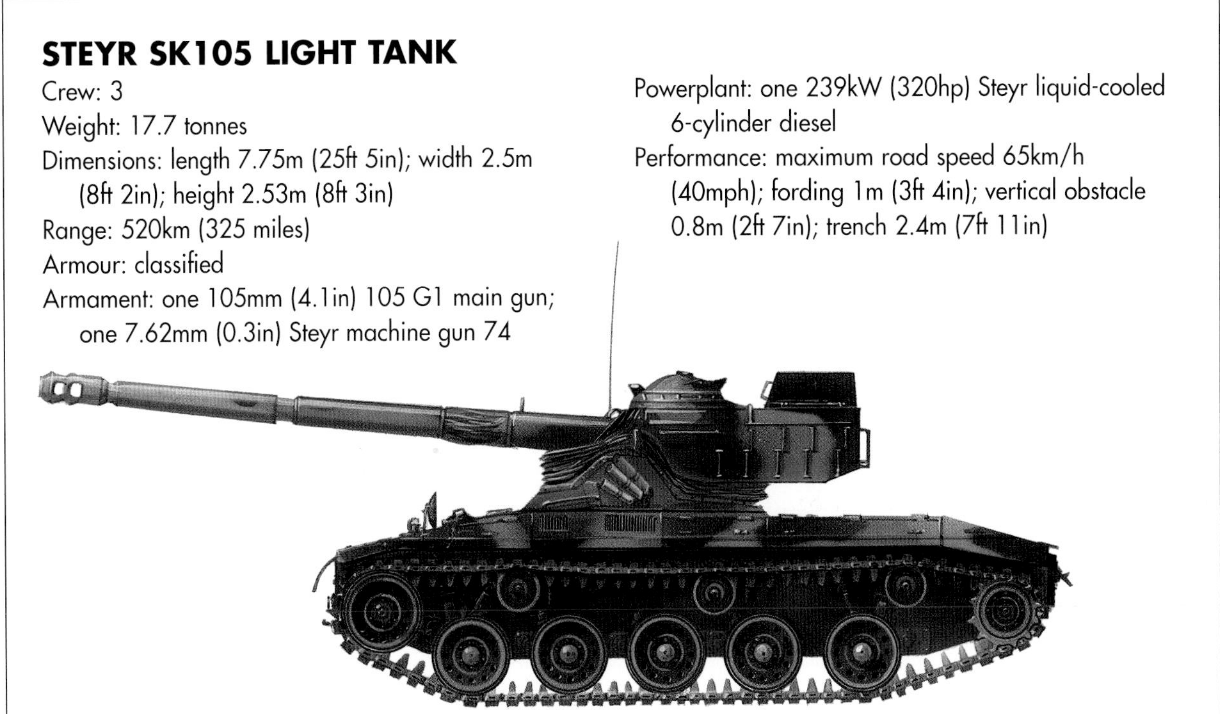

step in that direction, creating vehicles that can be quickly set up for a different role or even upgraded with new equipment by swapping in different modules. It may be that this idea will be applied to future battle tanks.

Is There A Future For The Tank?

There are those that claim that the day of the heavily armoured battle-wagon has passed, and that its role can be carried out by lighter, faster and cheaper vehicles. Certainly there are many situations in which heavy battle tanks are not the optimum solution.

Tracked vehicles were developed after wheeled armoured cars, largely due to the inability of armoured cars to operate where they were most needed. But armoured cars have developed hugely since that time. Perhaps they might be able to reclaim the battle-tank role from their tracked cousins? It is true that armoured cars are increasingly capable of undertaking the light-tank or tank destroyer role. Wheeled vehicles cannot

Infantry Fighting Vehicles (IFVs) are sometimes mistaken for tanks by civilians.

quite match the off-road tactical mobility of tanks, nor can they be so heavily laden with armour and other systems. However, they are cheaper and have better strategic mobility.

Getting tanks from place to place under their own power is a difficult prospect. Tracks tear up roads and a tank's road speed is rarely very impressive. In addition, there are serious logistics problems inherent in driving tanks to a new battle area. Large quantities of fuel are used up and wear can become considerable, increasing the maintenance burden or taking a proportion of the tanks out of service for repairs. For this reason, tanks are transported by rail or on the backs of wheeled tank transporters.

Wheeled armoured vehicles do not suffer from these problems. They can use ordinary roads more easily and at greater speed, with less wear on their running gear and smaller fuel consumption. This, coupled with a need for large numbers of lower-capability vehicles to fight insurgents or second-line enemy forces, makes the armoured car a viable alternative to the tank under many circumstances. However, it is likely that there will always be a need for heavy armoured vehicles for the top-end combat role, so the MBT is unlikely to disappear. Instead it is more likely to form part of a 'high-end/low-end' range of combat vehicles.

Simply trying to field as many top-end tanks as possible is inefficient. For one thing, few nations can afford enough of them and in many roles they represent massive overkill; using a sledgehammer to crack a nut. The alternative, using cheaper equipment in larger numbers, is effective in low-intensity warfare and when fighting an enemy without top-end capabilities, but it runs the risk of coming up against something the force cannot handle. An alternative strategy is to try to find some middle ground, using mid-range tanks that offer a balance of cost and effectiveness. This method runs the risk of failing at both ends of the spectrum – vehicles that are too expensive to be deployed in sufficient numbers and which may represent overkill in low-intensity situations, yet are not powerful enough to deal with a major threat.

The High Mobility Agility Test Vehicle (HIMAG) was an experimental project combining new suspension concepts with an advanced 75mm (2.95in) hypervelocity cannon.

The high-end/low-end philosophy aims to create a balanced force offering the best mix of capabilities for a given budget. Large numbers of 'low-end' vehicles are available to cover as much ground as possible, bringing to bear modest but still effective firepower in a lightly protected and inexpensive package. This is entirely enough to deal with most situations, and where more serious threats are encountered, the 'high-end' vehicles are deployed. In this case, high-end vehicles means state-of-the-art MBTs and supporting equipment capable of taking on the best that anyone else can field.

The tanks of the twenty-first century perform their tasks in a complex three-dimensional 'battlespace', with an electronic dimension to it as well. They are threatened by mines, infantry weapons, tank-hunting aircraft, guns, missiles and artillery-delivered anti-armour weapons. Battle tanks are designed to survive all this and continue doing their job, and as long as the other side has access to tanks that can function in this environment, something will be needed to fight them. For all the available antitank technology, the best counter to a tank remains another tank.

The future of the tank is thus reasonably assured. Light tanks will continue to act as scouts and handle low-intensity situations, while the top-end battle tanks deal with more serious threats. In this, the function of the tank has not changed. It exists to get mobile firepower into the battle area and to protect its crew and systems while they do their job.

So long as there is a need to deliver firepower at the critical moment and in spite of everything the enemy tries to do about it, there will be a need for tanks.

Glossary

AA Anti-Aircraft.
AAMG Anti-Aircraft Machine Gun, usually mounted on top of the turret of armoured vehicles.
AAV Assault Amphibian Vehicle. US term for armoured tracked amphibians used by marine corps, formerly called landing vehicle tracked or LVT.
AAVC Assault Amphibian Vehicle, Command. AAV with additional communications fit for unit commanders.
ACP Armoured Command Post. Armoured vehicle with extra communications gear used by commanders in the field.
AFD Automatic Feeding Device. System for feeding ammunition from magazine into breech mechanically.
AFV Armoured Fighting Vehicle. Generic term for military vehicles with armour protection and armament.
AP Armour Piercing. Ammunition designed to penetrate and destroy armoured targets. Term usually reserved for solid shot fired at high velocity.
APAM Anti-Personnel, Anti-Materiel. Dual-purpose round for use against soft targets.
APC Armoured Personnel Carrier. APCs, usually armed with machine guns, generally transport infantry to the battle before the troops dismount to fight on their own.
APDS Armour-Piercing Discarding Sabot. APDS projectiles are smaller than the diameter of the gun's barrel. Sabots (French for 'shoe') are placed around the projectile and fill the space between the projectile and barrel walls. Once the projectile clears the gun tube, the sabots fall away. APDS projectiles have a higher muzzle velocity than comparable full-bore projectiles.
APHE Armoured Piercing High Explosive. Thick-walled, hardened casing and small HE filling. Detonates inside tank.
Ballistics The science of studying projectiles and their paths. Ballistics can be 'interior' (inside the gun), 'exterior' (in-flight), or 'terminal' (at the point of impact).
Ditched A tank is ditched when the trench it is being driven across is too wide or the ground beneath is too soft or waterlogged to allow the tracks to grip.
DP Dual-purpose. When a weapon is intended for more than one job, or a round of ammunition has more than one effect, it is said to be dual-purpose.
FAV Fast Attack Vehicle. Light vehicle carrying MGs, cannon, grenade launchers or missiles. Used by Special Forces making raids behind enemy lines.
FCS Fire Control System. Computers, laser rangefinders, optical and thermal sights and gunlaying equipment designed to enable a fighting vehicle to engage the enemy accurately.
FEBA Forward Edge of the Battle Area. Loosely, what used to be called the front line.
Fording Depth of water which a military vehicle can wade through without flooding engine. Usually quoted as without preparation and with preparation.
FV Fighting Vehicle. Term used by the British army to identify vehicles accepted for service. For example the FV432 was Britain's standard APC for nearly 30 years.
GP General-Purpose.
GPMG General-Purpose Machine Gun. MG used as both infantry LMG and for sustained fire. Variants adapted as coaxial guns for tanks and as anti-aircraft guns on many different kinds of armoured vehicle.
Gradient Degree of slope up which a tank can travel.
Grenades Originally hand-thrown high-explosive and fragmentation bombs, but also applied to weapons delivered by grenade launchers. Tanks usually have some kind of grenade-launching system to deliver smoke grenades.
HE High Explosive.
HEAP High Explosive Anti-Personnel. Dual-purpose HE round which destroys by a combination of blast and anti-personnel effects.
HEAT High Explosive Anti Tank. Tank round or guided missile with shaped-charge warhead designed to burn through the thickest of armour.
HE-Frag High Explosive-Fragmentation. Dual-purpose munition suitable for dealing with troops and soft-skin targets.
HEP High Explosive Plastic.
HESH High Explosive Squash Head. British term for HEP.
HVAP High Velocity Armour Piercing. Armour piercing round fired at very high velocity, relying on kinetic energy to break through enemy armour.
LRV Light Recovery Vehicle.
MG Machine gun.
Muzzle Brake Device attached to the gun muzzle to reduce recoil force without seriously limiting muzzle velocity.
Muzzle velocity Speed of projectile as it leaves the muzzle. Air friction means velocity drops rapidly once in flight.
NATO North Atlantic Treaty Organization. Western alliance established to counter Soviet threat in Europe after World War II.
RMG Ranging Machine Gun. A machine gun coaxial with the main armament. The bullets have the same ballistic performance as the main gun.
Round One complete piece of ammunition.
RP Rocket propelled. Applied to tank ammunition, artillery rounds and antitank grenades.
RPG Rocket Propelled Grenade Launcher. Soviet-made infantry antitank weapons.
RPV Remote-Piloted Vehicle. Now equipped with real-time datalinks used to provide reconnaissance information.
RTC Royal Tank Corps. The world's first armoured formation.
Running Gear The transmission, suspension, wheels and tracks of a tank.
Shell Hollow projectile normally fired from a rifled gun. Shell can have a number of fillings, including HE, submunitions, chemical and smoke.
SLAP Saboted Light-Armour Penetrator. Machine-gun calibre high-velocity weapon designed to penetrate light armour.
Shot Solid projectile, usually armour-piercing.
Sloped Armour Angled armour – projectiles will either ricochet or be forced to penetrate diagonally.
SMG Sub machine-gun. Small fully automatic weapon often carried as personal arm by armoured crewmen.
Trajectory The curved path of a projectile through the air.
Transmission Means by which the power of the engine is converted to rotary movement of wheels or tracks. Transmission can be hydraulic mechanical or electrical.
Traverse The ability of a gun or turret to swing away from the centreline of a vehicle. A fully rotating turret has a traverse of 360 degrees.
Tread Distance between the centrelines of a vehicle's tracks or wheels.
Trench Field fortification which the tank was developed to deal with. Expressed as a distance in feet or metres in a tank's specification, trench indicates the largest gap a tank can cross without being ditched.
Turret Revolving armoured box mounting a gun. Usually accommodates commander and other crew.
Turret ring Ring in the hull on which the turret rides supported by bearings. The size of the turret ring affects the size of the gun which can be fitted: the larger the ring, the larger the gun.
TRV Tank Recovery Vehicle.
Unditching beam Heavy wooden beam carried on early tanks. Mounted transversely across the tracks, it was used to gain extra grip when the tank was bogged down.
VDU Visual Display Unit.
Velocity The speed of a projectile at any point along its trajectory, usually measured in feet per second or metres per second.
Vertical volute spring Suspension with road wheels mounted to a bogie in pairs on arms, pivoting against a vertically mounted volute spring, it is protected from damage by the bogie frame.
WAM Wide Area Munitions. New area effect munitions designed to spread intelligent submunitions over a wide area.
Whippet WWI term originally describing the first medium tanks, later to describe any light tank.
Zippo Track Vietnam slang for an M113 APC converted to a mechanized flame-thrower under the designation M132A2.

Index

Page numbers in *italic* refer to illustrations
Page numbers in **bold** refer to Head to Head comparisons
Service ranks are often the latest shown in the text